STONE
MIRROR

STONE MIRROR

Reflections on Contemporary Korea

David I. Steinberg

EastBridge

Norwalk

EastBridge

Signature Books

Copyright © 2002 by EastBridge

All rights reserved. No part of this book may be reproduced in any
form without written permission from the publisher, EastBridge.
64 Wall Street, Norwalk, CT 06850

EastBridge is a nonprofit publishing corporation,
chartered in the State of Connecticut and tax exempt under
section 501(c)(3) of the United States tax code.

EastBridge has received a generous multiyear
grant from the Henry Luce Foundation.

Library of Congress Cataloging-in-Publication Data

Steinberg, David I., 1928-
   Stone mirror : reflections on contemporary Korea / David I. Steinberg.
       p. cm. — (Signature books)
   ISBN 1-891936-20-4 (hardcover : alk. paper) — ISBN 1-891936-12-3
(pbk. : alk. paper)
  1. Korea (South)—Social conditions. 2. Korea (South)--Economic
conditions--1960- 3. Korea (South)—Civilization. I. Title. II.
Signature books (Norwalk, CT)
HN730.5.A8 S74 2002
306'.095195—dc21

                                                          2002151437

Printed in the United States of America

Contents

Introduction

If writing on some of the dynamics of Korean society and culture by a foreigner be hubris, then in this case at least it has been hubris delayed, perhaps even matured or fermented over time. The origins of this column go back about two score years when, in 1963 after I had been in Korea for the first time for only a few months as the representative of The Asia Foundation, the editor of the *Korea Times* suggested that I write op-ed columns telling the paper's audience what I thought of Korea. I felt this was utterly inappropriate as I was a neophyte, far more acquainted with other Asian societies than with Korea.

I recognized that such a request, this concern over what foreigners thought about them, might indicate a sense of Korean insecurity in their own position, certainly understandable in the wake of a brutal colonial period, three years of military occupation, a civil war that killed millions, and dire poverty as yet unrelieved. In those days, it was quite common for knowledgeable Koreans to come up to foreigners and begin a conversation by assuming how much the foreigner did not want to be in that cold, poor, benighted state—a point of entry that infuriated me as I had chosen to be there. But however much the Koreans may have been curious about my views, mine were still amorphous. I politely declined, and instead wanted to know, and attempted to find out, what Koreans thought of their own country. In the course of such explorations, and as a language exercise, for I needed short, essay-like pieces rather than novels or short stories, I tried translating Lee O-Young's popular *In This Earth and in That Wind: This Is Korea.*[*] I was fortunate in coming to Korean with a background in Chinese, which helped me understand Chinese characters even if it did not prepare me for the different grammatical structure.

These were a series of insightful and sensitive op-ed pieces on Lee's views of aspects of Korean society and culture, usually contrasted with foreign ones, that had been widely popular when they appeared in book form. At the time, such translations were rare, and as part of the learning process I attempted to write down my poor efforts for my own edification. As a result of unexpected interest by the editor of the *Korea Times* over dinner one evening, he offered to publish such, needless to say, corrected attempts. Some fifty of these pieces

---

[*] He was a professor at Ewha Women's University, and later became minister of culture.

were weekly staples on the op-ed page of the Sunday edition. They were later published as a volume by the Korea Branch of the Royal Asiatic Society in 1967 and went through a number of printings, and only disappeared from the bookstores a few years ago.

When I returned to Korea in 1994 in my second incarnation as the representative of The Asia Foundation, the new editor of the *Korea Times* suggested that I write a newspaper column on any subject of my choosing. I was at first reluctant, but with the encouragement of my family and The Asia Foundation, I thought I would try a once-a-month column. The editor at that time, Mr. Kim Myong-sik, suggested that once a week would be easier and more appropriate. I scoffed, but later learned that he was right for reasons that still seem obscure; whatever creative juices might have existed seemed to flow more evenly that way.

Next, if I were to write such a column, what would it be called? I considered various permutations of "east and west wind," something of that ilk, but found these either had been used by others, or were singularly trite. Sitting alone one day musing on the problem, I thought that I would look up my surname in the Korean dictionary and see what was there that perhaps might offer a clue. But I have always felt that naming things after oneself or in honor of people was somehow gauche (a highway might better be named "The Route of the Flying Hubcap" in the Chinese fashion rather than after some notable, and personal names on car dealerships and stores bothered me). But since my name in Chinese and Korean, given to me by the university I attended in China over half a century ago, translated as "stone," from the German "stein, " I thought there might be something appropriate. And so I found *sokkyong* (or in the new and infamous romanization system mandated by the Korean government—and this is the only time in this volume that such use appears—*soekkyeong*), or "stone mirror." On reflection (*sic*), I thought that this was indeed appropriate, as I was in fact holding up Korea, and myself as a byproduct of these writings, to a mirror with all the dire implications of nakedly exposing myself to the scrutiny of the English-reading world of Korea, and forever being associated with opinions I might have long since abandoned.

The *Korea Times* editorial staff gave me free rein; perhaps a bit too much, for although I appreciated the freedom to write on anything that amused, bothered, or delighted me, the editors treated my words as something akin to sacrosanct, neither questioning some ideas that needed rethinking or minimally rephrasing, nor correcting sometimes egregious grammatical mistakes, elliptical sentences, or spelling errors. I have come to believe that a good editor is a long-term delight even if a short-term pain. When once I was told by my research assistant that my opening sentence in a study I had written for the Department of State on irrigation was too convoluted, I replied that Thoreau's first sentence in *Walden* had nine commas. I was informed politely but firmly that I was not Thoreau.

Since the Stone Mirror column started in 1995, I have written over 240 published articles for it, as well as a number for the *Times* outside of my column, and some for other English and Korean papers in Korea, and some internationally, all in addition to my more academic writings. Obviously, this number would make a cumbersome and expensive volume even if all were worthy of reprinting, which in my judgment is not the case. I have subjected both family and colleagues to the excruciating task of grading my weekly "examinations" (I am sure my students would have enjoyed that turnabout) and winnowing down the number. The ultimate responsibility for the choice, however, must remain mine alone.

The problem was to pick those that considered something interesting about Korea, or offered what one would like to call some insight into the society. Those that were so topical that the references have become irrelevant or obscure have been eliminated. One always has one's preferences, and these have been included. I have added a few essays from other Korean journalistic writings because I felt they were particularly germane to some Korean issue. Such additions to the usual column articles have been so noted. I have also edited all columns for grammar, style, sometimes tense, and occasionally to add a thought that seemed to fit. The EastBridge editor has also cosmetically improved my presentations. Footnotes have been included to explain points that may have been lost over time, or to comment on why an article was included in spite of its temporal nature.

Almost all of these essays are about Korea, and if I am critical, I am as critical of my own as well as other societies. There have been many complaints of and by foreigners who "bash" Korea, based perhaps on their unpleasant experiences, prejudices, or perhaps personalities. This certainly has neither been my experience nor my intent, and my complaints about the society are intended to be constructive, and should be so construed, and focused on those aspects of improvement that at least some knowledgeable Koreans have articulated. It is important to explain that although I criticize many aspects of the Korean political system, I do so in terms of the generic issues and processes I perceive to be retarding some goals set by the Koreans themselves, and while avoiding support for or opposition to any specific party or group. Once a state minister of another country asked me why I wrote so critically about his society and not of Korea; I promised to send him, and did, a variety of what I regarded as my more trenchant Korea essays.

It is certainly not my intent to advocate American or foreign solutions to Korean problems. I strongly believe that Korean society will over time develop approaches to cope with many of the problems discussed in the following pages. Whatever may evolve, I feel sure it will be distinctively Korean.

These essays do not contribute to the academic literature on Korea, and thus no doubt will be shunned by my university colleagues. Bridging the gaps between the state sector, academia, the nonprofit field, and popular informed opinion has been a lifelong preoccupation, and thus I make no apologies for the attempt, but only perhaps for the product if it does not fulfill my, and my readers', hopes. There will be other just criticisms. In less than a thousand words one is trying to make a point, and in doing so there is a tendency to make it both sweeping and broad. These generalizations are by their nature often gross, as opposed to being finely honed, and are unacademic. Yet they are there for a purpose, and one hopes the discriminating reader will understand that one is referring to tendencies along a spectrum, not absolutes, and if one is characterizing a society, one does not intend that these be predictions about any individual or institutional action or consequence. National character studies, originally designed to predict behavior during World War II, might have been popular half a century ago, but they have been remarkably discredited. Still, history is relevant. Mark Twain is said to have remarked that if history did not repeat itself, it often rhymed. Yet Dante Alighieri was right to put fortunetellers and soothsayers in a very low circle of hell, indeed.

Many of these essays are fixed in time—related to a regime or a problem prevalent at a moment in history. Rather than update some of these pieces, I have kept them as they were written (sometimes adding an explanatory note at the end), because they still are relevant or illustrate the permutations of an internal problem in Korea or in its relationships overseas. The reader, one hopes, will then get a sense of the breadth and enduring nature of some of these issues

I would like to thank Douglas Merwin, the editor of EastBridge, for his encouragement and help, and Mr. Kim Myong-sik, first of the *Korea Times* and later assistant minister of the Ministry of Information, for his faith that although I may be critical of an action by the Korean government or of some societal problem, I have affection for the Korean people and their well-being at heart. To my colleagues who have read and graded some of these essays, especially Professor David Chandler of Cambodia fame, I am grateful.

There are hundreds of Koreans and some foreigners who, by a chance remark or observation, a felicitous choice of phrasing, an idea that seemed particularly germane, a few sentences in some volume or newspaper, are inadvertently but anonymously included in this work as unindicted co-conspirators. I have mined their individual and cumulative wisdom unashamedly because I respect what they have said and think their views inform the discourse on contemporary Korea. But to have quoted them, perhaps not in the context they intended, would hold up some to intellectual scrutiny they might wish to avoid. So they remain remembered but uncited.

My family, my sons and especially my wife, Lee Myong-sook, bore the burden of these efforts and to them I am thankful; many of these pieces bear her suggestions for improvement, but perhaps she might reject many more as inappropriate; the mistakes of one spouse should not indiscriminately be placed on the other. The errors and sins of commission and omission are mine alone.

Having lived in Korea for eight years, and having taken innumerable trips there over four decades, I have great admiration for what the Koreans have accomplished. If over half a century ago, the American anthropologist Cornelius Osgood could write that there was no more important country about which Americans knew so little, today one might say that there is no more important country that has transformed itself so rapidly. Foreigners know a great deal more about Korea than once we did. This is attested to by the multitude of Ph.D. dissertations and volumes in English and in other languages on aspects of that society. These essays may contribute little that cannot be gleaned from perusal of more academic studies, but one hopes that these short, digestible pieces offer the reader quick glimpses of aspects of Korean society that will help explain what makes Korea what it is.

This work is dedicated with affection to the people of Korea, whom I hope will be sympathetic to the intent of this volume and my concern for their welfare, and for whom I hope the new century will be far better than the last.

Bethesda, Maryland

July 2002

Note on Korean Usage
and Romanization

Korean surnames generally precede given names, e.g., PARK Chung Hee, except when usage establishes a different pattern, e.g., Syngman RHEE. Married women retain their maiden names. The romanization system used herein is a modified McCune-Reischauer system and uses no diacritical marks, such as that indicating a short "o" vowel. Most of the place names are those that have traditionally been used in foreign publications, and not the new ones approved by the Korean government in 2000.

Stone Mirror

1

Korean Mores and Customs

Each society varies in the degree to which one is beholden, and in what particular aspects. In the Philippines, if one does not hire one's relatives, one is socially disgraced; nepotism is socially defined. In the United States, if one does, it is a case for comment (Jack Kennedy and Robert Kennedy, for example), and if one is an official, the move is subject to all kinds of sanctions. One American in the foreign aid agency went to jail because he hired his wife.

One of the most obvious expressions of familial cohesion and beholdenness are the *chaebol* structures, but these are simply clear and powerful manifestations of something far more widespread in the society. How far one is beholden is a question. Is the issue simply one of asserting concern and sympathy about a person's situation—one to whom one is beholden—or is there a real commitment to intervene on that person's behalf? It probably varies with the circumstances.

I have sometimes been asked by friends to intercede in college admissions in the United States. Americans understand, at least generally, that one could only ensure that an entrance application is not overlooked and is given careful scrutiny, but that one could not control the corporate process of admission. Some Koreans, on the other hand, somewhat naively believe that because one was a member of a faculty or had friends on other faculties one had far more power than one really had, and that if one did not control the process, it was because one did not wish to fulfill the obligations imposed by friendship.

Once an American graduate school dean called me in Korea to complain that a Korean dean had written three exactly the same letters of recommendation for each of his three staff applying for the same fellowship to the United States. The American did not know why the dean had done this and whom to choose. But the Korean dean had fulfilled his obligation by writing appropriate letters of support for each, and could not be faulted by any of the parties concerned.

There is a constant debate at both practical and theoretical levels in the United States on the degree to which elected politicians should be beholden to their constituents, to the forces that provide funds for their campaigns, or to their own conscience, if there are tensions among the three. Should, in other words, an elected politician vote his or her conscience or follow the polls or the funding interests? The issues are often opaque.

How beholden is a politician to his or her party? When should a politician vote the political party line? In the United States, there are often splits within the party, and conservatives and liberals within the same party often end up on different sides of an issue. In England, some votes are regarded as "free," and members of Parliament vote their conscience. In Korea there are rarely splits. When I once suggested that the voting record of each legislator should be published so that the public would know how he or she voted, my Korean friends indicated that I did not know how the National Assembly worked, because everyone voted with their party. One was reminded of the musical H.M.S. *Pinafore,* in which the admiral, while in Parliament, "never thought of thinking for myself at all," "voted at his party's call," and "thought so little they rewarded me by making me the ruler of the Queen's navy."

How far is one beholden if one receives a gift? The answer may vary by amount, occasion, and nature of the relationship. It will certainly change by society. If one is beholden for future favors, when does the gift becomes a bribe?

This issue of Beholdenness even extends to international relations. As an "elder brother" in the Confucian analogy of international relations, the United States is supposed to act as a sympathetic, understanding, and protective kin, even though modern diplomacy does not accept that concept. One Southeast Asian ambassador some years ago complained to me that the United States was not acting like the elder brother in dealing with his country in rice trading, thus protecting the economy of this younger, therefore weaker, brother.

In Korea, nationalism requires equality in international relations, but many feel that the United States, as an elder brother in the Korean-American relationship, has a special, familial obligation to play the protective, understanding role that an elder brother has in the family. This can have dire consequences. Thus, from this viewpoint it is inappropriate to push too hard on market openings, to criticize publicly, and to be too strident in negotiations. Much of the criticism of the United States in relation to the Kwangju massacre of 1980 was not because the United States did anything, but because—as elder brother—the United States did not forcefully intervene to prevent the Korean government from doing what it did. An elder brother would have protected the people.

Emotional beholdenness is thus quite important from the personal to the international realms. When it operates internally in any society, its people determine how extensive it should be and under what circumstances. When it operates across cultures, however, there are often misinterpretations that can have disastrous effects.

March 1996

On "Cash Only"

Financial transactions around the world take place electronically. National sovereignty sometimes cannot contain or even monitor the movement of capital in and out of various societies in this form. In much of the West, an individual may be paid by electronic deposit to a bank, and may carry a number of credit cards and deal in cash only to pay tolls on roads or to buy something as inconsequential as an ice cream cone or a pizza.

Americans rarely carry large amounts of cash even if they can afford it, and most serious transactions take place by check or some other means that enable both parties concerned to keep a record of the transaction. In the movies, at any rate, only the Mafia deal in cash.

Stories in the Korean press and on television related to scandals describe or picture cardboard fruit or *ramyon* boxes stuffed with W.10,000 notes as political or other kinds of contributions in houses or placed in the trunks of cars. This raises a number of interesting questions. It seems that Korea is one of the few countries in the OECD where cash in the magnitudes indicated is both common and indeed, under certain circumstances, may be legal.

I belong to a society in which cash is limited and receipts are critical. Offices are audited, and there have to be receipts for expenditures over $25, and in many cases for items costing much less. If my organization makes a gift or donation, such as at a funeral or a wedding in Korea, then I must explain that it is customary in this society to pay in new notes and that there will be no receipts. Checks are a convenient means to ensure that most transactions are duly noted, and, as many companies suggest, "Your check is your receipt." But one does not give checks in Korea at weddings or funerals. And it has been virtually impossible to have personal checking accounts.

Receipts are unusual in Korea, except at the major hotels or other places frequented by foreigners. Even most doctors do not give receipts, and then only if cajoled into doing so for foreign insurance purposes. No receipts may mean that the transaction is not recorded, and thus taxes are avoided. This underground activity in Korea is variously estimated at from 20 to 40 percent of the whole economy.

The previous administration has forced all higher-level civil servants and political appointees to declare their assets, and if they had no valid explanation for their wealth, they were dismissed or requested to retire. This was a positive reform, but is there an annual recheck of these assets? One assumes that wealth had to be substantiated with some sort of paper trail.

Where is the paper trail in political or other donations? If any government is serious about reform of corruption, then it would be quite simple to begin reform by two uncomplicated laws. The first is to decide that no political donation of any size or amount may be given in cash. It must be done through an individual, institutional, or bank check with the donor's name clearly indicated. Then, at least, transparency would be more evident. Political parties should also be required to publish in the press or in some manner available to the public a list of donors and the amounts provided. The maximum donation allowed is a separate issue.

The second reform would require that no individual could receive such donations, which would have to be made in the name of a political party or institution and deposited in some institutional bank account. If a donation went to an individual, it would be a prima facie case of bribery or corruption.

The United States has recently faced serious abuses of the political donation process, as we all know and as the press has reported. There are urgent needs for reform there, and one can only hope that a bipartisan effort will now be made to do so. There have been measures to tighten up regulations on what government officials can receive in terms of money, goods, or services, and these are welcome regulations, although the political party reforms have yet to be instituted.

In Korea, the problem is more acute. *Ttok kap* (lit., "the price of rice cakes," but actually payments made to an individual to oil the societal and institutional gears and relationships and to enable things to get done) is legal in Korea in amounts that are, to an American, more than substantial. In themselves, they are not considered bribes for there is no specific return on that investment, but rather the creation of good will—essential for social and institutional survival.

The *ttok kap* system needs reform, but it is deeply ingrained in this, a gift-giving society. Giving gifts can be innocent and charming, but an understanding of the motives behind such actions is needed. Forcing a system of checks and receipts would be an easy step forward, and would also probably increase revenue to the government as less of the economy would be underground.

March 1996

On Citizenship and Employment

Citizenship by definition is highly nationalistic. A flurry of news and editorial activity of late is evident over the issue of whether there should be a requirement of Korean citizenship, and against dual citizenship, both for those assuming government posts and for the families of those who occupy higher public or private positions. From the editorial content, it seems many Koreans are unhappy over Koreans and their dependents holding, or having held, foreign or dual citizenship. This debate, as in so many in Korea, has taken on strong nationalist overtones. It is both inappropriate and impossible from afar to comment on specific cases, but the generic issues are important and deserve further discussion.

There would probably be near universal agreement that any government has the right to ensure that its privileged information and official representation be kept in the hands of those with assumed and demonstrated loyalty—that is, citizens of that state (foreigners may be "honorary consuls" but rarely real ones). But as international trade becomes ubiquitous, in this new era, we are also witnessing extensive movements of peoples with important consequences for citizenship. All children born in the United States, for example, are automatically considered U.S. citizens. They may keep dual citizenship with some other country, attained by virtue of their parents, until such time as they must pledge allegiance to one state or another, for example, when a person goes into the military.

But what about that person's dependents? This has become a sensitive issue in some countries. The military junta in Myanmar (Burma) has decreed that Aung San Suu Kyi, the Nobel Peace Prize laureate, cannot be elected to public office because her (now deceased) husband was British and her children hold foreign passports, although she is a Burmese citizen. This appeals to a highly nationalistic, even xenophobic, strain in that society, but it is hardly a model of good governance in this modern world. I believe that the citizenship of the dependents of U.S. government officials, who themselves must be a citizen or hold a "green card," is irrelevant in terms of employment.

It is significant that in Korea the issue of nationality comes up not only in the case of government appointments, but also for those private appointments that are in the public eye. That the president of a state university be a citizen is understandable, although I would question even that, for one would have thought that state secrets have no place in an academic setting where access to knowledge is supposed to be open. But what about private universities? That there was something of a public outcry in Korea over this in the past seems, at least to a foreigner, as inappropriate.

The supplementary argument is that a minister's family should be citizens because familial involvement would enable the official to understand the problems facing his or her official charge, such as education or health. This seems spurious as well. Would a single person who had no children be excluded from the post of minister of education? Let us remember Kim Ock-gil,* for example. Would a foreign minister's family have to have lived abroad to allow him/her to qualify for that post? Would any government want to limit appointments to official positions on the basis of familial involvement in the field of the official's responsibility? I think not.

The cases that have been brought to the public's attention have involved some Koreans who hold or have held—or whose dependents hold—U.S. citizenship. Although every state should have the right to protect national security, today it is the U.S. connection that is in the limelight even though the principle may apply more broadly. The American relationship is, for better or worse, important for the present generation not only because of security concerns or trade or investment, but because of the extensive educational and employment opportunities in the United States for a large number of Koreans who have taken advantage of those possibilities. As editorials point out, there are a large number of well-educated Koreans, many of whose families were partly educated or lived in the United States for considerable periods and who may have acquired American citizenship.

* Former President, Ewha Women's University, and later, Minister of Education.

ically give one the ability to speak ex cathedra, because one has the moral authority simply by virtue of holding that position. It is assumed that such decisions carry moral weight. Morality and power are thus intimately intertwined. A person is worthy simply because of the title and position occupied. So a title on the door means power galore. Thus not only is compromise difficult, because it is a retreat from morality, but even admitting error is also a problem, except when it is a part of a ritual cleansing act that sometimes is required when one individual, the "fall-guy," is forced to take responsibility that really belongs to an institution or someone higher up on the power scale. Thus a minister must resign if there is a tragedy in a field under his authority even though he was not a party to the problem. Taking such responsibility is regarded as a noble gesture.

On the other hand, surrender is more appropriate than compromise because even if one has lost the metaphorical battle, one has at least kept one's virtue intact because one was forced into that position by overwhelming forces beyond one's control. One has kept to one's principles. In that case, *myongbun* (introducing a moral argument to make an individual or institutional excuse) is invoked to give a publicly acceptable reason for the abandonment of the position.

Perhaps leadership in any institution invokes a sense of authority that, in a hierarchical society, is not easily subject to questioning. If a professor's opinion in Korea is challenged, then the moral role of the teacher is diminished or evaporates.

This makes it difficult to run a modern institution that is able to adjust to new needs in a contemporary world in which change is both ubiquitous and unavoidable, and must be addressed for organizational survival in either the profit or non-profit fields. If change is not authorized from the top, because it is very difficult for it to percolate up from the bottom, and if a present position has been invoked as sacrosanct, then surrender (in the business field, bankruptcy), may be the result.

Societies generally share this problem of how gracefully to compromise, or retreat, or better how to avoid the necessity of retreating by first not predicating positions as infallible. Korea seems to have a more acute version of this virus than some other societies.

This is not an isolated issue, but involves how authority and hierarchy are viewed in the society, and thus is intertwined with fundamental values. So changes are likely to be slow, but until they come, we may see a continuous series of events that create a set of problems for any group in the society—problems that might be better addressed through compromise rather than confrontation.

February 1997

On Lying Flat on the Ground and Not Moving

Koreans have an expression *pok chi pu dong,* which literally translates to lying on the ground and not moving. Although each of the words derives from the Chinese, the expression is said to be particularly Korean and rather modern, almost slang, although it sounds classical. If one heard this without context, it would seem as if one were describing a dead or comatose person for whom sympathy or anguish would seem to be the proper response; one would consider calling an ambulance. This is, however, far from the truth.

The expression is in vogue these days in Seoul. I have heard two quite different interpretations of it; the first implies a type of fear, and the second a kind of sabotage.

Each new administration that has come to power, either through elections or through revolutions or coups, has conducted what has almost become "ritual purges" of some of those that were associated with power in the previous group. Often these purges involve those who made illicit financial gains, or at least so they were accused, or were perceived to be or were somehow out of touch with what quickly became the new orthodoxy. So if there were a national policy problem that a new administration inherited from the previous one, those associated with the earlier one could be accused of fostering the problem or benefiting from it. This attitude, rarely discussed in the textbooks on Korea and its political life, is nonetheless real. It is, of course, prevalent elsewhere, but the issue is the degree to which this is a problem.

What is the practical effect of the ritualization of this attitude? It means that those who are in office when a new government comes in feel insecure or threatened, and they become exceedingly careful in maintaining their positions. After all, this has become especially important in a period of bureaucratic "downsizing" and early (unrequested) retirements. This is true in many administrations worldwide; in the United States we do not say we lie down flat, but we "keep our head down"—I am not sure whether we are kneeling or crouching.

These real fears, which are based on historical precedent, mean that those who must administer policies but who are not members of the new political team take every possible step to prevent future problems and the blame attached to policies that either lose fashion or produce deleterious results. The natural reaction under these circumstances is inertia—take no initiative, make no suggestions, and even administer as few things as possible. They do only what is routine to avoid being noticed. As Americans say, they keep "out of the loop" of decision-making or implementation.

In personal terms this may be a wise policy. It reduces work and stress and may protect the future employment of those who are so prescient. But in terms of public policy in both the long and short terms, it is disastrous. In the immediate period, policies are not implemented if the decisions to do so can be avoided, and over a longer term innovation, initiative, and experimentation are frowned upon. It is just at this juncture in Korean history, under globalization and intense international competition, that Korea needs to have increased productivity—whether it is in products or in administration. But this attitude stifles all of the above.

To a senior policy advisor or politically appointed administrator, this attitude takes on the guise of the second meaning of the term—sabotage. Thus, the argument goes, the well-thought-through policies of the new administration are being undercut by those down the chain of command who do not carry out the policies mandated from those on high. This means that new policies, whatever their merits, will have less chance of success, and there are likely to be serious deficiencies, with poor political prospects, in the future. So those people who adopt the attitudes associated with being immobile in administration are subverting the administration.

Now the sad aspect of all of this is that in a sense both attitudes are right. True, poorly administered, perhaps more accurately unadministered, policies will have little effect except to backfire politically over time. But exposure on the "cutting edge," as Americans like to say, of policy may be a form of hara-kiri. If one is a mid-level official, one is never sure which will apply. So rather than trying to steer a perilous passage between the Scylla of sabotage and the Charybdis of administration, one lies down and hopes it all goes away.

Although this tendency is probably present to some degree in almost every administration in every country, in Korea it seems particularly acute. Both attitudes are understandable because of a political heritage that too vehemently rewards orthodoxy and treats political outsiders with suspicion. Years ago, during the Park Chung Hee period, foreign observers were amazed by the alacrity with which policies were implemented, even down to the village level. These policies were not always sound, and many were actually deleterious, but their implementation was never in doubt. Today there is a different world in which administrators try to avoid such actions.

Still, there is a second expression in Seoul these days; rather than *pok chi pu dong*, it is *pok chi an dong*, which translates into lying on the ground with only one's eyes moving. This is said to be a new mode, in which one lies low, but watches carefully to see what the trends are, trying to ascertain the situation while not taking any action unless absolutely necessary.

Self-preservation is a natural trait, but it is one that if carried to extremes can destroy Korea's competitive edge in the world market in which it must exist, and can set the stage some years from now, when a new administration comes into power, that it will adopt the same attitudes, continuing the ritual purges and fear that seem to have become pervasive. The spiral may continue to rise even as governments shift through democratic procedures; this would be detrimental to the society as a whole.

In bureaucracies, initiatives are rarely encouraged, except at the top. Activities continue because to stop them would require a new decision—so bureaucratic inertia is prevalent. Someone needs to break the mold and encourage administrators to perform at the highest efficiency and with zeal tempered by common sense. All groups in Korea, public and private, need innovation and efficiency.

March 1999

On Privacy

Privacy is a concept culturally determined. Each society has its own rules, and they differ profoundly one from another. There are various types of privacy, including the physical, mental, informational, spatial, let alone the major public policy issues of what the government might want to know about you, how that information is gathered, and what you are prepared to tell it. In the computer age when unverified data from myriad sources can end up in a central file and affect your credit rating, insurance, medical benefits, or job security, privacy becomes an important issue. And it is not just the government's or business' role that should be of concern.

In Korea, the government believes it has the right, in loco parentis, to watch over what people read or write when the state feels the social order might be threatened. Although this may sound very modern and authoritarian, it is in fact very old, and has its origins in Confucian concepts of the government as father, and the people as children who must be protected in their own best interests. There were in 1990, after political liberalization in 1987, some 376 books banned in Korea.

But there are other kinds of privacy, more mundane and less intellectually intrusive although they may lead to misunderstanding or embarrassment. In my society, to ask how much one receives as salary would be considered impertinent, but not in many other cultures. If I ask about someone's children or wife I might be accused of being intrusive in one society, but if I do not ask in another, I would be thought of as cold and unsympathetic. In the United States, of course, if you ask about someone's spouse you never know which number spouse you or they are referring to. It would be impolite there to ask, "Are you still married to so-and-so?"

When I have gone into an examining room in a doctor's office in Korea, on a number of occasions other staff or even patients wander in while I am being examined. I am terribly embarrassed not because of anything inappropriately exposed, but because I had expected the seclusion that a doctor's office would bring. So too, coming from a medical family I remember the silence with which my father would greet inquiries from his own family about his patients, but I have been told in Korea that often this might become the topic of cocktail conversation.

Most Americans want and seek the solitude of a private bedroom, and after even a few months, infants are encouraged to sleep alone—of course where the parents can keep an alert, real or electronic, ear on them. This is supposed to breed independence, I suppose, and self-reliance. In Korea, a child is never left to sleep alone. This is a type of bonding. Group-sleeping of parents and children or siblings together is more the rule than the exception. Although it may be a matter of available space in poorer households, it probably runs deeper, and there may be very positive reassurances that such group-sleeping brings to those involved. Privacy in Korea may breed loneliness. Isolation is to be avoided.

Social space is also required. I knew a highly placed American whose career I believe was limited because he had the habit of getting physically too close (in some vague, American sense) to someone with whom he was conversing, and as his confidant tried to back away, often into a corner, this person continued the diminution of physical space until the talkee felt about to be devoured. This had nothing to do with sexual advances, but what might have been appropriate in another culture was not in the United States.

In some cultures, one invades space with hand gestures while one talks; in others, using hands while speaking is considered rude and even aggressive. Psychologists have studied that in some cultures the hand gestures are usually sideways, and in others toward the person spoken to. To mix them up is considered inappropriate, and can convey the wrong signals.

Privacy ironically is also social. Japanese men sometimes used to ride trains and change their outer clothes in public. Because culturally they were not to be observed, they were indeed not seen, socially speaking. I have gone into the outer office of a Korean executive, whom I can see in his shirtsleeves working at his desk in his inner room. He sees me, and his secretary announces me, but he will not acknowledge my presence until he has stood up, put his suit jacket on, and then we formally meet. An American might acknowledge his visitor even as he also puts his coat on.

When the Peace Corps was in Korea, it had a very high rate of early return. When sociologists tried to find out why, they discovered the lack of privacy for any foreigner, but especially for women, in rural Korea at that time was exhausting to many. They were often continuously followed by children as if they were on display in a zoo, or so they felt. It would be both normal and appropriate for an older female family member to scrub the back of someone younger, as if they were in a public bath; it is giving a helping hand.

Although Americans prize privacy, they can be garrulous about their private lives far more than most Koreans under certain socially appropriate conditions. Talking freely and intimately to bartenders is part of American and other Western folklore (Albert Camus's novel *The Fall* [La chute] is essentially such a conversation), and Ameri-

cans tend to demand verbal clarity in relations that in other societies
would be opaque.

In few cultures are the rules rigid. In one society, allowing one's
children modest independence does not necessarily mean that children have complete freedom. I imagine there are discussions in many
American homes as to whether a parent should explore a child's
drawer, or read a diary, or open mail, and if so, at what age (if ever)
this should cease. In Korea, I think that the chances are far greater
than this would continue without any qualms, and would be more acceptable to the children.

There are no rights or wrongs in this issue of individual privacy,
but the recognition that there are differences is a step toward being ac-
commodating to the views of ones friends and associates from across
the cultural divide. Pardon me while I shut my door so I can be alone.

June 1996

The God of Time

In Javanese culture, they say that the god of time is also the god of
death. As one gets older, one recognizes that both are closely related,
and that the wisdom of the connection, although expressed in a manner that may be unfamiliar to many in Western cultures, has depth and
elegance of expression akin to poetry. Much of our life is spent growing, but simultaneously decaying.

But death and time are related in many forms beyond our individual lives and in far more complex ways. Time causes the decline and
death not only of individuals, but of institutions, regimes, states, and
societies. They also die or fall, and not just like the Roman Empire;
perhaps it is better to say, in a non-Marxist sense, states do wither
away. General MacArthur in a famous speech to the U.S. Congress
after he was dismissed from his command by President Truman, said
that old soldiers never die, they just fade away—something he personally seemed to have little intention of doing. T.S. Eliot wrote that
the world would end not with a bang but a whimper. Institutional, and
sometimes personal, death becomes, then, a slow process, often painful—the institutional equivalent of cancer.

But in modern society, to continue the analogy, the god of time
may also be the god of continuance, if not of life. This is especially
true in bureaucracies. To stop an activity once it has been started may

even be more difficult than beginning it in the first instance. In this case, then, bureaucratic stasis may give continuing life (if not vitality) to an institution or a program. One well-known American once asked me what the strength was in official Washington circles of a particular activity in which he was interested. When I replied it was bureaucratic inertia, not the value of the effort, he was not pleased. How many archaic elements of a bureaucracy continue to exist long after the rationale for their operations have faded away. Even "sunset" legislation, which forces review of activities after a certain period, often does not succeed in ending the existence of a variety of programs and groups. To argue that some activity should stop could be interpreted to mean that it should never have begun. Even small bureaucracies, public or private, have tenacious holds on their little empires, as we all know.

But continuing an activity may allow the form, which may have had little substance, to evolve into a reality that captures its initial intent.

Consider elections in Korea. For so many years, they were necessary as, essentially, showmanship or sleight of hand—they had to be held, for both internal and external public relations and window dressing, but their essence was founded on manipulation and collusion between the state and, often, pliant voters who did not understand the importance of what they were doing, and were willing to be swayed by money or intimidation. Constitutional or other laws were irrelevant—ignored or breached. Force and deception were often employed to ensure that the results would conform to governmental orthodoxy. If the issue was in doubt, then the locus of the elections could be changed—from direct to indirect elections, for example, that would ensure centralized control. This process was often an elaborate charade in which, at least publicly, many connived.

But the very fact of holding such elections over time, their protracted life during a period in which the population began to demand more from their government in terms of pluralism, gave the public the expectation that such elections could be meaningful, and put pressure on the state to respond. As the society evolved and an understanding of the importance of such events became accepted, elections became a requirement not only of form but of substance. Whether stringent laws prompted compliance with the spirit of the elections or whether changes in public attitudes prompted enforcement of the laws may be subject to debate, but there is no question that elections have transcended their early, simply confirmational, role.

It is virtually inconceivable that Korea could return to the period of managed elections. There is vibrant pluralism, private citizens' groups monitor the results, and there is far more transparency in the process, although some areas seem occasionally shrouded. Urbanites carefully follow politics. This indeed is progress.

Political parties are now the problem—they remain highly personalized even after fifty years of the Republic, and little change is visible. Perhaps we need to appeal to higher authority since so little progress has been made in their operations and maturity; we could use not a new Javanese god, but a Korean one who would be god of time and political parties, a deity who could begin to transform them into meaningful entities, or if that doesn't happen, speed their decay. Local deities have always held an appeal, and since politics is an all-consuming indoor sport, perhaps the second most popular, in Korea, we may have to go up the hierarchical and mystical ladder to get change.

Ironically, it is the Javanese, a people noted for nonconfrontational social attitudes and discreet indirection, who have expressed so baldly the relationship between the time and death. Americans, noted for their confrontational society and "in your face" attitudes, have preferred to avoid discussing the most obvious of associations. Perhaps we in the West need to adapt to the concept of a god of time—a special deity reserved not only to time and death but to life as well, and which would embody the relationship between growth and decay. Time may not heal all wounds, contrary to the saying, for it destroys as much as it allows for creation, but it does give pause for perspective and reflection, and in these rapidly evolving times that is at least something.

July 1998

On "The Future Isn't What It Was"

Paul Valéry is said to have remarked that the future is not what it was, and if that sounds like a conundrum or a statement by baseball's verbal contortionist Yogi Berra, it really is neither. Although fortune-tellers do not have high social status and are said to be assigned to a low circle of hell, we all seem to be engaged in trying to predict the future. After all, political risk analysis is a growth industry all over the world, academics try for tenure by coming up with an elegant theory that will explain the future as well as the past, and Nobel prizes have been awarded for neat scientific explanations and predictions. At a more mundane level, we invest in the stock market or join a company thinking that the future will conform to our anticipations. Our hopes are usually positive. Although we cannot pick our parents, we do pick our mates based on expectations, and we try to influence our children's futures to be better off and to conform to our norms, however liberal or conservative they may be.

We have grown to be comfortable in our expectations of the future even though we recognize that we are in constant change— change that is accelerating at dizzying speeds and at seemingly geometrical progressions. Although we may be subject to what has been called "future shock," in a sense most of us feel we can live with those shocks.

This is in part because we have come to believe in constant progress as we think it will make our lives more convenient and comfortable. If something is new, it will be better, as advertisers constantly remind us. But progress as a concept is itself relatively new—perhaps a couple of hundred years old and then a product of the Western intellectual tradition. After all, if the theory of evolution is true, then what evolves reaches a new, usually more complex, stage of development, better adapted to its environment, and we equate complexity of organisms with growth and progress. We take adaptation of the species and transform it into a societal phenomenon; material change becomes social hope. The West has essentially conceived of history as linear—constant movement. Christianity produced the concept of the second coming of Christ, bringing the kingdom of heaven, which is a kind of progress. This idea was lacking in traditional Korea; Buddhism was quite different, in spite of some messianic sects in some Buddhist countries.

In many parts of the world, the future was predictable because social relationships remained relatively constant, class was a given, mobility was limited, and if one played one's cards properly, one could reasonably predict where one would be in a couple of decades. In many older societies, including Korea, the idea of progress was traditionally inappropriate—for this would be in violation of the Confucian norms that predicated a golden age of long- past sages.

For the modern Korean there still is a concept that the future is predictable in spite of the vast changes that have taken place in Korea in half a century of independence. The Korean War, the evolution of the class structure, and the economic development that afforded Koreans their rise from poverty and vastly affected the society, have all altered both the future and the conceptions of it. Although few predicted these results, there has grown up in Korea ingrained concepts of where the society was going, and how it would get there.

Increasing affluence was a given, virtually at all levels, over the past generation. Aspirations for one's children were based on a constantly evolving society in which all ships rose with the rising tide of the good economy and Korea's more prominent place on the world scene. Even politics were improving as elections became more meaningful, and society in general was felt to be more stable even if class mobility was on the increase.

But the financial crisis has changed all that. Yes, a small group of the moneyed class and the nouveau riche still maintain their financial status, even if it buys less in imported products. But financial change coincided with political change, or some would argue the former caused the latter. But both together have produced consternation in some circles. After all, politics was considered to be predictable; for an indefinite future the "ins" were supposed to remain "ins" even if the leader had to change. We may remember that the formation of the Democratic Liberal Party in 1990 was specifically designed to emulate the longevity of the Japanese Liberal Democratic Party—both proved to be ephemeral in keeping their parties in power.

We know that the economic crisis has devastated the middle class, whose futures now seem as uncertain as they had previously appeared to be fixed on an upward trajectory. Politics is now as fluid as economics, and they reinforce each other. But now the anticipated future will not be the same as it once seemed, and living with the uncertainties of life will be an added burden. Even if we are assigned to a lower circle of hell we will want to try and find and predict a secure path through the uncertainties of the future.

October 1998

On Retirement—The "Slippered Years"

This felicitous phrase of the Victorian Anthony Trollope evokes images of the elderly gentleman padding around his home without shoes, not needing or wanting to get properly dressed—perhaps enmeshed in a bathrobe to accompany his slippers, dependent on his re-maining family, and not willing to encounter the external world as a participant. In Western societies the scene is often real, but it is usu-ally one in what we may euphemistically call "advanced retirement," as if it were part of life's curriculum. Others would call it old age, oth-ers awaiting death.

This is not only a Victorian attitude. At one recent U.S. govern-ment-sponsored retirement seminar, a consultant discussed the sav-ing accruing to the retired. For example, he said, there is less need for dressy clothes after one stops going to work. Some would say, on the contrary, that the older one gets, the better and more carefully dressed one ought to be to compensate for the desiccations of age.

Retirement in the United States often creates the opportunity to en-gage in a second career, sometimes quite removed from the vocation of one's life. There are then those who prefer to volunteer their ser-vices to community and social or civic groups. One cousin read to the blind; one friend volunteered to help organize local nonprofit groups, and another helped publish a UN-related newsletter.

At whatever age one retires, there are some today who picture life differently. In the United States, some want to move to warmth, per-haps to make up for the cold of aging, so they go to Florida, Arizona, or southern California. They plan to go fishing, play golf, garden, or perhaps just watch television. Some close to family want to spend time with grandchildren.

In Korea, retiring to where the family is seems to be important. Al-though apartment living does not often allow the extended family to live together as they once did, many Koreans pick their apartment lo-cations to be near their children. I have not met many Koreans who come from rural areas who want to retire to a simple rural life. Per-haps Kim Ock-gil, former president of Ewha, was an exception when she moved from Seoul to the provinces. No one I know has moved to Cheju to be warmer. It may be too removed from the mainstream, and perhaps there are psychological remnants of it as a Chosun Dynasty place of exile. It is nice for a honeymoon, some might say, but I wouldn't want to live there. When Koreans go to Los Angeles, it is not for the climate, but for jobs or the children's education. Also, when one retires, one has more time and thus needs more friends.

I sense no movement to escape the urban problems of Seoul by moving out. Many Thai now want to retire in Chiangmai and even

Chiangrai, once very remote, to escape the urban degradation of Bangkok. But perhaps Seoul, like Paris, is too much the hub for people to want to live anywhere else and give up the excitement of the metropolis, if once one has lived here.

Although Koreans are proud of their *kohyang*, or hometowns, they seem to go back for *chusok* (the Korean harvest festival or the equivalent of the U.S. Thanksgiving) or perhaps the Lunar New Year, but not to live. There is a strong nostalgia for and perhaps a filtered, idealized memory of rural life that might be destroyed by continuously living without the amenities of urban dwelling even with all of its attendant problems.

When Koreans retire from a university or government service, in contrast to Americans, they seem to undertake positions only if they are in the same field to maintain their prestige. So a professor might establish a new research institute that will allow him or her to pursue an individualized intellectual bent, while a former public official might become an advisor to a company or a ministry. People seem to want institutional attachments, even if self-created, and ones that continue to reflect their exalted status.

The exception to this pattern is in the military, where officers generally retire when young. Many in the past have become consultants or advisors to major corporations. This is not because they know the business or industry, but rather because through the years of military government and influence, a retired professional military man would naturally have extensive contacts with other military figures from the Military Academy or individual units. With the importance of individual, personal relationships for effective operations in Korea, these individuals often play critical intermediate roles in enabling industry to work effectively. Foreign firms have also employed these people in advisory positions. What will happen with the eclipse of the military in public life is an interesting question. Of course, in the United States, military and government officials often become consultants when they retire, but the law prohibits them from negotiating with the government on contracts for a number of years. U.S. law may be too loosely worded, for the intent is often subverted through evasion.

In Korea, the real problem may be with the cabinet. The shelf life of a minister in Korea is very short—perhaps about a year. We are now into our fifth prime minister in the Kim Young Sam administration, and cabinet reshuffles seem to be the fashion. It is akin to performing magic—it transforms perceptions, or so it is believed. Real power, however, lies in the strong presidential system.

Although there is enormous depth of talent in Korea, the rapid change of cabinet members strikes the outside observer as a waste of talent. What do former ministers do when they are retired? Few can go back to teaching, if that was their original profession, as universities seem reluctant to rehire them, and their positions have been filled. Some may go into politics and run for the National Assembly. Some establish their own institutes to attempt to continue to play policy roles.

Part of the problem seems to be that one administration does not want to employ persons, however talented, who were closely associated with a previous administration. This is different from the problem in the United States, where a few manage to bridge the divide between Republican and Democratic administrations. The issue in Korea is not party, because loyalties are personal in nature, but persons who are identified with the entourage of a national leader by working for that administration.

But in Korea and the United States, and in many other countries as well, finding effective roles for those who retire will become more important. They are a resource useful to the society, and often underutilized. They have experience and perspective, as well as training and skills, and it would be a loss if they were not effectively used. In Korea, it is possible that their roles may be more effective than in the United States, as age here is given more respect.

I personally have retired several times already—and hope I have a couple of more opportunities to do the same. Not for me the "slippered years."

February 1996

On Buddhism and Violence

There are two kinds of professors who study religion: those who specialize in the classical texts that were or became the fundamental core of the philosophical basis of a group and the essential sources of doctrine, and those who explore the place of a particular religion in its sociopolitical, economic, and cultural setting. When one crosses the disciplinary line and interprets the texts as influencing modern behavior, or uses contemporary standards to reinterpret classical texts, there are often problems.

The difference between each approach is profound. When we turn to the Hindu Vedas, the Koran, the Old or New Testaments, or the various Buddhist scriptures we may arrive at conclusions that are totally at variance from those reached by societal specialists who see the practical evolution of the ideals and ideas of an earlier period. The rise of capitalism in Europe, the Crusades, and the Inquisition are not to be found in the Sermon on the Mount (did the meek inherit the earth?), nor is the violence associated with the takeover of the Chogye Temple in Seoul in the Buddhist scriptures. Although it may be important intellectually to cross both time and disciplines to understand fully religious beliefs, it may be disconcerting. A Western professor of Buddhism who specialized in texts on first traveling in Burma is said to have cried a great deal of the time because the popular Buddhism so evident and vital there had so little to do with the ideal.

The other-worldly aspects of Buddhism are well known. The goal is to seek nirvana, the release from endless reincarnations and thus the suffering associated with human attachments, either through one's own self-discipline, as in the Hinayana (Theravada) school of Buddhism practiced in Southeast Asia, or also through the intervention of "saints" (Bodhisattvas), as in the Mahayana school, which is the Buddhism of Northeast Asia, including Korea.

But this other-worldly ideology has misguided observers as to the reality of how Buddhism (as indeed have all major religions) has become secularized in the contemporary era. Buddhism was, and is, a political force, and one involved with the very mundane aspects of control over wealth and power, as the dispute over control of the extensive assets of the Chogye Temple in Seoul so vividly illustrates.

Buddhist monks have led violent demonstrations against Muslims in Burma, were critical forces in the nationalist, anticolonial activities under British rule, and some have been in revolt against the military. They have been involved in assassinations in Sri Lanka, and in Korea in the classical period there were "warrior monks." Monks were also engaged in violent activities in Japan, and these are but a few illustrations.

The ideals of Buddhism are noble, and have been of great appeal to the intellectuals of many different societies because they represent a purity of principle that in a confused world has great meaning. True, Americans in particular, perhaps because we seem to prefer instant solutions to complex problems of any kind, have made Zen Buddhism something of a fad, corrupting and shortening the discipline required in Zen to attain the instant revelation of truth that in that sect is a product of long and arduous thought and practice.

Korea is experiencing a burst of religiosity. Most obvious to foreigners has been the growth of Christianity, which in Korea means Protestantism, making Korea the world's premier country in the rate of expansion of that belief. The multitude of churches all over Korea, and not just in Seoul or other major cities where the lit red crosses on myriad steeples dot the night landscape attest to this expansion, which has carried over to Koreans in the United States where churches are the prime organizing focus of the overseas Korean community life.

But this explosion of religion has not been limited to Christianity. Buddhism has also expanded, and donations to the Buddhist temples and sects, of which there are said to be eighteen in Korea, with the Chogye sect by far the largest with some 10 million adherents, has been extensive. The control of the assets of temples and activities are a major financial attraction and source of temporal power to some within the Buddhist community. As one travels around Korea, the amount of temple renovation and building is remarkable. Whether this continues in the wake of the financial crisis is a question, but especially in times of social and economic turmoil and uncertainty, a return to religion is often evident, and Korea and all religions are no exceptions.

Having spent many years in Theravada Buddhist countries, I admire the discipline of the proper monks there who did not marry, abstained from food after noon, did not eat meat, avoided liquor, and were not supposed to be involved in even the handling of money (although in the modern world this is increasingly difficult). To see them early in the morning, at dawn, walking often as a group in single file with bowed heads through the streets or villages offering the opportunity for others to make merit by providing food to them is a profoundly symbolic sight. Westerners call this "begging," but that is incorrect—the monks are providing a religious service to the people, and rarely eat the food so provided.

Monks marrying, as in Korea, and engaging in wholly secular lives is thus disconcerting. Some say this was a product of Syngman Rhee's lack of Buddhist insight. I attended an elegant dinner party in

Seoul at which a monk ate well, drank scotch, and ended the meal with a fine brandy; to me it seemed to corrupt all the principles on which Buddhism rested. Monks riding in the most luxurious cars and eating at fine restaurants are common sights in Seoul.

To see the recent violence associated with the control of the Chogye Temple in Seoul, and reported internationally by various television networks, is disheartening. Greed and the struggle for power are just what Buddhism tries to overcome among its believers. How tragic that those who profess to lead in this beautiful religion should so corrupt its ideals. And, by mixing the classic texts with modern conflicts, I am guilty of combining the ancient and modern, and although I may not cry like my professor friend in Burma, I feel a profound sense of loss.

January 1998

On a Liminal Society

In a sense we are all liminal people. We stand on the thresholds of new eras, whatever age we may be. These eras may be personal—a wedding, a funeral, the onset of a new educational or occupational experience, the preparation for our own inevitable mortality.

There are those that are institutional as well. Organizations for which we work or on which we depend for some goods or services are in constant flux—on the edge of some new need. Change is one of the few things on which we can rely, so organizations that cannot adapt to the liminal needs of new times will suffer, and most probably wither away. But people react differently to needs than do organizations.

But eras and times change, and thus whether we like it or not we are all liminal—living on the edge of some development that will probably profoundly affect our lives. For some it is the information age or globalization, or in some countries urbanization, to mention just a few of the many forces that oblige us to react to change.

Being a liminal person—on the verge of a major transition, let alone multiple transitions, is disquieting. The memories of our past, especially those pleasant, whether they be of people, events, places, or occasions, are disrupted. We want to return to where the events are clear and distinct, where the outcome is predetermined, where assurance is affirmed, and where our role was positive or benign. This is true in societies as in people, and where we may unconsciously shade and color our memories to create for ourselves our personally appealing versions of our own history, so societies also create from fact their mythic histories, and then train new generations in these myths to perpetuate the mixed reality and illusions of the past.

Korea is a particularly powerful example of a liminal society. Few countries in the world have changed in so many ways so quickly. The catalogue of changes within the mature lifetime of those still alive would be voluminous. To an outsider, these changes have come so rapidly that the psychological adjustment to them must have been difficult. It is perhaps the essential unity of the Korean people, where ethnicity and language and culture are intertwined in a single group—a virtual national family as the Chinese characters so indicate, that has made these transitions, even those that have occurred with trauma, to have been undertaken without sundering the society.

Yet the ferment is continuous, and the pace of change may increase. Globalization creates internal strains in adjusting to a Korea in which Korean goods and services are competing against the world, and sometimes initially not very successfully, where once they were carefully protected to the psychological advantage of many, the profits of a relatively few, but at high cost to everyone in terms both of innovation and expenses.

The new era of liminality, to coin a word, will increase the pace of change. It is not simply that a wider spectrum of Koreans can go abroad, picking and choosing where they want to go and what they want to see, but that back in Korea the forces intruding on their lives will be ever greater. Their products will change, the way they receive services may differ, the roles played by their local and national governments may alter, and their social relations may be transformed. In the accumulative influences of all of these events profound senses of disquiet may be unleashed that any single change would not make.

What will happen when unification comes, whenever that may take place? We are continuously on the lumen of unification, and for years we have discussed, argued, analyzed, prayed, and held seminars on this subject. Yet each change seems to bring us a modicum closer to the possibility, and however it may take place, and whenever it may happen, it seems virtually a historical necessity.

When such an event happens, even if it is later rather than sooner, it will create anxieties with which the society will have to deal. And those will not be easy times.

At those times, societies and individuals will search back to strengthen and, if they do not exist in sufficiently clear form, create myths that will enable the society to cope with profound change. This will likely take the form of heightened nationalism, which can be both productive and destructive. This need not only be official, but society will demand, perhaps unconsciously, these reinvented forms.

We can see the process today. The stress on Korean traditional holidays and customs that were a generation earlier decried or ignored in official circles are now being rediscovered by official agencies of the government. This may be a good thing, for the tendency to disregard the customs of the past loosens social moorings that need to be retightened.

To recognize that we are on the edge of change is to begin to cope with change. And it is this that one hopes will occur in Korea.

April 1997

On *Myongbun*

Myongbun seems to be an important concept in Korea. People tell me it is used continuously in a variety of contexts, and people invoke it for a number of complex purposes. The Korean dictionary is only partly helpful. It indicates that it means "decent behavioral limitations that one must observe morally; one's duty; justification; ostensible reason; plausible excuse." The problem for a foreigner is that this definition contains elements that are antithetical in some foreign cultures. In the United States, in any case, one's moral duty is often in conflict with one's plausible excuse or ostensible reason. We do not seem to have a word in English that encompasses both.

Sometimes the word seems to be used in a public relations sense: "What kind of a *myongbun* can we use to justify or explain that action?" people say. In this case, one is trying to cover over with a moral patina an inappropriate or selfish action that would provoke public rancor. The American would interpret this as a "spin" or a twist on reality to present a picture to your advantage. This is often performed by a "spin doctor" (a public relations specialist), usually in the employ of politicians or parties, who attempt to find a publicly acceptable rationale for something that was patently different in motivation or just silly or inept. We would be wrong to so translate the term as *myongbun*, because "spin" implies plausibility, but not necessarily moral justification, and is often at odds with a balanced appraisal of the situation. *Myongbun* must imply a larger good, something that relates morally to the society and not just the individual.

So a party or a politician using *myongbun* would appeal to some sort of social benefits derived from it. In an individual, it would imply altruism in some manner in society or national purpose. The story told me was of a Korean who could not stand his job, but could not leave by just telling his supervisor (as an American might), "I hate this job so I am quitting." That would destroy the credibility of the supervisor as well as that of the employee—a "lose-lose" situation. He would rather find the right opportunity, and then approach his superior and say that he feels it is moral duty to give his junior employees a chance at this position, and thus he will resign. The boss is not fooled, but everyone acts with grace and in the broader public good. It is, publicly, a "win-win" situation. If a child retaliates and harms someone who has injured the child's parents, this is *myongbun* justified in a society where filial piety is deeply ingrained. One senior Korean was recently offered an important overseas post he did not want to accept, and could only refuse it on the basis he could not leave behind or take with him his aged mother. General Kim Chang-soe turned down a politically dangerous position in the Yi Dynasty on the basis of his parents' needs.

Some say that Korea's dealings with Japan are a kind of *myongbun*, because Korea is demanding that the Japanese apologize and take moral responsibility for acts committed during the colonial period. There is a moral, national indignation in Korea's position in relation to any Japanese issue. In a sense, North Korea's consistent use of the term *juche*, self-reliance or autonomy, in its explanations of foreign affairs, is a form of *myongbun* because the very term to North Koreans is supposed to conjure up moral and even religious awe, although the outside world would not agree. At a national level, the United States may use its equivalent concept in some foreign policy situations because public morality is important to the people, whatever the facts. So the United States went to war in the Persian Gulf to prevent aggression rather than to ensure oil supplies.

In a sense, then, *myongbun* serves two important purposes in Korean society. It clearly indicates a concern over face, or a socially acceptable situation with which no one can find moral fault. Koreans, I would argue, are more concerned about everyone's face if they are in-

volved in a delicate situation, while an American would be more concerned about individual face, although face is important in both societies although Americans sometimes prefer not to use that term.

The second point is that *myongbun* implies the collective, both
from the face-saving viewpoint, but more importantly in terms of social unity. One must appeal to the broader, social, collective "*uri*-ism"
or "we-ism" by which Koreans relate to each other even if they are involved in factional disputes. The ultimate *myongbun*, or moral justification, involves the whole Korean people.

We recognize that there is a sense of public social decency and ethics that must be preserved in Korea even if individual acts may be
selfish or despicable. Overall, even though such explanations may be
manipulative, they maintain the fiction of a social good. The political
sophistication of the Koreans is both broad and deep, even if for much
of modern history it has been unable to be expressed. I think most Koreans would recognize the public relations nature of *myongbun*, but
the fact that the term continues in popularity and is transparent socially even as it is designed to be socially opaque speaks well for this
aspect of society.

Americans demand candor and brutal honesty, which I believe are
virtues. But this is often a product of youth and idealism, not bad
things when the implications of right and wrong are clear and distinct.
As one ages, perhaps the grey areas and ambiguities seem to grow. So
there are occasions when the social veneer is important, and bluntness
will destroy more than it achieves.* The fact that the public good must
be invoked even in personal cases of *myongbun* is a good thing. Is that
in itself a case of *myongbun*?

July 1996

On "Roasts" and "Face"

When someone senior retires or leaves a job, that person's colleagues
often have a party in which the person is "roasted." That is, the person
is on the "hot seat" (is uncomfortable), as the Americans say. He or
she is subjected to good-humored discussion or even skits concerning

---

*   In 2001, President Bush's condemnation of the North Korean regime
as "evil" no doubt reflected his strongly held beliefs, but in negotiations Koreans often demand *Myongbun*–and this was lacking.

his or her interests or likes or particular quirks of personality. Sometimes a satirical piece is written for the event, and old tunes may be exhumed and filled with new, satirical words about that person. Often the person will join in the fun and lampoon himself. This also happens at a national level when the White House correspondents get together to have an annual satirization of the president and his administration, in which the president participates, often making fun of his own foibles.

This poking of fun at people in positions of some authority by those subordinate to that person or who have been in some manner colleagues or associates seems to be a particularly strange American custom. This is different from the political cartoonists or satirists who write or draw for the press, because there has been no intimate and continuing association between the subject and the writer in contrast to those around the one "roasted."

The need for humor and levity seems essential in American society to ease the tensions associated with emotional relationships, either personal or institutional. Even at funerals we will often speak fondly of the humorously touching incidents in the deceased's life even as we solemnly pray for his departed soul. Even President Nixon, probably the least approachable and entertaining of recent American presidents, recognized this trait in the American character and appeared on the television program "Laugh-In" in which he had a cameo performance in a skit entitled "Sock It To Me." Americans, including their leaders, somehow expect not to be taken seriously all the time.

This seems a remarkably strange custom, especially when contrasted with Korean practices. The American usage on the surface seems to deprive the person of "face"—of respect for accomplishments, status, age, or position. Yet Americans as a nation, in institutional settings, and personally also have a strong regard for face. We seem to believe that face in American society is somehow increased by participating in such fun and games, because to do so demonstrates that you are a "regular fellow" and a good guy. In a sense it helps support the egalitarian ideals of American society however much they may be lost in actuality. We are all equal at such moments no matter what the social and financial gaps. If one is too serious, that is a political drawback. Vice President Gore's political campaign suffered because he was viewed by the public as too serious and wooden no matter how knowledgeable he may have been.

In Korean society, however, the situation is quite different. When one reaches senior status in age or position, one is expected to act with the demeanor associated with such elevated dignity, and not to have that position questioned publicly, even in jest. We often see senior people assume the deportment and manner that accompanies elevated standing in the community. Of course, close friends can joke about personal traits with each other, but this is usually done in private or in a small inner circle. And when one goes drinking, then all the rules change and under the guise of being drunk one can say things that otherwise would be inappropriate. In Korea and Japan, getting drunk is a release and one is not held responsible for the remarks or actions of that time. In the United States, however, getting drunk often provokes remorse for having said the wrong thing or having acted inappropriately, in addition to the puritanism associated with being drunk itself. Some say that American youth have no such regrets, but it is evident among those more mature. The American sense of guilt and of the need to be in control of one's emotions and life probably contribute to the need for a release through the "roasting" process when the heat is turned up.

Most of us would find it incomprehensible if the Korean press together with Blue House staff and the president himself were to gather together for an evening of iconoclastic and sometime fairly ribald fun. Comradery would rather be expressed, were such an event ever to happen, through the singing of songs, but not satirical ones made up for the occasion. At the summit meeting in Pyongyang, the singing of the unification song was an informal and poignant event, indicating a warming of relationships, but certainly not a roasting in which the heat is increased.

Korean friends, whom I have known from their early maturity, in public act appropriate to their age after their *hwan-gap* (sixtieth birthday). Their demeanor becomes more serious, their walk somewhat more deliberate, and the aura that surrounds them exudes authority. It would almost be sacrilegious to break up such a manner by levity.

All this means simply that the societies are different, and any attempt to transpose one into the other would likely make everyone extremely uncomfortable. It is when one crosses cultures that these differences become evident. Senior Americans may be charged by Koreans with acting in a juvenile manner, while Americans may believe that senior Koreans act officiously. If these are the worst of our inter-cultural problems, we probably are in reasonably good shape.

October 2000

On the Rule of (Only Observed) Law

Bishop Berkeley (1685-1753), the Irish philosopher, asked it first: if a tree falls in the forest, and there is no one there to hear it, does it make a sound? This caused considerable debate in intellectual circles at the time, because it is impossible to prove either conclusion. It is, however, not simply idle speculation.

I thought of this very early one Sunday morning when I was driving in Seoul. I was following another car, and there were only the two of us in the vicinity, in itself a rare occasion. The other automobile successively ran through four red lights at crossstreets and pedestrian intersections because there was no one there (except me—the silent observer of the speeding parade) to notice.

As an analogue to Bishop Berkeley, I wondered whether in Korea people obey the law even if there is no one around to observe them? It seems evident that they do not, at least in traffic, if no one is there to enforce the rules. If they do not obey the regulations in traffic, may we draw conclusions from this for the society more broadly? What about obeying other laws?

I read somewhere that a foreigner asked an American whether he always stopped at stop signs and red lights even when no one was about. When the reply came back, "almost always," the foreigner remarked that Americans must really believe in the rule of law, for the law was there to be observed even if there were no observers. I am not as sanguine about Americans as I would like to be in this case, but the story has the ring of general truth. That is not to deny the prevalence of crime in the United States.

I was struck some years ago reading an academic study of the business sector in Korea under Syngman Rhee and under Park Chung Hee. Under Rhee, according to those Korean businessmen interviewed, enforcement of regulations was like the Korean proverb—"three days cold and four days warm," indicating that regulations were enforced for a period, and then laxness set in, and business could get away with evading the rules. This, they said, was not true under President Park.

We seem to be in the "warm" period now, where traffic rules are not enforced, and observable traffic violations on any one trip are too numerous to count, even when the traffic police are in view.

The questions I have are not primarily about traffic in this essay, but about the concept of law more broadly. The West talks about the "Rule of Law," preferably in capital letters to indicate its importance and universality. But this is a mistaken concept when generally applied. True, there is a rule of law where law is essentially the codification of social norms and/or aspirations, is impersonal, and is uniform and predictable. There is a continuity of legal tradition in Europe, which is lacking elsewhere.

In many societies, indigenous law was supplanted by foreign religious law (Islamic, Buddhist, Christian, etc.), and then colonial law, and now international law—the legal tradition was less strong because it was discontinuous. Law is often used to oppress or justify or perpetuate inequalities in all countries. The law is ignored both because people feel they can get away in doing so, and when such laws are promulgated or enforced by regimes that are considered as illegitimate. So breaking the law under Japanese colonial rule could be considered a nationalist act in Korea. Circumventing the regulations under dictatorships could be thought of as espousing democracy.

Where law is limited in any of these categories, then law is disregarded or flouted whenever there is no one around to monitor or enforce it. This essentially says, in other words, "I obey the law when it is in my interests and I want to." Under these circumstances, the resulting myriad interpretations of law lead to chaos.

In most societies, rank has at least some privileges, but there is also the expression "noblesse oblige," indicating that rank also has its obligations. One of those obligations is to obey the law. In the United States, when a senior person flaunts his or her power by denigrating or avoiding the rules, that person is subject to far more popular criticism then an ordinary person who does the same thing. Thus, there may be the ideal of equality before the law, but not in the court of public opinion. We tend to forgive the unfortunate lawbreaker if there are mitigating circumstances, such as poverty, deprivation, abuse, etc. Perhaps this is because of the peer jury system, under which people generally tend to want to temper their judgments of others.

In a sense, this is the opposite of what happens in Korea. Having power is often equated with being above the law, and when people evade the rules and are not caught, they appear to feel both lucky and superior. Also, when a high-ranking person here ignores the rules, the people are more apt to be forgiving than, for example, those in the United States. On the other hand, when the upper classes ignore the law here, they are sometimes castigated by the top echelon. Park Chung Hee said that educated people who jaywalk should be punished more severely than those uneducated because they should know better. So much for equality before the law. One Blue House official, when confronted with the fact that a Korean president had broken a law, immediately responded that the law should be changed.

But democracy, whatever else it does mean, does not mean anarchy destructive of social cohesion and civility in traffic or business, or in any other relationship. Those who argue that individualism in making your own traffic or social rules indicates democratic governance miss the point. One may argue whether individualism, or what degree of individualism, is socially desirable or possible in any particular society, and whether human rights should primarily be considered as collective or individual. But for everyone to make his or her own traffic or other regulations indicates attitudes of extreme arrogance, which is the antithesis of democracy. One needs to maintain that just rules need to be obeyed even when no one is watching.

So even when the tree falls and there is no one there to hear it, whether it makes a sound is less important than whether we act as if it did.

May 1996

On Trust

How much trust exists in Korean society? This is a matter of some importance, and the subject of debate because there are scholars who maintain the trust is an essential ingredient in both the democratic political process and economic development.

The argument has been that if civic trust exists—that there is social space between the citizens and the state and that citizens trusting each other for defined purposes can band together for some common concern and petition the government for change—this is an important element of democracy. Thus citizens groups—the nongovernmental organizations—are a force for pluralism in the society as they mitigate the concentration of power in the hands of any central government.

But banding together for some perceived common goal is a kind of social trust for specific purposes. If this trust is absent, then civil society is weak and democracy becomes more fragile. So too trust is essential for economic growth: for internal loyalty within economic organizations, external belief that contracts will be honored, in supplying goods on credit or consignment, and that the state will play by predictable rules of the established game. If trust is absent, then organizations are tenuous and may be built around individuals and not ideas or programs, and factionalism becomes a primary force.

Many foreign academicians would argue that trust is very limited in Korea, while some Korean scholars have disagreed. That some forms of trust exist is not normally disputed. The question is how far does it extend and how deep does it lie. Some conceive of trust as a series of concentric circles radiating out of a center. The primordial trust is the core family, and then beyond it the extended family and the clan. Perhaps then trust extends to one's classmates, first at primary, secondary, and then university, or if one has passed a civil service or foreign service examination, or graduated from the military academy, to those of the same class or year. An examination of coup leadership would point to the validity of at least some of these claims. Certain types of trust rest with one's geographic cohorts, especially it seems in employment and in election matters.

Trust is generated, or attempted to be generated, through the analogy of the family. Governments treat their citizens like a father his children, and indeed this is a millennium-old analogy from the Shilla Dynasty, and is based on Confucian principles as developed in China. Thus one is supposed to trust government as one would trust one's father. In modern social science terms we would say that this is to generate political legitimacy. Many say that big businesses are paternalistic, and so try to engender trust and loyalty on the same basis. Some critics of businesses in Korea claim that they are more like military units than families.

The stage beyond trust is loyalty, and this is a critical element in Korean thinking, in government slogans, and in the general concepts of morality. *Chung* is a vital force in annual government slogans. But that loyalty is generally not interpreted to be loyal to ideals or even institutions. Loyalty, because of the personalization of power, becomes loyalty to an individual and not necessarily to that person's ideas. Thus loyalty to the state is transformed or interpreted as loyalty to, and trust in, the head of state, and disagreement on issues of substance may, and often are, interpreted as personal disloyalty. Thus power becomes even more highly personalized.

Once, years ago, when a new head took over control of an organization, I was asked by one of his subordinates whether I was loyal to the new leader. When I replied that I was loyal to the ideals of the organization, eyebrows were raised. Under such circumstances, one is not to be trusted. In the United States, there are often resignations from government by individuals who may disagree with state policies, but these are usually couched in more nonconfrontational modes—one needs to spend more time with one's family, or there are personal reasons, etc. (indicating the strong individualism in U.S. society, as the reasons for such resignations in Korea or elsewhere might have been stated in the interests of some collective good). Very rarely do we see resignations attributed to blatant disagreement on policies or programs, and I believe it is disquieting that we are not prepared to stand up publicly for ideals. Trust needs to be institutional and ideational, as well as personal.

August 1997

On State-Business Relations and the Dried Squid Sellers

Around the most egregiously compacted traffic jams in Seoul at intersections, where red lights seem as interminable as a consignment to purgatory and green lights are as ephemeral as the pink cherry blossoms of spring, a curious phenomenon occurs. Out of nowhere, like mushrooms springing up in the rainy season, the fuming drivers with *han* (pent up frustration and anger) accumulating exponentially and stomachs growling will note the almost magical appearance of people selling dried squid to those motorists who feel forever doomed to remain stationary until their next incarnation.

The dried squid sellers are perhaps a particular Korean phenomenon, but they symbolize a ubiquitous issue. Whether Seoul traffic is better or worse than other cities is not the point. The sellers live off traffic problems that no doubt were not anticipated even in the best of planning of ring roads and synchronized traffic lights, let alone in the haphazard growth of populations, affluence, and automobiles. The sellers are entrepreneurs, but of a special sort. They have acutely recognized an opportunity and a ready market for a product that they can sell with little investment of funds but with considerable energy and lightness of foot.

These sellers have no interest in urban planners trying to end traffic jams and ensure a smooth flow of vehicles to save time, money, and energy. Rather, if they had a little more community consciousness, they might even form a nongovernmental organization to defend their livelihood with the logo, on the English model for royalty, "itinerant purveyors of fast foods to the elite." That is, they would like to see these traffic problems go forth and multiply, as they say, thus increasing their financial opportunities and expanding their entrepreneurial skills.

The dried squid sellers are a metaphor for those who earn their livings from the misfortunes or needs of others, and who are against reforms because it would break their rice bowls, as the proverb tells us. Their counterparts are prevalent everywhere, but especially in governments at all levels. Low-level and honest bureaucrats turn to the myriad regulations that governments have instituted to protect the citizenry of the state with some, let us assume, potentially beneficial objectives. The explication of these regulations, their exposition and interpretative massaging, the search for nuances and the exploration of loopholes become more than just the satisfaction of inhibited intellects; they are the very marrow of bureaucratic existence.

They say that to open a plant in Korea the approval process takes an average of 530 days and 382 documents through 54 government agencies under 27 legal statues, while in the United States it takes 145 days, 188 days in Taiwan, and 284 days in Japan.

Take away these regulations, smooth the flow of regulatory traffic, make life easier for all those who must less than patiently await bureaucratic pleasure and interpretation, and one has eliminated the position of that no doubt hardworking official.

This assumes the probity of the bureaucrat. But entrepreneurs are not only found in the streets with packages of dried squid in their arms; they are also found behind desks. The regulations await interpretation and those dependent on these rulings become impatient, even if their causes may be just. Impatience, let alone devious plans to circumvent regulations, and these bureaucratic traffic jams then become an explosive mixture that easily lends itself to corruption.

The bureaucratic inbox is filled, and one's application is at the bottom. To move it miraculously to the top, thus speeding the plans to be fulfilled, or the ignoring of the small print of some regulation requiring a license here or an inspection there, has created a new market—a buyer and a seller, so to speak, in which a monopolistic constipation has been formed that only money or favors will allow to burst open.

In another country, before deregulation of import and export regulations, a deputy minister said to me that his Ministry of Trade was "a den of pirates." Each official, interpreting his own special cove of regulations, could extract tolls from all those who passed his way or sink their entrepreneurial ships.

There is a worldwide need to eliminate the regulatory pirate coves, and retrain the dried squid sellers of the bureaucracy. But there is also a need to ensure that the entrepreneurial regulators who prey upon the needs or misfortunes of others do not allow the entrepreneurial regulatees to run rampant, and ignore the social rules of the game. This is a fine line, and where individual actions of government may create inappropriate opportunities for private gain, perhaps the nongovernmental group watchdog organizations could perform a useful role monitoring traffic, thus assisting all in this delicate balancing act of state-business regulations.

July 1996

On Sumptuary Laws and Regulations

Many societies have attempted to force acceptance of codes of dress or consumption to enforce either hierarchical distinctions or frugality on the part of elements of the society. And as authorities have tried to prevent conspicuous consumption, the people have in various subtle and not so subtle ways sought to evade the regulations to demonstrate their social standing in whatever group was important to them.

In medieval Japan, for example, there were regulations that outer garments of individuals at various court levels could only be of certain colors and materials, but the edicts did not mention regulations on the lining of these clothes. So under the austere exterior there flourished the rich, proscribed materials that could be discretely flashed on the proper occasions. Today, with many students in American schools striving for peer social recognition by wearing very expensive clothes and jewelry, resulting in thefts and fights, many schools are prescribing uniforms. Many parents are said to be in favor of such dress codes.

In a modern society, how much should a government at whatever level dictate patterns of consumption? Part of the issue relates to how we conceive of the role of government, and how we regard personal privacy. These are, of course, culturally determined.

The Confucian, or if you prefer, the post-Confucian societies, such as Korea, have a tendency to intrude into private living patterns far more than most modern Western societies (strict Middle Eastern societies interfere far more than Confucian ones—witness the Taliban in Afghanistan, life in Saudi Arabia, or see what orthodox Jews want in the state of Israel). This paternal role of government gives them the unstated authority to do so. This is, however, not a one-sided dictatorial pattern, because the people seem to accept this role of government, and on many occasions seem to welcome its involvement to a degree that many in some Western societies would question. In times of national emergency, however, most governments would exhort their citizens to be thrifty and prudent and supportive of state endeavors, such as rationing or otherwise limiting consumption.

Korea historically has set standards for consumption for at least five hundred years. In the modern period, however, these regulations or hortatory requests to the people have been pronounced. When they come from a high enough level, they have the force of edicts even if the suggestions were originally informal. Since Independence, there have been regulations about how much one can spend on a wedding or on funeral rites or ancestor worship, mixing barley with rice to save rice consumption, sending flowers on certain occasions, and other such regulations. The Family Ritual Law of 1969 was strengthened in 1973, and even as recently as this year there were guidelines on how much a wedding should cost. Buying foreign products of certain types and costs was frowned upon in recent times. The government claimed that these were private moves by concerned citizens, but their origins remain obscure. This had widespread nationalistic appeal, at least among groups that could not afford such items. Western economists decried such antiforeign actions that limited trade, and many did not understand that this was part of a long tradition.

Although I am of the school that wants maximum freedom, I am concerned over the current trend for ostentatious living—the "brand-name society," and conspicuous consumption that is today so evident in Korea. I feel the growing destruction of Korean group solidarity as class and economic status become as important today, and as visible, as they once were in traditional Korea when the *yangban* (gentry) reigned. The potential political implications are profound. However unfortunate shared poverty may have been, it created more group solidarity than income levels that are highly differentiated and that continue to widen.

The World Trade Organization and the OECD entry require that Korea import as freely as it exports, although many sections will open slowly and tentatively. And as we have seen, much of these imports will be luxury goods. So external controls are off, and it is up to the Koreans themselves to deal with their demand for luxuries, both internally and externally derived. One hopes that they can do this without depending on edicts from above.

How Koreans will acculturate to the concept of the new freedoms they have won while coping with the increasing perception of widening income disparities and set their own, social limits on conspicuous spending is an internal matter. Growing class differentiation is an important issue for the future, and one that cannot be ignored for too long without peril to the society.

November 1996

On the Masks of Youth

It is sad to relate, but as I walk down the streets of Seoul I feel I am viewing a new phenomenon—the prevalence of a new form of Korean masked dance or a type of Korean beige geisha with dark lipstick. The Japanese geisha traditionally used extensive makeup to create a white mask that obscured the texture of their faces. Korean young ladies are doing the same, only in some beige or off-white tones.

Whether one is viewing an anchor woman on television, a younger academic teaching at a well-known university, or just young ladies who are shopping downtown, one cannot help but be struck by their makeup. It is pasted on in such quantities that one feels that they have put on a lifelike mask from some masked dance drama or noh or kabuki play. It is the young who seem to do this, and they are the ones who have nothing to hide.

There have been complaints in the Korean press about the growing popularity of imported cosmetics as part of the boom in the sales of luxury goods. Statistics indeed show that the use of cosmetics in Korea is per capita about four times that of other countries, so both foreign and local firms view Korea as a lucrative market. Although others may be able to tell the difference, to me the effects of all cosmetics are virtually alike. It is ironic that one of the purposes of such makeup is to look like no makeup was applied. What concerns me is its indiscriminate use.

Seoul is filled with women whose features are charming, whose skins are porcelain-clear and far more delicate than most Western women, and who are thoroughly fashionable and self-assured. Why do they do this?

I cannot believe they do this to please men, but rather because of some arcane feminine fashion that allows them to attain their own glamorous standards or that gives them some cachet among their peers. As women, I believe, dress more for other women than to please men, so they perhaps put on makeup for some related reason. I am not sure for whom men dress.

The use of makeup has become so widespread a fashion that I hear that middle and high school girls, who are not allowed to use makeup in school, when they go on group field trips with their schoolmates and are away from the rigors of the classroom and parental supervision will put on extensive makeup as well. How young does one start?

What is lost is the bloom of youth—one of its most attractive features. Although growing up in many societies is not without considerable trauma, the freshness of youth, its enthusiasm and vitality, are some of their great assets. As one gets older, one feels this perhaps more, but the vigor of youth, its idealism, its willingness to champion causes they believe are just or desirable, are in conflict with the cosmetic syndrome, as we might call it. For if youth cares more about how they are viewed, can they really be the conscience of society, as they exclaim?

This kind of fashion consciousness worldwide and across genders produces uniformity in dress and styles—the very thing against which many youth wish to rebel. The cosmetic masks that are so prevalent make it difficult to tell these people apart. The maintenance costs of supplying the daily paint must be considerable. We have read in the press that Japanese school girls engage in escort services with much older men so that they can have the funds to buy the fashionable things that they want and that give them peer status. Who pays for all these cosmetic expenses?

Now, boys have their own set of problems, and are as much subject to their own set of peer pressures as girls. They may want certain designer clothes, and their haircuts, even eyeglasses, tend to be of a oneness that is depressingly uniform, so they too are part of a more generalized problem.

In the United States, I used to complain about young people who became blasé too early in life. They had experienced too much, and as a result by the time they were prepared to go to college they had been so indulged by overly anxious parents that they treated life as if it held no interest and they had seen everything. This I felt was deplorable, because youth to me should be exploring and enthusiastic, excited about life, and constantly seeking for new knowledge, rather than feeling that by their late teens they had done everything worth doing.

Do cosmetics mask not only the lovely features of a young woman, but her emotions and her enthusiasms as well? Professional clothes models never seem to smile—they are unreal, perhaps intentionally; they wear another mask—of studied indifference. At least the emotions of Koreans cut through the layers of insulation. It would be so much nicer if the naturalness could be more explicit.

April 1997

On Those Who Deal with Subordinates

Most of us have experienced the haughty manners of bureaucrats who attempt to show their power through magnification of their supposed importance—from some clerk in a local government office to someone whose signature or *tojang* (seal) is required to move a piece of paper to the next rank.

The Chinese, in their usual pithy manner, have an expression for their ilk, and which is also used in Korean: *An ha mu in* (lit: below one's eyes there is no one [worthy of respect], i.e., supposed subordinates are not counted or treated with appropriate dignity). This is a problem of petty bureaucrats and minor administrative dictators. Alas, it is if not universal, then at least widespread across many cultures. Korea and the United States are no exceptions.

Those who suffer working under such local, petty tyrants are subjected to the worst kind of administrative degradation. They are constantly bureaucratically battered, undercut in even minor decisions, and made to feel personally and organizationally insecure. This is an objective assessment of their plight, for indeed they are insecure in relation to their supervisors both psychologically and administratively, and thus in their positions. Those tyrants act similarly to those outside who are regarded as inferior in social or administrative standing, and who are also made to feel insecure.

But in reality it may be the person administering the insults who may be even more insecure. This is reflected in their inability to listen to, let alone consider, alternative views—even those that may be supportive. They tend to micromanage, eliminating even modest inroads on their perceptions of their authority. They tend to consider their organizational functions as a kind of separate fiefdom over which they are the feudal lord or *daimyo*. They often regard their organization as a private preserve on which they can hunt as they choose. Their authority cannot be questioned, even indirectly. They continually assert their title and their privileges. Admirable British "understatement" is not in their genetic structure. If they were to allow debate or questioning, and if they were to delegate even a modicum of authority, they would be even more insecure. Perhaps a subordinate might claim their throne through competence.

In the olden days in some countries the newly crowned king might kill all those who might have otherwise claimed that prize—including half or full brothers. But even the Chinese emperor or the Korean king had the imperial censorate, whose duty it was (sometimes under peril of banishment or even their lives) to tell the king when he was wrong and to uphold traditional morality and social norms.

Such high-ranking individuals fear encroachment on what they regard as their authority. Because they are insecure, they do not want too competent an associate. So if they need assistance, and if their administrative span becomes too broad, then they would more likely pick two mediocre people to assist them rather than one really talented associate. This is a fundamental law concerning the growth of bureaucracies.

We have seen such tyrants operate at a national level, where their rules almost always end in abject failure or violence as they become megalomaniac in their exercise of power, and creating such resentment that they are often eventually overthrown. In the modern world, North Korea, Burma (Myanmar), Nigeria, Zaire, Haiti and other countries at various times have all felt the dire consequences of their rule.

But those petty tyrants often go unnoticed by the outside world. They rule petty kingdoms of no redeeming social value. We can be thankful that their influence span is narrow, although those who must endure their often-expressed wrath and ill temper may not be so sanguine. They cause no national problems, because normally their organizational span and influence are quite limited. But within their insulated universe they are tyrants, harassing their subordinates and acting as if they had sole authority. Yet, socially they are often amiable and even charming. Their education may be excellent. Their cocktail party conversations may even be stimulating. They may have reached their limited bureaucratic acme just because on the surface and away from their desks they appear so "normal," so appropriate to continue the institutional image and its internal culture. They are in a way a "stealth bomb," a hidden missile that can destroy the credibility of an organization by creating such intense damage that it becomes too late to stop the fallout.

We all have seen such people. They operate almost anywhere at the lower levels of the bureaucracy and in organizations where outside controls are rather limited. They are neither Koreans, nor Chinese, nor Americans. But when they operate at the intersections of cultures and are a link between differing, and not well understood, social systems, then their influence can be more detrimental. Those from each culture will tend to assert that the other culture is characterized by this aberration. How many foreigners have encountered an officious bureaucrat in some minor Korean office who insists on his exaggerated authority? How many Koreans have found Americans in a customs office or local government who are the same?

They are plentiful, if not ubiquitous, and the problem is that in the short run they are difficult to escape and there is little recourse to their often inappropriate decisions. But we must guard against them, recognizing that they are lurking everywhere. We must also guard against ourselves, for perhaps they are all of us, and there is the danger.

July 1999

On Aging Historically

When does one begin to feel elderly? There are more subtle indicators than those associated with atrophied bones and creaking joints. And when is one regarded as elderly? This is a different proposition, but not only when one is eligible for "senior citizen" discounts or even when young ladies offer to give up their seats to you on the Seoul subway.

At a recent conference in Korea, I was approached by a younger historian who expressed interest in interviewing me about events in Korea with which I was associated almost half a century earlier. My personal perspective, he thought, would be useful in his research on that period. I was, of course, pleased to have been asked.

Another colleague, who overheard this conversation, remarked with a certain oblique delicacy that I had reached the stage when I was interviewed by historians. This colleague was too discrete to call that a sign of advanced age, but we all knew what she meant. But even assuming that an individual retains acute mental faculties, a multitude of previous incarnations may lead to drawing on selective or romanticized memory. This is as dangerous to historical accuracy as it is a salve to individual egos.

People are prone to want to remember and to share those memories, and a remarkable number are interested in learning about them. We see this in the rise of autobiographies that are both selective and self-serving. The fascination of the reading public, as expressed through egregiously inflated advances from publishers for unbalanced versions of bowdlerized history, is one of the marvels of the age, as is the number of the public who read this drivel.

Now, to capture the past in the present, oral histories have become popular. To talk is easier than to write, and if there is a talented interviewer and sufficient time, much may be learned. This method allows those who have memories to be interviewed to recall their involvement in salient events. These need not be of national or international importance. The proliferation of paper and knowledge has meant that we are swamped in data and views, and many organizations cannot even capture their own history or past, let alone the subtleties of previous decision-making, because of the amount of material. Ironically, because the proliferation of paper has lead to the need to store the vast desiderata of the past in remote locations, much of the past is virtually irretrievable at reasonable cost. So as the technology has developed to solve storage problems and retrieve information, we have essentially lost the capacity to do so. Staff changes in a society, in which employment continuity is ephemeral, procedures shifts, and lost materials mean that organizations that wish to establish their past roles within their sphere and encourage their employees to have a certain historical esprit in their work now turn to those of advanced age to remember via oral history, so important gaps in knowledge may be filled.

Personal reminiscences are important for writing history, for official files often omit the dynamics by which decisions are reached. In the U.S. Department of State, there used to be a saying that the person who writes the cable makes policy, but how that decision is finally reached may not be officially noted but may reveal a great deal about a society, an event, and the personalities involved. This is rarely put on paper. Eminent figures often stipulate that the tape recordings of their memories be sequestered for a number of years until their death or that of those most intimately involved in the drama.

In Korea, the production of institutional histories is common. Often written and published under subsidies from interested parties, these are often glowing accounts of the founder or benefactors of the enterprise. It is also the duty of subordinates to write such accounts. The sale of the volumes is irrelevant. They simply are a means to garner prestige and preserve memory and history, they thus have some limited use if treated with caution. Perhaps the Confucian heritage for honoring the merits of one's ancestors and respect for the written word may also play a role in the proliferation of this phenomenon.

But personal memories are by definition incomplete and may also be confused and partisan. So those who also write history must treat with a certain caution the memories over the decades of even the most astute of observers, and weigh those against other, perhaps equally skewed, views, searching for both balance and truth. One oral history may be insufficient; several may tell an important tale.

So one will continue to be pleased to be asked by others to remember things past, even if it is not "When to the sessions of sweet thought...."

September 2000

On Philanthropy and "Philanthropoids"

The explosion of wealth in Korea has also lead to an explosion of philanthropy (from the Greek "love of mankind"). There are a multitude of nonprofit foundations operating in Korea. These foundations come in all sizes and shapes, and perform good works in a wide range of fields. They run universities, provide scholarships for the needy or the exceptionally talented, they fund health centers and hospitals, provide research funds, and they also support the arts and culture. Some are specialized, such as those related to the field of journalism or the media or that fund art galleries or museums, while others have a broader focus.

The eighty-nine company-sponsored foundations registered with the government had total assets in 1994 of about $1.4 billion alone, not counting other foundations. About 90 percent are located in Seoul, and sixty-six are registered with the Ministry of Education, and eighteen with the Ministry of Health and Welfare.

There are many other foundations as well. They come, as in some other countries, in two varieties: those set up by individuals and businesses that are autonomous of government, and those that are quasi-autonomous funded by government through a ministry or other means. The latter may be called quasi-governmental or quasi-private organizations (they are also called elsewhere 'quangos' (quasi-governmental nongovernmental organizations). In contrast to similar organizations in some other countries, these organizations have their leadership and trustees chosen by some governmental body.

All these foundations have become exceedingly important within Korea and in assisting both the substance and image of Korea and Koreans abroad. The availability of funds to do good works in Korea is thus no longer a problem, even if the individual tax legislation might be revised to encourage small, private donations to foundations.

There are, however, issues associated with their operations. The most basic question is: what should foundations do, beyond good works, however defined, and how do their personnel affect what they do?

In general, and there are obvious exceptions, foundations in Korea do what the government might do if it had the political will or more extensive resources, not what the state will not do. Thus, foundations—both those completely private and those quasi-public— play it very safe. They are adding significant resources to established and proper programs that are no doubt needed in Korea, but these programs are generally neither controversial nor cutting edge. They normally do not test new ideas or engage in innovations beyond what are considered to be acceptable good works. Whether they should be more experimental for the good of society is a question.

Second, most personnel of foundations are not professionals. Foundations everywhere are generally a new field, and especially so in Korea where most corporate foundations were founded after 1976. The leaders and executives may be important and prestigious figures from academia or from the public policy field, or in some cases figures chosen because of political connections. But few leaders of foundations can be regarded as professional foundation staff. This is in part because there are no schools anywhere that teach and no courses that one can take about how to give money away. One can study the various disciplines, or evaluation mechanisms, or the necessary accounting procedures associated with foundations, but not how to provide support in the most effective, timely, sensitive manner that will cause the least destructive impact from the support.

About forty or more years ago, someone made a distinction between foundation staff: there were those who gave away their own money. These people were called "philanthropists," a time-honored word connoting prestige and social conscience. There was also a new breed of executives who gave away, not their money, but other people's money. They were called, jokingly, "philanthrapoids."

Philanthrapoids were "humanoids" doing good by spending other people's monies for socially desirable ends. This was a new profession that has assumed importance in countries that have industrialized, because they have the most money and thus the most foundations. If we were to examine all the OECD countries, for example, we would no doubt find a myriad of them in the member states.

Even if the word "philantrapoids" (of which group I am surely almost a charter member, having spent my life doing just this for public, private, and university organizations) congers up laughter, or at least smiles, they have become exceedingly important. They are the backbone of staff who attempt to link the overall purposes of a foundation to the achievement of its purposes through appropriate activities. They have learned through experience how to take goals and translate them into distinct activities that support the achievement of these goals, and then to monitor the progress and ultimate success or failure of all of these activities.

Korea lacks these individuals. This is in part because the development of foundations in Korea is relatively new, but also because the organizations have not yet perceived the need for these individuals. So staff are rotated, and no doubt good things are done, but they are very much based on traditional needs. Evaluation is rarely built into planning.

There is a link between the conventional operations of foundations that support programs that are good but not innovative and the lack of professional staff. Sometimes it is sufficient for foundations simply to fill gaps that the government at any level cannot support for lack of funds. These are best pursued in emergency situations when rapid mobilization of resources is required to help solve an immediate problem and when the government bureaucracy is cumbersome, or when the government, for policy reasons, may not wish to be involved.

But there is another, more sustained, value to foundations that is not being realized. This is the innovative aspects of doing, not what the state could do, but rather leading the state by creating the path in new, needed directions. Professional staff are more likely to pursue innovative programs than are those who take positions for the prestige involved.

Korea needs to develop a professional cadre of trained foundation "philanthropoids" who will seek to make each appropriate foundation an innovative island that contributes to the solution to the new problems that Korea will inevitably continue to face.

Eventually, as Koreans feel more secure in their world position, one hopes that Korean foundations will expand their operations not only to cover Korea's specialized interests here and abroad, but also the needs of other societies simply because we all are humanoids, and, when we are able, should contribute to human needs beyond those of our own societies.

September 1997

On 386

Those of us who are of a certain age and are computer conversant, if not literate, may remember the era when the term "386" meant, in some arcane technological language, the speed of a certain genre of computers that were at the cutting edge of that technology. We had graduated from the older, slower, 286 machines into the brave new world of the 386s. Speed was with us, and word processing and other programs were designed that required faster and faster machines with more memory.

Since the cutting edge of technology lasts what seems to be a "New York minute," the vernacular that translates into a blinking of an eye since New Yorkers are said to be impatient and hyperactive, it was a very short time before we were into 486 machines. Those too could soon be found in the landfills and trash heaps of urban areas. We have gone through successive generations of machines in very short periods, and although the memory of the machines increases in what seems to be exponential degrees, our memories of the past are lost, littered as are the machines in the landfills of our minds. If we use fruit flies in laboratories to conduct experiments because their generational life is so short, and therefore we can get many generations included in a short period and thus demonstrate genetic change, the computer seems to be the technological equivalent. We have gone far beyond the hundreds of 286, 386, 486s in naming machine types, and now we have progressed beyond Pentium I and Pentium II, and now I see Pentium III in the advertisements. So if we think about 386 at all, it is only the Rip Van Winkles of the present age who have them, or even remember them,

But not so in Korea. There 386 does not have anything to do with computers, because Korean intellectuals seem to have more and better computers than my American academic friends. There, the use of the term "386," although drawing on the computer terminology, has a completely different meaning.

In Korea "386" refers to a generation, and one widely respected in the society. The "3" of 386 stands for the age–the 30's— of those of a certain generation, the "8" means they went to university in the 1980s; while the "6" means that they were born in the 1960s. If in the United States we have the "X" generation, Koreans have the "386" generation.

This is the generation that offers hope for Korea. They are the ones with the most modern education, ones who went through and participated in the move from authoritarianism to political liberalization, those who often were out in the streets in 1987 and earlier, who demanded that government fulfill the promise of Korean society. They also saw the growth of civil society and the mushrooming of citizens' organization banding together to demand of government and society the righting of social wrongs. They are also the ones who had more access to information about the world and Korea's place in it.

That generation is now of an age when they are entering the maturity of leadership roles in their chosen fields, and when they can begin to have an influence on the society. Some Koreans say they are heros to the younger generation, because they had to stand up for ideals and principles and sometimes fight for them, while those younger were born with the political equivalent of a silver spoon in their mouths, as the saying goes, and were handed political liberalization.

It is to this 386 generation that many look to ensure the expansion of pluralism and the deepening of democracy. They are the ones who have the memory, and are in positions to exercise influence, and have the maturity of judgment (in spite of the Korean penchant for the elderly). We hope that they can avoid the excessive displays of wealth and ostentatious living that characterized much of the earlier movement of Korea into industrialized status. Even more importantly, we hope that they will look to Korean politics and demand, as we enter the new millennium, that it move from its traditional malaise into which it has remained, and be reinvigorated with the spirit of service to the people and society, and Korea's place in the world.

October 1999

On the Relativity of Truth

Two letters in the *Korea Times* have pointed out a problem that foreigners have faced in Korean court or police actions. That is, what is truth, and how is it conceived? In some societies it is considered absolute, and in others socially determined. But it is often not so simple; what is true and clear in one sense may be false or obscure in another.

In the United States, when one goes into court one promises to tell "the truth, the whole truth, and nothing but the truth, so help me God" (or so the movies tell us). The implication here is that truth is imposed on society from above with a spiritual justification that, theoretically, society cannot break under penalty of hell or eternal damnation. The actuality may be far from the ideal, yet that ideal is significant and in general respected. It is reinforced by potential perjury charges if violated. I have a nonbelieving lawyer friend who, in court, will not "swear" (implying a higher being), but is prepared to "affirm" the truth.

We have recently seen this breakdown in the United States in the jury system, when jurors seem to have considered a "greater" truth imposed over a lesser one. In the celebrated O.J. Simpson trial, many African-Americans felt that justice, as interpreted as retribution for generations of discrimination and slavery, overlay and was more important than truth about a particular crime, and that even if he were guilty of that crime, he should be found innocent because of the racial discrimination that has existed for so long in the United States. So here, and in many other societies as well, truth is socially derived.

Truth may be absolute in some clear and distinct, often simple, circumstances, but at other times it is far more complex. Consider, for example, the famous movie *Roshomon,* in which each of the principals reaches different conclusions about the same event, and the viewer is intentionally left with ambiguous perceptions. We all avoid the truth in social circumstances, when we do not want to burden a casual acquaintance with our ills when asked how we are. Politeness takes precedence over truth.

In Korea, in the two cases cited in the letters-to-the-editor column, we see examples of relative truth when the issue involves antagonistic relations between a Korean and a foreigner. In one case, a Korean witness testified that a foreigner hit a Korean man first, but then recanted when questioned, saying that she said it because Koreans when threatened had to stick together against outsiders. In the other case, alibis were supplied by people for someone who was positively identified as the criminal, seemingly because the party aggrieved was a foreigner.

When Koreans were pitted against some foreign element, there often has been a strong sense of solidarity among them in spite of a long history of personalized power and factionalism. In the national and historical sense, this has been an important element in the preservation of Korean culture in the face of much more powerful neighbors. Today, however, this seems to be an anachronism in the light of Korea's position economically in the world, and the whole policy of globalization.

What accounts for this residual antiforeign sentiment in crises? Xenophobia seems to me to be a kinder word than racism. In Korea, culture, language, society, ethnicity, and—as the Koreans say—"race" and "blood" are all merged into a single nation-state without significant minority groups. In these unusual circumstances, the "we" and "they" syndrome takes on the tone of a racial argument, although it would more accurately be called an ethnic one.

Those of us who are foreigners and know, respect, and are committed to the well-being of the Korean people recognize that as someone grown up outside the system and different in all of the above categories, we will never be completely accepted in Korean society at large, no matter how much we may be respected and even liked among certain segments of that society with which we have close professional or social relations. We are prepared to accept that, and leave to the ignorant the prejudice that in some circles seems so apparent. But if individually and socially we must rely on the good taste and fairness of individuals, do we have a right to expect that institutionally there will be a measured response, where individuals are treated with a sense of fairness and not subject to discrimination? After all, Korea depends on its external relations for its well-being. We all recognize that there are often linguistic problems in such circumstances, but even more basic is the assumption of universal innocence until proven guilty.

This is not simply a private or individual matter, but affects public policy. There have recently been renegotiations of the U.S.-Korean Status of Forces Agreement (SOFA) dealing with jurisdiction of the Korean authorities and the U.S. military over those accused of being involved in criminal acts. This is a delicate subject, made even more delicate because of the infamous rape case involving U.S. military personnel and a Japanese civilian in Okinawa. The negotiations, which seem to continue endlessly and the details of which are obscure to an outsider, may in part be made more difficult by these cases, which seem not to be rare. The two cases cited above, as reported in the letters, continue to raise questions of how justice and truth are perceived. Even though these did not involve the military, and thus jurisdiction was not relevant, by implication it raises questions about justice when foreigners are involved, and thus which legal system should have jurisdiction, and when.

Foreigners everywhere will unintentionally violate local customs, alas; and local authorities will, also alas, interpret these acts in their own cultural lights. But if we cannot agree on a uniform code of culture and justice, we may need to evolve a uniform code of fairness. The problem is that the very term "fairness" is culturally determined.

January 1997

On the Brand Name Society

Korea seems one of the most brand-conscious of societies. The right names of products, stores, institutions, or even people are enough to encourage Koreans to buy, participate, or become involved. Cost does not seem to be a factor—in fact, the greater the expense, the more the prestige. As Korea has grown more affluent, the trait is even more pronounced, but it is not new. It has important social implications.

Most societies have their elite institutions and products. In England, there is great cachet when a shop can advertise "purveyors of xxx to Her Majesty, etc." A designer label increases sales and adds healthy percentages to both male and female clothing, as any Korean will attest.

Institutional names also carry weight: Oxford and Cambridge in England, the Ivy League in the United States, Todai in Japan, for example. But one wonders whether all the tailors on Savile Row are good, or whether all doctors in Harley Street are the best in their fields. Fifth Avenue has more than its share of poor stores.

In Korea, this brand name syndrome seems to have been carried to extremes. Sometimes it is because the most prestigious is in fact the best, or at least near the top in quality. Seoul National University comes to mind. Sometimes it is sheer ostentation, not quality, that sells. The more expensive, the better. Whether it is golf clubs or wine, it must have the reputation of being the best. One is judged by one's peers, or in Korea by one's peer families. This creates immense psychological burdens. So what one wears or where one goes or how much one has paid becomes especially important. A Seoul National University degree is a license for employment and even marriage opportunities. In the United States, we say that some family is trying "to keep up with the Jones'"—the neighbors. In Korea, it's the Jones' who are trying to keep up with you.

Americans like bargains, and they will buy false Gucci shoes or bags or phoney Rolex watches here or from some itinerant vendor around the corner from Fifth Avenue. But in Korea, the most important market for these transgressions of intellectual property rights is not foreign—it is domestic. One has never seen so many Chanel or Gucci handbags on any other street except in Seoul. This says something about the society and its values. This obsession is a permit to produce forgeries. Perhaps this is a modern, commercial equivalent of the Yi Dynasty concept of *Sadaejuui*, or "serving the great"—paying intellectual obeisance to China. Today it is to your favorite couturier.

One not only pays more for a brand name, but one seems to want to pay more to prove the prestige. Why else does Placido Domingo get several times more for appearing in Korea than anywhere else? If one goes to a restaurant, the host will rarely order *majuang* (Korean) wine. I suppose the ultimate "brand name" in Korean national prestige until now was the Olympics itself; the World Cup may take its place in a few years.

One buys a product one trusts, and thus the brand name is the means by which you can efficiently shop. So if foreign brand names have class, it is not only a matter of prestige, it may also be that there is a lingering mistrust of the quality of some locally made product. In fact, one might argue that it is the Koreans who mistrust their own products more than foreigners. This has serious implications.

Many Americans will buy products from mail-order concerns, where they only know the item they wish to purchase from a picture in a catalogue, but they trust the company for quality and to refund their money should there be any problem. Perhaps one reason why mail order is just beginning in Korea is because of this lack of trust. They say this is changing with credit cards, but Korean credit cards offer no credit—they are a means of instant verification of a debit. The user is not trusted to pay later, in spite of a national identity card system that should make escape exceedingly difficult. Why else is it virtually impossible for the ordinary citizen to open a personal checking account? Perhaps businesses, which do have such accounts, have name brand value, but people do not.

But in another sense people do have such status. If we take the concept of "brand" and extend it, we could say that certain Korean families and clans have very good "brand recognition." So to marry a child into one of these families is considered proper and appropriate.

Quality brands are important—for international recognition, for national pride, and for further trade. In the beginning of the export drive, exported products did not carry the name of the Korean manufacturer. They now do so proudly, and that is both domestic and international progress. But the future of the small business in Korea and the role of the conscientious producer who lacks name recognition need to be considered.

Too great a focus on expensive and obvious brand names creates social pressures—envy of those who ostentatiously display their wealth, as we have seen in some crimes committed last fall,[*] and psy-

---

[*]   A gang murdered a person on the basis of economic envy because she has the largest charge account at a fashionable department store.

chological stress on those who cannot compete but who are relatively successful in their fields. A couple of years ago the Korean Government was accused by the United States of keeping out luxury imports. The fundamental issue may not be imports, but all luxury items — what is the luxury associated with the brand name fixation doing to Korean society, and what implications does it have for the Korean political process? Is Korea unconsciously recreating the hierarchical class differentiation based on displays of wealth that was traditional in lineage? Let us buy for quality and associate for excellence. But let us do so for reasons inherent in our tasks or interests, and not because we flaunt our wealth so our neighbors will be impressed.

October 1995

On Aging in Korean Society

According to my trusty *Economist* diary, September 15 is a holiday in Japan—"Respect for the Aged Day." If one looks at the politics in Japan over the past decades, every day seems to fall into that category. Being a member of the geriatric generation has been an important qualification for political leadership. Although the average age of politicians in Korea seems almost a decade younger than those in Japan, aside from the special case of Syngman Rhee, there are calls for a new generation of political leadership here.

There has been great veneration for the aged in Korea as well, although there is no special holiday honoring them. Koreans bow and wish good luck to their elders at the New Year, and on other occasions. In turn, elders are expected to be benevolent, wise, and generous. They have some practical advantages as well. There are sometimes discounts for the elderly when purchasing some kinds of tickets. When I went to Hahoe Village in North Kyongsang Province two months ago, the young man giving me my discounted ticket remarked in his eloquent, if broken, English that in Korean culture they respected the elderly.

The older I get in Korea, the more people seem to give me public respect. As I still get up to give my seat to a lady on the subway—a vestige of my early training—I find in Korea people offering me their seats instead. I am called "haraboji" (grandfather) sometimes, and although I know it is meant kindly and almost as an honorific title, it gives me pause, as I do not consider myself to be decrepit.

But some Koreans say that perhaps I am mistaken, and that I get preference not simply because I am older, but because I am a foreigner as well. Koreans, they go on, today esteem the elderly in their own family or among their friends and their social circle or foreigners, but much less so in society as a whole. That traditional virtue, they say regretfully, is past.

There is some alienation on both sides of the generational equation. If the aged generally are honored less, they are also less able to participate in the almost kaleidoscopic changes that rapid growth and modernization have brought. Their frustration is understandable.

In fact, some Korean critics of their own society claim that it is not the elderly alone who are denied respect, but Koreans treat other Koreans outside of their own particular circles with great indifference and even contempt. It is not, they argue, a matter of age, but a general, society-wide denial of *in,* or "human heartedness."

Still, Korea is a better society for the elderly. If the United States is an easier place in which to live longer because of the quality of medicine, it is a difficult country in which to grow old. It is a youth culture, as many have remarked, where the elderly are marginalized, effectively consigned to the "sunbelt" resorts where they have developed some localized political power. Although manufacturers and advertising agencies have discovered a large elderly market in the United States, and strong national lobbying groups protect the perquisites of the aged, the culture calls for what is young and new. Age itself garners no respect as the old are neither deemed wiser nor productive and are considered passé. With families highly mobile, dispersed, and unable (or unwilling) to care for the older generation, the symbol of aging is the old age home—a sad, lonely, and sorry commentary on the society.

In Korea, the elderly act their respected parts. I have walked in Korean rural areas with an eminent Korean agricultural economics professor of exactly my age. He approached the villages with a mien and gait suggesting dignity and accomplishments befitting his age and status. His step was measured, his attitude kindly but knowledgeable. He knew his role as he had known villages all his life. He was the Confucian gentleman reflecting the poise in his secure social standing.

I, on the other hand, strolled in with the nonchalance of the American youth, browsing in rice paddies, curious about a house or two, tripping over a farm implement here, a low fence there, perhaps unconsciously reflecting the youth culture from which I have sprung. I was inquisitive, but not dignified.

But Korea is a youthful society. When one goes to Myongdong or Taehakno, one hardly sees an older person. Vibrant youth fill these areas. Although the aged proportion of the population is increasing, there seem to be whole sections of the city given over to youth. As I sit in my car waiting for a light to change at Chongno, I count those crossing the street at the cross walk, and almost all are young. The older men seem segregated in Pagoda Park.

But as Korea has become urbanized and industrialized, and as birth rates fall, the society as a whole is aging. An increasingly larger percentage of the elderly can no longer live with children in small apartments, and indeed a growing percentage cannot rely on their children for financial support. Until recently, a son was the family's social security; traditionally, a son who passed the examination system was the family's means for continued social status and prestige.

There are both differences and similarities in the activities of the youth and aged in Korean and American societies. If one goes to a museum or an art gallery in both countries, there will be a representative group of both ages. But if one goes to a classical music concert in the United States, the audience will largely be the elderly. If one goes to a similar concert in Korea, however, the audience will generally be composed of the young. In the United States it does not seem to be a question of money or leisure, for rock concerts are more expensive. In Korea, concerts cost as much, and often more, although many of the young go free. In the United States, the older groups may have been more exposed to that art form, while in Korea it may be youth who appreciate it.

Although incomes have risen and aspects of city life are more comfortable, there are many urban problems that threaten the quality of Korean life. But still for the elderly, at least for now, life is better here than in many other societies. So many Koreans abroad not only want to come home to be buried, but to live their last years remembering what life was like for the elderly when they were young. They may be disappointed now that such respect has diminished, but at least it is still residual here.

October 1995

On Solitaire and Solitude

Lately I have discovered a new element in my computer. My strength, and my weakness, is that I rely on my computer, but essentially I use it for writing, both for business and pleasure. I have become quite adept at word processing, which I first learned on the DOS system, and which, because of familiarity, I am reluctant to change. I am not interested in computer games, but my computer also has a "windows" program, although not of the most modern kind, and on that program I have rather recently found that I can play solitaire, a card game, by definition, for singles.

I don't play cards any more, although when I was a student we would sometimes play for very low stakes, and I found in my primary or middle school days that one could play solitaire. I often did so at that time, but do not remember playing it again until recently.

Card games do not interest me any more, or more accurately do not interest me for more than a few minutes to fill time plagued by ennui. But it started me thinking. Although there are many sophisticated games for those who wish to concentrate in a serious manner on what they are doing, such as bridge, which requires a prodigious memory of everything that went before in the game, or poker, in which bluffing is important (and which tells us a great deal about the societies in which this is popular), we have developed a number of popular card games that are solely for one person. This also says something about that society.

There is one use of cards for the solitary player in both the West and Korea. That is for fortune-telling. So some people, I am told, will look into the cards to see what kind of day they will have, or whether they will meet someone attractive of the opposite sex. But that is a different function than simply passing time alone.

Korean card or other games most often involve more than one person. Two seem especially popular. *Hwatoe* is a card game played vigorously, and *yut*, which has nothing to do with cards, is perhaps the most exciting of family games, and the most physical of this type of indoor sport. Perhaps there are card games in Korea that may be played alone, but I know of none that are really popular. It seems a characteristic of Korean society that fun is always in groups—almost never singularly. Whether one plays cards, drinks, climbs mountains, or does almost anything, Koreans seem to regard it as more fun if there are other people around. If one is alone, then perhaps one is meditating in some Buddhist temple. Otherwise it is *shimshim hada*, or boring. Confucianism, among all major schools of thought, is the ideology of social interaction par excellence, not of other worldliness or contemplating the infinite, whatever that might be.

Although there is a Taoist element emanating from China in traditional Korea, which does tend to place the solitary individual in relation to nature, or at least is so illustrated in classical paintings, it seems less stressed than in China itself. Koreans, I would argue, are social beings.

I have not heard any Koreans call one of their compatriots a "loner"—one who seeks solitude as a good rather than as a state to be endured. We hear the term used in the United States quite frequently, although it often occurs in a somewhat pejorative tone, as when a neighbor comments to the press that such and such an individual, suspected of some crime, was a "loner." While it may not be completely accepted in some communities in the United States, it seems a more common occurrence. That Americans are also social is indicated that solitary confinement in prison is regarded as the worst of punishments.

The writer, the researcher, the artist, and even the felon are essentially loners when they are "engaged in their employment or maturing their felonious little plans," as the Gilbert and Sullivan operetta tells us. Even the reader is so isolated, if not physically then intellectually. But there are few writers and artists, and even readers in some societies are in less supply as television, which can be a group activity, takes over leisure time.

I am in favor of groups and their activities, but I do seek solace in solitude if not solitaire—how else could one write these columns?

June 1996

On "Working without a Net"

The most exciting parts of a circus are the trapeze artists who zoom far above the heads of the viewers and perform all sorts of turns and leaps from rope to rope with grace and obvious daring, sometime alone and sometimes with one or more partners. They make Tarzan swinging from vine to vine in the old movies look positively senile.

The audience is even more excited when, in some instances, the artists perform without a safety net below them to catch them if they fall. They literally in those circumstances do take their lives in their hands with their every movement.

So the safety net has become a protective symbol. We say that the welfare system is a kind of social safety net to help those who cannot manage ordinary living on the tightrope of life, although we may disagree about how wide the mesh should be, and who should and should not be allowed to fall through.

"Working without a net" has thus become a metaphor for living dangerously—taking chances without any fail-safe position. These days we often seem concerned about fail-safe factors in case things don't work out as we planned, but operating without a net creates high tension and drama.

I thought of this when Korea finally won co-sponsorship of the World Cup. The daily reiteration of the prospects of the Cup concerned me. I had been worried for some time, because long ago Korea seemed to have crossed the political and public relations Rubicon concerning the Cup. Here was a society, indeed a whole nation, completely mobilized to win sponsoring it. Virtually everyone seemed involved with pins or stickers; it was in much of the advertising, and in the media in general. I telephoned one high official a month or so before the decision to ask for an appointment, and he said it would be better after the resolution on the World Cup, as he was too busy working on it. I had also spoken with a major figure involved in Cup activities about two months before the decision was due, and I asked him what would happen if Korea did not win the World Cup. He replied that he could not even contemplate that alternative.

Korea is said to be a nation of risk-takers according to foreign observers. This is apparent in many aspects of society. But taking risks is different from being gamblers, as other societies are sometimes known, whether fairly or not is another issue. Gamblers hope for a lucky day or streak of luck even when the odds are vastly against them. They bet; what is involved is sheer fortune or *palja*, but no hard work except to watch the roulette wheel or the dice. Koreans also take great risks, which may be considered a type of gambling, but it is quite apparent they do not simply rely on luck, like picking the right lottery ticket number. Koreans are prepared to work at their objectives, and they enter the fray with great vigor and enthusiasm even when the betting, by outsiders, is against them. After all, an entrepreneur is by definition a person who is prepared to take risks.

There are many examples. In the late 1960s, President Park Chung Hee bet against all foreign donors, including the World Bank, which wanted to cut off economic assistance, on constructing the Seoul-Pusan expressway, which they all felt would be outrageously uneconomic. President Park insisted and was proven correct. The state went against all foreign advice in building POSCO (Pohang Iron and Steel) at a time when bankers said there was a glut of steel on the market. Observers questioned Korea entering the automobile export market, and today on its expansion.

The same applied in computer chips and a host of other decisions many of which laid the foundation of Korea's present prosperity. Similar commitments are made every day at lower economic levels, and although the failures must be many, the successes are also apparent and striking. Working to achieve, and taking risks to do so, is apparent in the educational process in Korea, where much— years of work— is staked but the potential rewards are very great indeed. The increasing degree of mobility in Korean society is an indication that risk-taking does often pay off. What is more apparent in risk-taking than migration, which is taking risks in a foreign environment—exponentially difficult, but at which the Koreans work exceptionally hard.

Why is there such a tendency in Korea to take economic or other risks? Koreans seem to do this more than either the Chinese or the Japanese, or at least they are better known for it. Some have said that it may be a product of hardships, epitomized by the Korean War, in which everything was going to be lost in any case, and risks had to be taken to survive. Perhaps. Yet the voting patterns in Korea indicate that people now vote conservatively—they do not seem to want to take chances losing their hard-gained middle-class status. Even risk-taking in marriage, itself perhaps the greatest risk of all, is mitigated by parental involvement. If they don't want to run risks in politics and social life, why do they do so in so many other fields?

The basic reasons for risk-taking to the degree apparent here remain obscure. Let us hope, whatever the reasons, that the North Koreans, if they share the same trait, will confine their risk-taking to their internal realm, not on foreign adventures.

July 1996

On Satire

Satire is the honored Western literary tradition, dating back to the ancient Greeks, in which human vices or follies are held up to public scrutiny and ridicule with the purpose of exposing and publicly censoring such activities. The word derives from the Latin to be full of food; this root also produced the English "saturate." It has nothing to do with "satyrs," which comes from a different source, although some satirized may feel that those producing the satires are indeed satyrs.

The satiric tradition goes back to Aristophanes and continues through the Romans, such as Juvenal, and in English through Jonathan Swift and beyond. To qualify as satire a work should be serious. A few insults hurled at someone or some action does not qualify, and a political polemic against some person, group, or institution lacks the subtlety that is associated with satire, although this distinction is being lost. Criticism alone is not satire, although they are related as satire is indeed critical. A newspaper columnist normally does not write satire, but a poet, dramatist, or novelist may.

Satire is a form of social commentary with the general aim of improving someone or something through criticism that may be direct or oblique. It requires a degree of social and political distance between the satirist and those satirized. The necessary distance is, of course, difficult to measure, and will vary by time, by subject satirized, by publishing venue, and by the degree of directness of the attack. If the effort is too indirect, it is ineffective; if too direct, in some societies one could lose one's head.

Satire is common today in some form in most pluralistic societies. It is often directed toward external people or issues when the state will not allow internal debate on important problems. North Korea does not seem to allow satire of any internal action by the government or of its leader; Burma (Myanmar) does the same. Satire in Burma is directed only toward the opposition and the external world, and then only within government prescribed limits. The tradition in the West is for most satire to be directed against the established norms, social conventions, or the authorities, although theoretically this not need be the case. But to be effective the target of satire should be well known.

What is the tradition and state of satire in Korea? Although there was a strong heritage of criticism in the Confucian court system, and indeed the Censorate was established on a Chinese model to provide the monarch with a theoretically independent source of advice and admonition, there seems to have been little literati satire that has come down to us. Of course, there was a plethora of criticism in the poetry and court documentation of each period, for with factionalism as important as it was such criticism would be expected. But it would be stretching the definition (which indeed is a Western one and thus may be limited) to call this satire.

There was, however, a strong tradition of satire, but its locus was neither in the court nor in the upper classes, but among the peasantry. The masked dance traditions (for several survived in Korea) were essentially satirical dance-dramas that provided a socially acceptable form of satire of the most biting kind. It was often directed toward the yangban (gentry), who controlled both power and wealth in the local communities, and toward the Buddhist monkhood, which was often regarded as corrupt. It was an outlet for protest, but because it was not directed at specific individuals it was locally tolerated. It is now regarded as an important cultural contribution to the Korean heritage.

There are, however, no great works of traditional Korean literature that may be classified as satire, although many contain criticisms of aspects of society.

The colonial period is different. A great many novels and poetry appeared that were obliquely satirical of the Japanese authorities, and those Koreans who associated too closely with them. In a sense, the unjust colonial experience allowed, even encouraged, satire to flourish even as the Japanese authorities attempted to control information and public expression of criticism.

Satire since independence has a mixed history. Certain types of criticism and satire were allowed under the dictatorships, but others were not. If the government wanted to make a point, it might allow satire of foreigners, especially the Americans and their troops and those who associated with those troops. But these were kept under government scrutiny.

Internal satire was severely controlled. We can remember the poet Kim Chi-ha's poems about the five thieves that were banned by the Park Chung Hee regime and the poet himself jailed. More specifically, it was illegal to criticize or satirize the head of state (or of any head of state for that matter). In other words, the social distance required to produce good satire was severely restricted, which in itself seems to have produced even more demand for outlets to express concern or indignation about aspects of the regime. Satire may not prevent street demonstrations, but a lack of satirical ability may increase their intensity and frequency as the only means of expressing protest.

Today in Korea there is a greater degree of freedom than at any period in Korean history. That does not mean that there are no limitations on satiric expressions. Although the Constitutional Court in October 1996 ruled that prior censorship was illegal, according to the recent press it still continues. "The concern [over control] has recently turned into a reality when the Korean Public Performance Ethics Committee virtually banned the screening of a romantic movie by declining to grant a rating to the movie on the grounds that it contained lines blasphemous to a state head." Blasphemous? The Head of State as local Deity? Perhaps even more importantly, self-censorship is evident, and this inhibits the production of some of the most pungent forms of satire.

Satire has been a powerful force for reform, and an effective means for expression of disquiet and criticism of activities and events. The state has historically generally placed some limits on satire, whether for political or legal purposes (such as libel or slander, which are defined by each society differently). If we postulate that no society or individual is perfect, and thus there is always room for improvement, satire is a means to bring to public attention the inadequacies and injustices of the time. We should therefore be encouraging satire as a template by which we can measure the need for reform and change. Its suppression at any level can only retard progress.

June 1997

On Going to Intellectual Heaven

"When good Americans die, they go to Paris," or so the brother-in-law of the American poet Henry Wadsworth Longfellow is said to have remarked in the nineteenth century. Oscar Wilde countered that when bad Americans die, they stayed in America. Such was the allure of Paris, known as the city of light, at least for the American and even British literati and the aspirants to that status, and indeed for many in the upper class. Paris was the hub of glamour and intellectual vitality, an informal image that lasted until World War II. George Gershwin could write *An American in Paris*, and the city sheltered Hemingway, Fitzgerald, Henry Miller, Gertrude Stein, Joyce, Beckett, and a host of other writers between the wars. Somehow London, which might have been thought as the home of those who wrote in English, did not work.

Of course, Paris was also considered risqué. Henry James, in his *The Ambassadors*, has an emissary from a straitlaced New England town sent to Paris to "save" a young man from its enticements. Even today that popular image has not completely been eclipsed. As a satirical song goes, "The French don't care what you do as long as you pronounce it properly." It was said to be the home of debauchery, but there may have been more prostitutes in Victorian London than in Paris. No, whatever the reputation of Paris as a center for licentiousness, that is far from reality. The attraction of Paris has not only been the city of, sometimes, breathtaking urban beauty, that city of light, but intellectual light as well. That was even more important; it meant intellectual freedom and removal of the strictures and constraints of Western, especially American, "small town mentality" that often permeated major Western centers, at least until the social mobility created by World War II. In spite of considerable autonomy, there was a great degree of social and intellectual conformity. Paris remains a center, perhaps the center, of the Western intellectual tradition, and the French government has assiduously attempted to foster that image. That intellectual freedom has been a hallmark of this city and culture for a very long period indeed. One may visit the graves of Voltaire and Rousseau in the Pantheon to remind one of this importance.

All this has raised the question of where, emotionally, good Korean intellectuals might want to go when they die. Where is the inspirational home of Koreans, where they would feel at the font or hub of their tradition and culture—where they would be traditionally inspired and yet have the freedom to explore? Is this an inherent contradiction? One hopes not.

Some Koreans, when asked, have said that it is where the mountains and the water are in proper harmony, but they are being literal, referring to grave sites that are in conformity with the proper traditions of geomancy, or *pungsoo* (Chinese, *fengshui*, lit., wind and water). Others might call on a Christian heaven. But when asking the question one hopes for a cultural and emotive reply to the Korean intellectual tradition, not a physical or religious response.

Tokyo and Kyoto are out for all Koreans, even though many of the, now elderly, elite were trained in Japan and are quite at home in aspects of that intellectual tradition, even if they will not publicly admit it. Beijing, even if the source of much of what became Korean culture, does not seem to have that attraction. Those Koreans who have spent much time in the West or may feel quite comfortable in that society and may think fondly of that experience, but this would be a distinct minority position. Perhaps the Japanese might feel Kyoto was such a center, and the Chinese at least once might have felt Beijing (or perhaps old Beijing in imperial times—the new Beijing is intellectually stultifying) was their cultural spiritual home.

Perhaps the answer lies simply in the uniqueness of Korea in spite of a host of foreign influences such as those from China, Japan, and the West. All these influences have been important. They have shaped Korean history, its bureaucracy and political culture, its laws, and indeed many of its aspirations. Yet it seems to have left a core of "Korean-ness" that finds, for many intellectuals and perhaps for the masses as well, a spiritual home safely in Korea—a home where spiritual influences are melded with the physical—with the Korean-ness of its sky and mountains.

One may not hear much about the *minjung* movement these days in Korea, but that does not mean that the search for Korean roots, as distinct from the foreign, even neighborly traditions such as Confucianism that have been absorbed into Korean society, is not still vital. It may have been overtly more evident than in the 1980s, following the anti-Americanism spurred in part by the Kwangju incident of 1980, and later by the political liberalization of 1987, yet it is there waiting to be revitalized or perhaps become more apparent. One may expect that the influences of globalization, which will seem to diminish further or even threaten the Korean core culture as foreign influences continue to spread, will produce a reaction that will foster this nationalism. When reunification finally comes, whatever its form and content, it is likely to increase the Korean consciousness of the validity of this tradition.

But the idea that good Americans go to Paris was not only because it was a font of Western culture, but because there was the freedom there to spread one's intellectual wings that Americans felt could not be done at home—even in the land, as the Americans say, "of the free." So for the intellectual, this is a vital element of that quest.

Pyongyang is an exceedingly unlikely site as a Korean intellectual heaven; its intellectual orthodoxy stultifies. So it seems that Seoul, or an imagined Seoul free from the very different but often binding intellectual strictures of the nineteenth and twentieth centuries, may be the place where good Koreans will intellectually want to go when they die, but physically they will want to return to their *kohyang*, or old hometown. But intellectually Seoul may need further freedoms to win that appellation—the spirit, and social acceptance of that liberty, beyond what the Korean Constitution literally provides—in essence, a new Seoul of intellectual light. But then, where do bad Koreans go? The old Seoul of restrictions and repression?

January 2002

On Summer and Togetherness in Korea

Whether togetherness is a natural or acquired state I will leave to others to determine. There are, however, certainly differences in defining privacy across cultures, and in Korea it seems a rare commodity, at least for many foreigners. Its absence assumes more visible form in summer when people are outside. Korea is one of the most densely populated countries, and it has a relatively short summer respite from the all-too-constant rigors of schoolwork, since the major vacation is in the winter—perhaps a holdover from the period when heating buildings was too expensive. With an increasing affluence that allows vacations, transport, and travel, the confluence of Koreans in search of summer fun reaches heights few who have not experienced it can imagine.

Of course, Americans have their Coney Island and other resorts around major urban areas, and they flock to the beaches in astonishing numbers to be grilled in the sun. The French all seem to take their vacations at the same time. But Koreans seem to delight in closer proximities that defy the American privacy scale. Having fun is *with* people. They seem to avoid solitude and to gather at designated resort areas, often renowned for their scenic beauty or their pleasant beaches. There collective humanity congregates amid a welter of haphazard and juxtaposed buildings and sheds that are to pass for summertime beach accommodations.

Virtually touching each other, inns, restaurants, stalls, and shops seem unplanned and are jumbled together to make quiet impossible. Such togetherness does not come cheaply. At one west coast beach resort, a one-*pyong* (six-foot-square) pink wooden "coffin" on stilts with a small window and undersized door (water and toilets are located elsewhere—somewhere, and there is no furniture) rents for about $35 per night and virtually abuts the next "coffin." One can sleep a number of people in it. It is all part of the ephemeral beach scene.

And a scene it is, with a good bit of convivial singing and loud speakers, awash with copious quantities of alcohol in various forms, making it for the less-than-outgoing a littoral on one of the lower circles of hell.

The mountains spread out and are thus more inviting. Reforestation has succeeded in Korea, and one can find moments of sylvan beauty and solitude in remote sites. Not, however, if you go to a famous temple located in some secluded spot. There the detachment that once gave rise to meditation is overwhelmed by visitors in appropriate mountain gear, busloads of school children, and the eating and drinking establishments, both permanent and mobile, that arise on the periphery of devotional sites. The temporal has invaded the spiritual, and there is no escape. The old Korean expression, indicating what one may get away with, applies: "If you have *nunch'i* (lit., "eye measure," sizing up the situation), you can even eat pickled shrimp in a Buddhist temple."

Vacations, outings, and hiking all seem to be good excuses for eating and drinking. Koreans are not only gregarious but their society is also most certainly a food culture, a hospitable one where friendships and relationships of business and pleasure are associated with food and drink. One climbs a mountain to view the scenery, to be sure, but with others both for the pleasure of friends and sharing an experience, but also to be able to cook and eat out. After all, symbolically, all *p'anchan* (side dishes eaten with rice) and *ch'ige* (soup or stew) are communal dishes.

A few years ago on a trip to Korea I decided to walk in the mountains for a few days between academic conferences. I picked a lonely looking spot on the map, and decided to go by myself with a simple backpack. My wife was much against it, fearing I would slip and fall, lying undiscovered alone, uncared for in some inaccessible fastness. My Koreans friends all felt the situation would be *simsim hada*, or boring without anyone to talk to. But solitude is a learning experience.

The first leg of the trip was easy; the express bus was efficient and comfortable. The second leg, the *gun* (county) bus, was easy to get on but difficult to get off. The driver decided that I could not possibly want to alight in some remote village I had picked off the map, but that I really wanted to go to a famous temple some thirty kilometers away where all the outsiders went. In my poor Korean I finally convinced him that I did indeed want to descend. When I got off, the local policeman decided that I must have made a mistake and really wanted to go to the temple. He was being kind and concerned, but puzzled that I would want to be alone in the mountains.

I started up the path toward the mountains, passing through a few villages that became more scattered as I proceeded. When I reached the last village the trail seemed to end. I asked directions of some local housewives who were gathered at the end of the workday by one of the low walls. They insisted that I could not climb the mountain before dusk, and they determined that I should spend the night in one of their houses. So I was taken in by a family—a couple, their two young children, and a grandfather. I bathed in the mountain stream, and was fed and treated with unusual kindness before I went on my solitary way the next morning. I had virtually become a friend of the family.

In coming down the mountain and walking along dirt roads, trucks or cars would stop, offering me lifts to the next town, the drivers unable to fathom why an elderly (at least in their eyes) foreigner would walk alone on a hot summer day without his car having had some sort of trouble.

I have met with unfailing kindnesses in rural areas, and usually even in cities. There was spontaneous openness and hospitality. I have been offered cold rice and salted fish in the fields, and even *makkoli* (rice beer) at eight in the morning, a way for me to obliterate the rest of the day. But some, such as I, are lone observers of the passing parade, as someone remarked. In Korea, solitude and privacy are not seen as virtues of the Confucian *kunja* (superior man). As a foreigner, I am allowed some leeway, and my literally outlandish sins are often forgiven. But perhaps I am simply more of a Taoist by temperament.

August 1995

2

Ceremonies and Traditions

On "Black Is the Color of My True Love's Car"

I heard indirectly one day that a well-known hotel in Seoul did not want to valet park my light grey, medium-sized, bourgeois car in front of its lobby because it would lessen the prestige of the hotel. Only large black cars were acceptable, it seems. If you have a high position, a large black car is virtually required. In this case, too, black is beautiful.

I assume that this preoccupation with black cars goes back to a Japanese pattern, where decorum and conformity may be even more apparent than in Korea, and where black cars still seem to be the epitome of formality and fashion for the elite. In the late 1950s and early 1960s, in Korea, black cars were not a sign of the status of government officials. Most roads outside the city were not paved and one needed four-wheel drive. So it was black jeeps instead—a remnant of the Korean War days newly melded into an old protocol. This was then a real sign of status, but as roads improved, black sedans replaced jeeps for officials in the cities. The jeeps were moved and still remained for a long period as potent symbols of power for local officials in the countryside.

Americans are different. They like sporty cars and colors, and red is now said to be the most popular color, although government car pools have a variety of nondescript colors, except for the very top where black still reigns. Perhaps it is societal youthfulness, for I now see in Korea bright purple and green cars driven (usually) by what I would call the very young. It is, however, a far cry from the early days of automobiles. Then, Henry Ford, when asked by people for cars of different colors, said they could have any color they wanted as long as it was black.

The preoccupation with black is interesting, reflecting formality, and status as well, which includes money and at least potential leisure. One cannot help invoking Thorstein Veblen, whose book, *The Theory of the Leisure Class,* about one hundred years ago was a seminal volume in social thought and theory. He claimed that the elites in societies created images and activities that demonstrated that they had leisure, which was equated with money and status in those days. Extrapolating from Veblen, if, for example, you were an urbanite and had a tan, then this established that you had the leisure to take a vacation to get it, and thus were well off. Perhaps carrying a golf bag today has the same function. One need not even play—it is an outward display, like carrying an imitation Gucci bag. So having a chauffeur is a sign of the leisure class, but as black cars show dirt more than white ones, if you have a black car it means you have the funds to get it cleaned often, have a driver to clean it, or have the leisure to clean it yourself. One rarely sees dirty black cars in Korea.

It is historically strange that now black indicates formality in Korean society. One knows that when one has high-level official meetings, a dark suit—sort of "off-black"—is normally worn. The dark suit for men in Korea is what a "basic black" dress was for women in the West. Koreans pay more for black chicken, and black goats are a specialized and expensive taste for women—a kind of tonic.

But this fascination with black is contrary to earlier practice. Korean clothes are traditionally white, and white, not black, was the color of mourning, perhaps the most formal of occasions. Koreans were known as the "white-clothed people." Further, virility and status are normally associate with *yang*, which is symbolized by brightness and the sun and maleness, while *yin* is female, dark, and invokes the moon. So if one only thought abstractly about Korea from a *yin-yang* perspective on what kind of cars people would want, one might have thought that white would be the most popular color. So much for deductive logic from false premises.

Black in the West often was historically used to evoke evil and ignorance, although we are more sensitive to color issues today. Herman Melville may be the ancestral unindicted co-conspirator of my hotel doorman—he had Moby-Dick, the white whale, epitomize evil.

There is an old English folk song, "Black is the color of my true love's hair," itself interesting in light of the Anglo-Saxon blondness. In Korea, everyone's hair was once black, although tinting to "wine" color, really different shades of brown, among young women is, alas, prevalent. So for the conservatives and status conscious, there may be two Korean translations of the English folk song: "Black Still Is the Color of My True Love's Hair," and "Black Is the Color of My True Love's Car."

August 1996

On Names—Lost and Otherwise

A number of years ago Richard Kim wrote a powerful volume (*Lost Names*) poignantly recounting the forced elimination of Korean names by the Japanese toward the close of colonial rule in their effort to integrate Korea completely into the Japanese sphere. It is an important, evocative, and disturbing essay on attempted cultural genocide.

In a much less serious vein, Koreans have lost their other names in daily use as well. Foreigners are often struck that Koreans rarely use anyone's given name except among close friends, schoolmates, or family. One is generally known by one's title alone, or by one's surname with an appended title, "Mr."' or preferably "Dr." Wives are not named when talking to a third party, and the term "the person inside" or some circumlocution is used instead. I have the advantage of being called "Representative" (*t'aepyo*), but in Korea this may translate as either "representative" or "president," depending on the circumstances. It is sometimes embarrassing to receive an undeserved higher status.

When we get telephone calls at home, people generally introduce themselves by their home location, as if there were only one person living in that particular ward. I have often wondered what would happen if that custom were introduced in the United States. Women will also often introduce themselves on the telephone by saying that they are the mother of so-and-so. My problem is that I have trouble remembering names, even those of my distant relatives. Thus, I could never be a politician. This is in contrast to a Korean barber, whom I had not seen in seventeen years, and who greeted me by both name and organization after that lapse of time.

Americans have another problem with names—when do we use first or last names? We have no rules, so there is always some tension. Coming from Boston, which has a tradition of more formality and social distance, I tend to want to set the rules on when my first name and last name are used—first name among friends, colleagues, and so forth, and last name on all other occasions. This is inconsistent with the western part of the United States, which tends to be more familiar. I dislike it when a receptionist or a telephone operator whom I have never seen calls me by my first name.

Societies establish corporate name cultures. In some groups, the practice is for all professionals to call the head of the organization by his or her first name, but only in private or in solely professional gatherings. Support staff always use the last name appended by a "Mr." or "Dr." If the latter is used too profusely in peer groups, then it sounds affected. In England, I am told that professors never address each other as "Dr." or "Professor," but rather by the surname alone, as colleagues. Americans tend to use the first name more than the last name and title.

In some countries, a title is forever—once an ambassador or a colonel, always an ambassador or colonel. Of course, there are countries that really confuse foreigners. Burma has no surnames, so everyone, even in the same family, has an individual name, which they keep. One must be careful never to talk ill of anyone because you may be talking to his brother. Sometimes one only finds out who is related to whom when one reads obituaries. Burmese must invent a surname when they go abroad to register anywhere.

Of course, in Korea married women keep their own surnames, which causes foreigners some confusion when introducing them to third parties. Koreans tend to be tolerant of foreign mistakes in this regard. Married women retaining their surnames is relatively recent in the United States. In the early 1970s, a wife of a USAID employee in another country wanted to be listed in the U.S. Embassy telephone directory under her maiden name. It caused a major crisis, but of course she eventually got her way.

When Westerners began to translate Asian novels and stories, they had an early custom, now thankfully discarded, of literally translating everyone's given name, especially those of women. So we were told that "plum blossom" or someone did or said something. This was an attempt at exotica, and was cute in Western eyes, but misrepresented emotions and was destructive of personality and literary intent. After all, we do not translate English names, most of which have meanings; we would regard it as absurd. I do not want to be known as "beloved," which the dictionary informs me is the meaning of David. Do people unconsciously take on the meanings associated with their names?

In spite of the paucity of surnames in Korean, which is of some confusion to the newly arrived foreigner since about 22 percent of Koreans are named Kim and 18 percent named Lee or Rhee, etc., Korean names have the advantage of both collectivity and individuality. Which clan one belongs to provides additional information. One can sometimes tell the generation of a person in a particular family through the use of the same character as part of the given name, while the other character provides individuality. There are sufficient numbers of characters to illustrate whatever individuality and meaning the parents have in mind. Now, some parents avoid Chinese-based names, and go for purely Korean words. There are in Korea professional name-givers who help pick an auspicious given name. One can also go to a fortune-teller to get help in legally changing one's name or that of one's child to ward off possible calamities.

There are, of course, fashions in names, at least in the United States. Parents sometimes try hard to find an acceptable name that is recognizable but not too common only to find out too late that many others who have children in the same school have chosen exactly the same name. Other parents name their children after movie stars or other famous people.

Until a generation or so ago in France, you could not register a child's name unless it was a saint's name; luckily, there were many saints, but the couple who tried to name a newborn after Stalin were legally prescribed from doing so. In the United States, many people, both parents and individuals, custom design names by having unusual spellings or other tokens of individuality. I am dubious about the success of this. But Russell Baker of the *New York Times* once wrote that to succeed in the United States it was very helpful to have first and last names that were interchangeable— you were then clearly part of the Anglo-Saxon establishment.

I prefer the Korean mode—linking the individual to the family but providing individuality, and where women keep their own names. It provides a balance between collectivity and individualism.

February 1966

On Graying Gracefully

"Romance gray," said in English but pronounced with a Korean accent, used to be a popular expression in Korea. Never used about females, it indicated the attractiveness of the mid-career males to women, and the prevalence of males whose temples were naturally lightening and who had a somewhat wandering eye. It was, so it seemed, a light-hearted expression used not without a good bit of envy on the part of many.

The United States does not seem to share that attitude. It is, alas, a culture concentrating on youth. So some men have gone to great lengths to demonstrate their youthfulness by tinting their hair from gray back to its original color. "You look years younger," an approving (but domineering) wife says in a television advertisement. People say that such a youthful appearance will be both sexier and give the impression professionally that one is more successful, and thus perhaps should not be laid off in the rash of "downsizing" of industry. Television advertisements promulgate products that are said to do this with great ease and naturalness.

When President Reagan was in office, the press sometimes discretely asked about the rich, black color of his hair at his advanced age, but he always maintained that it was natural, although many had suspicions. His avuncular qualities probably would have got him elected even if his hair were white. I have always thought that actors were a special breed, and what they did to their faces or hair or teeth, or other parts today with liposuction, face-lifting, and hair transplants was a product of a particular subculture that tolerated, some might say demanded, such Potemkin-like human facades. Image, apparently, is more than substance. Perhaps it is also true of politicians as well.

In Korea, one might suggest, appearances are even more important than in the West, for they should socially portray happiness, success, accomplishments, prosperity, and good health. I sometimes notice men anew here as if I saw them for the first time, although I have known them for a number of years. I know their ages must equal, if not surpass, mine. Their impression at first sometimes struck me as odd, and I wondered why and how they had changed until I realized, quite suddenly, that their hair was black. Perhaps it had been gray, or even white. I had noticed the change back to black, even though it may have been gradual, because I had not seen them for some time. I know quite a number of people who now appear younger, far younger, than I.

This trend has social implications in Korea. People tell me that if your boss has black hair, then it would be discreet for you to have black hair as well, because it is not appropriate, and even impolite, to appear older, and thus give the impression of being wiser, than one's superiors. The boss might feel uncomfortable giving orders to one who could, visually, be his father. So if the head of a company has black hair, most of his senior subordinates may feel it necessary to have the same.

This apparent new need for the appearance of youth in Korea struck me as odd. Here was a society that was quintessentially Confucian, where the "superior man" was older almost by definition and was the ideal, and where age normally confers status and prestige. It impressed me as quite a remarkable shift that members of the elite were attempting to appear younger. Society was changing, and perhaps this shift in attitudes says more about how Korea has moved than all the statistics and social science surveys. Perhaps the Korean syndrome is not the Western Potemkin approach, but a "pre-temps-Kim" attitude.

Today, however, this trend may be on the wane. Those of us who watch television news have observed recent changes in President Kim Young Sam, and the chief executive often sets the style. People tell me that before he became president, his hair was gray. Then it became black, but now he appeared before the April 1966 election as more relaxed and more approachable, and one cannot help but notice that there is a tinge of "romance gray" appearing around his temples. It softens his appearance and is more natural—perhaps more appealing to the public. He seems to be one of us. A Korean president always seems serious and austere, and perhaps this change portrays him as more humane. Will his associates now follow suite? What about other politicians? A number of leaders are at least as old as he, and their hair is all black, or so it seems from my color television. Does "romance gray" translate into "political gray?" Or into "political gravy?"

I used to feel as Proust did in his *Remembrance of Things Past* when after many years he returned to society to attend a gala party. He could not understand why everyone had changed and appeared so old. When I saw old friends after a long absence, I would think to myself, "My, how he has aged," thinking mostly of gray or white hair, little realizing that my daily shaving bouts with the mirror in a way prevented me from the shock of sudden recognition of personal deterioration. In this case, familiarity breeds not contempt but insulation.

Women are different, in that many societies, by depriving them of rewarding livelihoods, have herded them along paths that have forced them to rely more on looks than inherent abilities, and thus their preoccupation with "keeping up face," to mix metaphors. But I see among young women in both Korea and abroad the denigration of what the Victorians used to call "their crowning glory," their hair. So

Western women become blondes, so they say, because "gentlemen prefer blondes," according to the novel, and "blondes have more fun," as one advertisement used to claim. This goes back to the Renaissance. Because there are a multitude of natural hair colors in the West, they may be slightly altered to regain existing color or change tone a bit.

In Korea, we see a different, disturbing trend. Here young attractive women, almost all of whom have naturally similar hair color, give a russet tinge to their otherwise lustrous black hair, for me degrading a beauty that was an asset. They may wish to appear different, but instead they then appear all the same in their fadishness. But should the color of one's hair, eyebrows, and even eyes match, complement, or contrast with each other?

As an observer of the passing hair parade, I don't have to worry. I have too little hair to count, and to try to wash out sparse "aged white" with "romance gray" or youthful brown would be a wasted effort.

April 1966

On Lee Tai-young and the Status of Women

Lee Tai-young, honored in her lifetime, deserves recognition after her death. She died on December 16, 1998. She was in her way a pioneer—for women's rights, for the rights of women in the professions, for children, for justice and human rights, and for the family.

Every woman who came after her and who entered into professions, such as law or engineering, previously excluded to women, owe her a debt, for she led the way as the first woman to enter law school and as the first woman lawyer in Korea. Every family that gets into trouble in Korea and that must go to Family and Children's Court for redress is also indebted to her, for she alone sparked the founding of that court in 1963, and thus fostered justice and expanded its cause in Korea. She moved a patrimonially oriented society into greater consideration for women and children, and through them, to us all.

Those foreigners who do not know Korea may not understand what a quiet pioneer, indeed revolutionary, she was, for she indeed led a revolution in women's rights through example. Now, in the United States there are many women in law school, and they are the majority in a great number. But when Lee Tai-young started her career, there were not only no female lawyers, there were few lawyers at all, and not one woman had ever been to law school. Those trained at law schools went into the bureaucracy or became judges or prosecutors. Civil-dispute settlement was not the confrontational experience it is in many countries of the West—intermediaries and middle men or the clan settled matters away from the courts, for it was commonly thought at that time that going to court meant one was a criminal. Rule and the exercise of power, in public or private, was theoretically in a Confucian society through moral example, and law was a means of punishment, not dispute settlement. Even though gender equality was mandated under the various constitutions of the Republic, these provisions were never enforced, and often legislation conflicted with those noble aims. President Syngman Rhee refused to grant her a license to pratice law. Even later, when court appearances were more common, the judges often encouraged out-of-court dispute settlement. It was not seemly for women to complain about domestic issues to outsiders, for status and face were lost.

But in those cases where no informal adjudication was possible, the Family Court was a critical innovation on the Korean scene. The abuse of women and children, so prevalent in the society, was (and to a large degree still is) covered up and ignored, so that the Court gave people an avenue of redress that was theretofore unavailable and socially inappropriate. Without the Court, the subjugation of women would have continued even longer than it has. It is to the credit of a foreign organization, The Asia Foundation, that as early as the 1950s it recognized the problem and supported some of the activities of Lee Tai-young that led to the formation of the Court, as well as supporting a wide variety of other legal activities that fostered concepts of the role of law in Korean society.

Lee Tai-young, both personally and through her husband and family, often found herself in opposition to those in power. This was not because she was against legitimate authority, but because the arbitrary, thus illegal, exercise of authoritarian governments that undercut the rights of the citizenry were anathema to her.

We should remember her as a major contributor to human rights in Korea and as a pioneer for equality and the expanded role of women in her own time.

January 1999

On Women's Rights and Tradition

Although Korean women have equal rights with men under the constitution, and considerable legislation supports and specifies those rights and provisions, there is still a substantial body of Korean male and female opinion that is not anxious to enforce existing laws, and indeed in many cases subverts their intent. Laws call for equal inheritance and equal wages for equal work, but we all know that these are only occasionally honored. If the lack of high- level government officials, except for one specialized bureau concentrating on women's affairs, may be attributed to a male-dominated bureaucracy, the great paucity of elected women at any level, including newly inaugurated local governments, demonstrates that this is not imposed from above, but reflects some important sentiment from below.

One often hears Koreans say that the women's rights movement is a Western concept inflicted on Korea, and that it is alien to our (Korean) society. Some say that it is, in effect, a form of cultural imperialism. Other Koreans continue to maintain that we Koreans should not upset our traditional values, in which women are honored in the household even if they may be discriminated against outside. Many would also assert that Koreans must reestablish their traditions and return to their roots and protect their culture.

There is a major sentiment, and indeed a movement, in Korea to do just that—rediscover the roots of the Korean tradition. It is the *minjung* ("masses" or "people's") movement, which decries foreign influences and wishes to search out and restore traditional Korean cultural practices. This has both very positive and very negative impacts, while it is in some tension with the government's policy of globalization. It has revived traditional Korean music and folk art, and given a fillip to many worthy and important aspects of Korean culture. Its negative side is in denigrating foreign influences, whether they are positive or negative, and irrespective of their origins—Western, Japanese, or Chinese.

Those who proclaim that women's rights and the movement for it are foreign do not, in fact, understand the roots of Korean history. The movement may have foreign precedents, but the problem in Korea is self-imposed. The current deplorable state of women's rights in actuality, as opposed to their present legal status, was a foreign influence, imposed by Koreans on their own society. It entered from China and was destructive of earlier, indigenous, and more equal Korean women's basic rights.

Before Confucianism became the enforced ideological mold that shaped Korean society, as the Chosun (Yi) Dynasty (1398-1910) became established, women were far better off than they have been until modern times. Research has shown that in the Koryo Dynasty (918-1398), and well into the middle of the Chosun Dynasty (until about the early seventeenth century), women inherited equally with their brothers, and women could perform the critical ancestral rites that were considered the fundamental role in establishing status in the family and in the society. As such, they were the equal of males. As the rigidity of the Confucian family took hold, however, all this changed, and women were denigrated in the inheritance process and no longer were allowed by edict to perform these required rituals. The result was the rise of adoptions of male heirs as women's roles were degraded.

So those women and men who advocate and struggle for truly equal treatment for women should not be regarded as socially subversive elements who attempt to undermine Korea's traditional social values and patterns, but rather as advocates who attempt to bring Korea back to a more gender-related humane period in Korean history when women held more power and influence than they hold today. Better women's rights should be part of the *minjung* movement.

Some Korean men do not understand this, and they continually degrade women unconsciously while maintaining in doing so they are really strengthening traditional Korea. They are, instead, strengthening a Confucian tradition which in Korea became more rigorous and rigid than in China itself—more Catholic than the Pope. Sometimes they think of themselves as honoring women, when this is not really the case.

It is true that women have critical roles in society. They run the households and are in virtual charge of their children's education, which they pursue with great vigor and single-mindedness. Their influence extends beyond the home as well—what is called the *chima param*, the wind of women's skirts.

Some years ago, while traveling around rural Korea evaluating agricultural projects with two Korean professors and an ardent British feminist, we were in a state of perpetual argument over the status of Korean women. The Korean professors maintained that they really respected Korean women, but at the same time women had limited skills that prevented them from assuming more important roles. The feminist obviously disagreed. As we passed rows of women up to their knees in cold water transplanting rice seedlings while two men stood on dry land holding a string to ensure the women planted in straight rows, the professors said this string holding was a skill that women could not perform. The feminist became more and more incensed. Finally we came to a remote village where the professors rushed up and insisted on showing her a small shrine, with an inscription that they said they wanted to translate for her. The text read: "This shrine was established to honor a certain Ms. Kim who in the Imjin War [1592] carried her father on her back away from the Japanese invaders and thus saved his life. This shrine is dedicated to a filial daughter." The professors then said, "See how we honor our Korean women!" The British woman replied, "And what would have happened if she had carried her mother?"

February 1997

On "Rooting Out Evil Confucian Vestiges"

O tempera! O mores! A generation or more ago, when East Asia was studied in Western universities, Confucianism was regarded as an evil vestige that hindered economic development and social progress. It was said to be anachronistic, harking back to a previous golden age that the present and future could never equal. So progress was theoretically inimical in the Confucian worldview. But times change and with them academic ideas, as well as other, more mundane, fashions. For the past decade or so, a revisionist interpretation has been prominent; Confucianism has been touted as the force behind the East Asian "economic miracle" because it stressed education and a bureaucratic meritocracy. Lee Kuan Yew introduced Confucian values into the Singapore educational system, and later, when the issue of "Asian values" was promulgated, he used it to justify strong governments that inhibited democratic political rights and preserved societal order.

Now, President Kim Dae Jung, a strong critic of "Asian values," wants to eliminate the evils of Confucianism in his bid to create a "spiritual rearmament movement." These evils are said to be authoritarianism, collectivism, conservatism, cronyism, social hierarchy, and rigidity. These forces, I believe, have indeed been deleterious and important in Korean history, but we should not confuse the decay of the Yi (Chosun) Dynasty with the basic tenets of Confucian thought or neo-Confucianism, many of which were noble, anymore than the Sermon on the Mount or Thomas Aquinas reflect the rise of capitalism and greed in Western Europe.

The issue may be more the question of the structure of Korean society onto which Confucian forces were appended and into which they were amalgamated. These reinforced concepts of social hierarchy, for example, which had been important elements of pre-Confucian Korean groups and which became virtually solidified in the Yi Dynasty, and were quite in contrast with Chinese society. Social mobility in China was theoretically possible, if in fact extremely limited in practice. After all, ideally in Confucian thought anyone from any social class could become a *kunja*, a "superior man" or gentleman, if behavior and concepts were proper, and in China the examination system in theory was open to all males in the society even though it was effectively limited to those with sufficient funding to acquire the leisure to study. In the Yi Dynasty, however, *yangban* or gentry status was the determining factor in qualifying for entry into the system. Korea was thus subjected to a self-perpetuating elite intent on pursuing its own parochial interests—the powerful used it to their own advantage. The hierarchical system was essentially petrified, with residual fallout still evident in contemporary society. One of the psychic tensions of traditional Korea was that between the intellectual egalitarianism of Confucian thought and the structural, hierarchical rigidity of Korean life. There was a type of cognitive dissonance, never resolved, between these two opposite ideas.

The issue of cronyism, or if one prefers, the collusion between the state and the business sector that has led first to the spectacular economic development under the "East Asian model" and then, or simultaneously, to egregious corruption, is not a Confucian problem. It relates directly to the unarticulated but widespread concept of power as finite and personalized, with sharing or compromise a zero-sum game in which one party must lose. This is typical of many traditional societies, and still lingers today. Thus power remains centralized in an individual (the head of any institution) in a central government reluctant to give authority to the periphery, or in a *chaebol*. This is an essential reason why political parties are nothing more than their leadership and their entourage: they stand for little, do not perpetuate themselves by training younger, future leaders, and any loyalty they may engender rests with their leaders, not their ideas.

Korea was, in the term of the eminent German sociologist Max Weber, a patrimonial society—one with highly personalized concepts of power and authority with entourages formed on the basis of loyalty to individuals, and the resulting material and psychological benefits that the leaders dispense for such loyalty, rather than to ideas or institutions.

Assuming that one wishes to eliminate the "evils" associated with a tradition that encased the Yi Dynasty, which are still relevant, perhaps we should not look to eliminating the remnants of Confucianism, but rather discuss reforming the society as a whole, including residual, pre-Confucian legacies.

The concentration on humanism rather than the supernatural is an appealing aspect of Confucianism. But individualism has not been its forte, as Kim Dae Jung has indicated. Personally, I feel a closer affinity with the individualistic and amorphous aspects of Taoism with its emphasis on nature. But Confucianism in theory has much to recommend it, although one wishes it were gender equal.

September 1998

On the Seriousness of Humor

Dignity is usually associated with a serious mien. Important ceremonies seem to require a purposeful calm and solemn deportment befitting discussion of weighty matters. Few things in most societies are more serious than death, the dead, and their memorializing. For religious, magical, or sentimental reasons, dealing with the deceased requires us to be respectful, and thus grave and somber. Without such concerns we perhaps might bring otherworldly retribution on our collective heads and shoulders. And we will sometime be the one so memorialized; so, as they say, turn around is fair play.

Korea clearly illustrates this tendency. Not only are official pronouncements and speeches given with the due ceremony such occasions seem to demand in that culture, but memorial services are occasions where even a shy smile would be inappropriate. In a Korean memorial service I once attended, a critical element was the reading of the deceased's curriculum vitae. This was impressive, for the departed was indeed eminent with a long and successful career, but the ritual was, for the outsider at any rate, superfluous for we all knew him and what he had accomplished, and the speech was markedly boring—strewn with dates and titles of positions, with little sense of his humanity.

Americans have a peculiar culture. We do memorialize the dead, and we are somber and attend such services with gravity. Yet we most often demand a solemnity edged with a lightness of touch, empathy with uplifting, humorous stories of the deceased that bring warmth from the edge of the grave, for the event is more for the living rather than the dead. On such occasions, the older generation usually dresses appropriately and darkly, although among the younger elements this custom seems to have been lost, with bright colors in evidence. There are exceptions. In walking by Saint Patrick's cathedral in New York a few days after the enormous and traumatic tragedy of September 11, 2001, all around the block were hundreds of men and women all waiting to enter for a mass for the departed. I have never seen so many black suits and dresses, a sign of the importance of what had occurred. That was too searing for casual clothes or smiles. The collective trauma affected the American penchant for a light touch. But in the short sketches in the *New York Times* of those who died, their unique personal and often slightly humorous traits were included.

Normally Americans want to smile. At a recent memorial service I attended, we heard not only of my colleague's attributes, successes, and accomplishments, but also about his amusing customs, his abilities, and yet his warm and engaging peculiarities. This was intended not to demean him, but to allow the living to remember the dead with fondness and intimacy. In American culture we seem to need this. Humor seems required. As the after-dinner American speaker at a banquet will usually begin his or her speech with a joke, we want in death the intimacy of a smile with, or at least on behalf of, the deceased. The story goes that a Japanese speaker at an American banquet was told to begin his speech with a joke. He started out by telling his audience how he was instructed, but then said that since he was Japanese he would not commence with a joke. Everyone laughed.

So humor is important to Americans, at all levels. President Bush joked on fainting and falling after eating a pretzel, for he must have known if he did not treat it with humor, others would to his eventual detriment. That is a form of self-depreciation—to bring the exalted down to our level. And that too is an American syndrome—the need for egalitarianism. The deceased are not granted that liberty, so we must do it for them. Of course, there are occasions when humor is not appropriate, but that is not at a funeral.

The humor in the United States or lack thereof in Korea is not a religious issue, for Christians in each society act differently, perhaps on the basis of more primordial loyalties, without losing their divine invocation. Perhaps it is a question of the regard that Koreans have for their ancestors—a pious trait often lacking in Americans. We may or may not revere our progenitors, but we have little need to ensure that, if we do not make verbal or material offerings to their spirits, they will not haunt us in some emotional, if not literal, sense.

So in cross-cultural Korean-American relations in funerals and other somber events, we must balance two distinct and opposite cultural needs while navigating the bridge over the River Styx. Perhaps Charon can tell us how.

January 2002

On the Ties That Bind

A man's role, status, position, taste, and attitudes toward life and society are physically indicated by his clothes. But more specifically, they are represented by one's choice of neckties, for it is the part of male apparel that is most individual and changeable, since other attributes of men's attire remain relatively constant.

Clothes are important in Korea—more important here than in the United States, although we have a saying that "clothes make the man." The Koreans have a proverb that "clothes are like wings." The meaning is that they transform a person, but perhaps not necessarily into angels. The Korean adage does not elucidate on this issue. The Koreans do not seem to like casual dress—the new American custom of "dressing down" (without ties, for example) in the office on Fridays is unlikely to catch on here. Even when one climbs mountains or plays golf, one dresses up—stylishly for the occasion.

Clothes in Korea even have political or moral implications. When a person is arrested and goes on trial, they must wear prison garb even though they have not yet been convicted. This puts the defendant at a personal and social disadvantage, because he or she must feel demeaned and the public probably assumes guilt by mode of dress. When one is convicted in the United States it is usual for one to wear prison clothes (O.J. Simpson wore a conservative suit throughout his trial), and then not necessarily in minimum security prisons.

One former high official said that when he went to important meetings, not only was a white shirt necessary, but that a white shirt with a button-down collar was considered inappropriately casual. In Korean, the term "white collar" in transliteration is used. Colored or stripped shirts are beyond the pale. If we look at the cabinet meetings on television in Korea, there is virtual identity in the suits and shirts, but only some individuality in the ties.

Along with many, if not most Koreans, I have spent an inordinate amount of time watching television news concerning a variety of tumultuous events in Korea. I have viewed important people as they are arrested or taken in for questioning, pausing for photographers on a taped line set by the media in what seems almost a ritualistic stand before entering a building or in the lobby so that they are recorded for posterity. They usually appear stalwart and dignified, thereby implying innocence, in contrast with the petty criminals or even the figures from the Sampung tragedy, who often cover their faces or look down, avoiding the camera as far as possible, in what many would interpret as the same as guilty expressions or attitudes. How different the members of the political elite seem, I thought.

In musing about what I was viewing, I began to ask myself some questions. If I were forced to trade places with any of these figures, how would I approach society? How would I want to appear? How dignified would I want to be, and what would this convey to the viewing public? In other words, how should I dress and what kind of tie should I wear? This is a kind of surrogate indicator, as social scientists would say, of the kind of image I want to project to the public, and how I feel about myself at such a critical moment.

Of course, I must assume it is not always the principal figure who chooses his tie. A trusted aide or spouse may do that instead, but we must suppose that the male does have individual veto power in any case. In the Wodehouse novels about Bertram Wooster, Jeeves—the ultimate gentleman's gentleman—invariably won in disputes over the choice of clothes or ties. Sometimes my wife will change the tie I have placed out for the next day because she feels it will go better with my suit or make me look smarter or more chic (I maintain that is

3

Food and Hospitality

On Pizza

[On the proliferation of pizza in Korea]

Greetings to all who ne're have said
This is my own, my native bread.
From far off Tuscan hills extol
The wondrous pizza to distant Seoul,
Where, taken like a sudden wind,
So many young Korean *kind-*
er give up *kimchi*'s piquant taste,
To call for pizza in all haste.
And to their parent's great regret
Prefer a pepperoni pizza set.
From every ward (in Korean—*dong*)
To pizza parlors many throng
And Pizza parlors proliferate,
It seems as many as their plates,
And foreign names are all the rage
Astonishing a Confucian sage
Who in wonderment resigns
Himself to rampant neon signs.
Marco Polo, from Venezia
Didn't take the rounded pizza
Cathay bound; but brought noodles
(neglecting struddles).
Thus we have Venetian pasta.
To this we must cry "basta!"
Is turn about fair play
Where Italy now holds sway
In fairest Seoul?
Over fifty foreign names proclaim
Pizza's glory and domain
Over burgers, chicken, and *pindaetok**
Believe me, friends, it is no joke
When Piccolo, Party, Park, and Drama
Vie with Cosby, Combi, Copa (not Cabana)

*   Korean mung bean pancakes

A Deli Pizza (or is it Delhi?)
Sinks like anchors in the belly.
Alas, all Seoul it inundates,
And *panchan** it adulterates.
So, my friend, where will it end?
I lack the skill to so portend.
Pizzas, pizzas overpower.
But where is Godfather and Leaning Tower?

June 1995

On Excess Food

Any foreign visitor who goes to a Korean restaurant for lunch or dinner is always impressed by the quantity of food and the seemingly myriad dishes proffered to the affluent guest. It seems the more dishes presented, the better. There is considerable prestige involved in serving and being served all those dishes. Quality is important, authenticity is necessary, but numbers are evidently required. Small and few are not beautiful.

This is in quite some contrast with what seems fashionable in the West, The nouvelle cuisine stresses taste and presentation, but in most modest sized servings. People in the West seem now to prefer smaller amounts of food, perhaps because they are more concerned with their waistbands and their cholesterol.

In many restaurants, if one does not finish a significant portion of a dish, one can ask (at least in the United States) for a "doggie bag" to take home the remains of the day's food. Now, there is an established fiction, which no one believes, that the food will go for pets. Everyone understands that this is not true—the guests will eat it at a later time. Some say that this pattern is especially prevalent in Chinese restaurants, and although this is true, it also occurs in those that serve Western food. Even elegant continental-style restaurants engage in this practice, and have special containers for such remains.

Now, the question is asked why Koreans do not do the same thing? It may happen, but I have never seen this at any Korean restaurant. It is one thing to avoid this when the society is relatively affluent, although perhaps Americans have a tendency to be *yamche* (stingy).

* Korean side dishes eaten with rice.

But now when, as today, Korea is in economic trouble and general standards of living have dropped for the Korean middle class, could such a tradition develop?

Some say no, because the nature of Korean food does not lend itself to being taken home. This is true of some more liquid dishes, and many of the smaller plates that accompany any proper Korean meal. But this seems a partial explanation, and something else may also be operating here as well, and may be more important.

Koreans seem to have a far more highly developed sense of status and role than do Americans. They take seriously the prestige that accrues to their position in society, and will not jeopardize their public images by acting in a manner that will destroy that image. If, for example, a Korean intellectual is laid off from work, he generally would not take a non-intellectual job to support his family, as would most Americans. Indeed, such determination to support his family would rather be considered commendatory, not demeaning. An American would not be diminished by such actions.

So Americans will ask to take home excess food from a restaurant serving, perhaps because they are somewhat *yamche* and also because in their eyes this does not diminish their status. But Koreans have a far stronger sense of such status, and thus do not want to appear stingy or mean, and should seem to be either affluent or magnanimous, or both. After all, to be otherwise is not the way of the *kunja* (the morally superior person).

Yet all this food at Korean restaurants goes to waste. Koreans are taught not to eat everything on the plate because you will appear to be too hungry or poor, but American children are taught just the reverse—clean your plate, as countless mothers have cried to their children.

So in this time of lower economic standards will Koreans change? Probably not, yet the untouched food from restaurants would feed hordes of hungry people. Perhaps we may see the beginnings of "doggie bags" in Korean restaurants, but they had better develop a new name and a different rationale for them.[*]

December 1998

---

[*] Korean press reports in March 2002 indicated that the total food thrown away in restaurants in South Korea could feed all of North Korea, where famine struck much of the population in the 1990s.

The Koreans have a saying, "There is nothing to eat, but eat a lot." It is a charming phrase, but we all know it really means, "There is more here than you possibly can eat, but since you are the 'king' for the meal, enjoy it. I treat you as important, and will expect that you will some day reciprocate in some appropriate manner." This is not so different from many other societies, which is why U.S. government officials are now prohibited from being treated by those with whom they negotiate business. In Korea, the real meaning of eating well has to be understood if you are to savor the flavor of the society and its economics.

January 1997

On Coping With Visitors

An American acquaintance, a noted figure who came into Seoul some time ago, telephoned me about his schedule here. He gave me the names of a number of distinguished Koreans with whom he was planning to meet in the two days he was in town. They were indeed eminent persons, knowledgeable about the Korean and world scene, influential in policy and society, and delightful companions in addition. By coincidence, the morning he called I had breakfast with another well-known American, more of an academician, who also told me of his schedule, which included many of the same people. Two days prior to that, a third American had given me the same names on his schedule. The Americans were all the "usual suspects," Korea-wallahs or aficionados, who are constantly concerned with affairs Korean.

These Koreans are also the [eminent] usual suspects—those who are well known in Korean policy circles and who interact with ease and grace with foreigners. They are well informed and kind. But this confluence of hospitality and dialogue prompted me to ask: when do these eminent Koreans get any work done? They seem barraged by foreigners, all of whom want to see the same people because they are knowledgeable, important, accessible, and speak good English. Korean good humor and kindness perhaps motivated their willingness to meet, and because Korean hospitality is intimately bound to food, to host lunches and dinners. But the strain on the Korean psyche (let alone their individual and institutional pocketbooks) must be considerable. Of course, foreign visitors think that they are getting special treatment and information, but in fact it is as if they were on a group tour with individually scheduled appointments.

Foreigners are bombarding Koreans. They are smart enough to do so when the season in appropriate, and not only in Korea. In December, just in time for Christmas shopping, when much of the United States is cold, and when the tropical weather is most cool, Americans like to go to Thailand on official business if they can. Spring is a favorite time to visit Korea, as is fall, and during those periods hotel rooms in the upscale establishments are hard to find, for international conferences are held during the same period. So as the swallows return to Capistrano on schedule every year, so the international specialists return to Korea. I must admit to being an unindicted co-conspirator in this regard as well.

Koreans do the same when they travel abroad. They do not concentrate on only a few Americans or other foreigners because the ones they want to see are scattered in different cities, the institutions are diverse, and all Americans speak the local language. They also want to see other Koreans. Koreans living overseas, especially those who do so in conjunction with or after prominent careers in Korea, are often deluged with visitors. Such overseas Korean residents must, to be socially acceptable, offer hospitality to Korean travelers, and sometimes other services are required. A Korean friend in Honolulu got an unlisted telephone number because he was often called late at night from the airport by arriving Koreans who then expected him to get out of bed and pick them up at the airport, and then, of course, feed them a good Korean meal.

We know that one important function of Korean embassies in proper climates is to arrange golf courses and tee times for prominent Korean visitors. At least in those instances there is an element of relaxation in the relationship. One sometimes speculates that the primary function of all embassies overseas is to take care of visitors from the home country. Even as a mediocre player, I once was dragooned into playing tennis with a visiting U.S. senator who demanded a game, but there were no available embassy players.

I don't know how much time an eminent Korean spends with foreign visitors who are only peripherally related to their actual responsibilities. I believe that it must be a significant percentage of their working day, and one wonders how this might subvert their official duties.

There was an old adage that travel was broadening, and not only of the waistline with new and exciting foods and in the Korean case with luxuriant hospitality, but through new mental gymnastics that such experiences provide. Perhaps this may still be true. But there may be a corollary to that view, or perhaps a new theory of administrative efficiency. One might call it the "Stone Mirror Theorem." That is, in upper management levels of government, administrative efficiency decreases in direct proportion to the number of foreign visitors who visit a national capital. The more visitors come, the less time is available to spend on the work for which the government is allocating salaries. If such work involves foreign policy, we might posit that foreign relations will deteriorate in direct relation to the number of influential foreign visitors received. Presuming an optimum use of limited time, such visits inhibit the efficiency of work performed. A government, then, might want to encourage group tours to the Secret Garden, but discourage the peripatetic foreign elites in their Korean peregrinations.

Of course, every government has a number of "foreign handlers," those whose job it is to deal with foreigners because their linguistic abilities are considerable, and their charm is persuasive. But my friends want to see those who are involved in policies, not performance. And so the problem remains: does travel really improve policy formation?

May 1997

On Diffused Reciprocity

Every society has its own means by which social associations beyond family are solidified. Even among family members, these relationships often need strengthening. This is often done through some tangible expression of greater closeness through the presentation of something physical. The offer of hospitality through food is one common means that both creates an informal atmosphere leading to closer ties as well as placing the guest in some sort of bond, which may, perhaps, be simply released by returned hospitality of a similar type sometime later.

But other bonds are not so ephemeral. Some attempts to cement ties are taken with a very long perspective. And some involve very large amounts of money. So we must make a distinction, as does Korean law, between bribery, which is the specific use of a public position for private gain, and is usually short term in completing mutual benefits and is illegal, and what the Koreans call certain social courtesies, such as *ddok kap* (literally, the "price of rice cakes"), by which is meant the transfer of something of monetary value from one person to another to establish a generalized relationship of moral obligation that may not even be defined, or in gratitude after some event has occurred. Some academicians call this "diffused reciprocity," because there is no quid pro quo established, but there are expectations of mutual support. The Japanese term is *nemawashi,* or "root-binding"; it is a good term because it has in its literal meaning the connotation of a lengthy relationship. The concepts are all very similar: one is giving something to, or performing some favor for, someone in order that a close, but unspecified, tie is established that will prove helpful to the giver, and perhaps the receiver, at some indefinite time, perhaps long into the future. In a sense, one picks a relationship with someone who is felt to have potential for the person doing the giving. Of course the receiver must also feel the connection might mature into something important. These mutual ties are solidified by the *ddok kap,* which are funds that grease the social skids and allow life to continue on an even keel with developmental possibilities.

A professor may do something for a student, without feeling the need for recompense but perhaps partly based on his or her role as professor, and partly on the possibility that twenty years later that student might become an important person, and it may be a small investment in time and money to secure a relationship that is enduring. An employer may do something for his staff, something extra and more personal than a company bonus, to receive in return ill-defined but important loyalty. But these are somewhat different from *ddok kap.*

Korean law traditionally recognizes that *ddok kap* is a part of the Korean cultural system, and that funds, even very substantial funds that might be larger than the average annual income for a middle-class American family, transferred under this system of diffused reciprocity may not be legally punishable.

When does diffused reciprocity become focused reciprocity, and thus by definition bribery? There can be no unequivocal answer to such a question. That is what some recent court cases have been about in Korea. It will depend on the previous relationships between those involved, the present or anticipated links between the individuals, the amount of this potentially returnable reciprocity, the expectations of the parties concerned, and even the views of outsiders of the propriety of the relationship.

But law and belief systems may be quite different, although the gap seems to be closing in Korea. Although many, perhaps most, Koreans would believe in the generalized system of establishing relationships and the exchange of tangible products in the process, they are concerned even when there is no direct evidence of bribery, that the circumstances of the relationship and the benefits that would so obviously accrue to the parties involved means that the system has become corrupted.

The levels of corruption in the society at the highest levels have become so vast that a sense of cynicism has set in that virtually establishes guilt by profession and association. Many believe that people in certain fields are virtually corrupt by definition—that is, to be in a certain field requires corruption to survive. This undercuts the efficacy of government and institutions, and is detrimental to the society as a whole. In large part, the wave of nostalgia for former President Park Chung Hee, which ignores his gross violations of the human rights that Korea ostensibly espouses, is based on his apparent lack of personal corruption.

Every new government that has come to power in Korea has engaged in purges of previous regime staff and those closely associated with them. These purges have been based on charges of corruption on which an outsider has no evidence. But one must expect that whoever wins the next presidential election in December, there will be a new purge of the civil service or government corporations, perhaps some of the business staff closely associated with the previous government, and even politicians themselves.

Although these purges have been based on the concentration and personalization of power in the Korean political system, and thus those who have been defeated or replaced are outside the pale of proper treatment, the expectation of corruption even lends a sense of justice to the process.

Probably all of us believe in diffused reciprocity to some degree, and often unconsciously cultivate relationships in the vague expectation that they might be helpful sometime later. The question of gift-giving, which is such an important element of Korean social patterns, becomes enmeshed in the development of these relationships, and contributes to some of the most critical problems that Korea faces today.

It is, of course, for Koreans to work their own way out of this system. But present Korean practices present certain conflicts with foreign legislation on bribery, which in many cases are more strict and encompassing. No doubt these will be resolved over time, but one has reasonable assurance that whatever evolves will be distinctly Korean, while taking into account international practices. In the process, however, there may be a great deal of gnashing of teeth and anguish before some modus vivendi is worked out to society's general satisfaction.

August 1997

On Gifts and Gift-Giving

Koreans personally are the most generous of gift-givers. Americans are not, even though they do not perceive of themselves individually as any the less benevolent, and indeed for charities and other relief and humanitarian activities they may be munificent to the point of gullibility. But in Korea, Americans are often considered *yamche,* or stingy in a somewhat cute manner, as, for example, when someone asks you for a match and then asks for a cigarette. This is not because Americans are parsimonious, but rather because they do not understand the rules of the Korean gift-giving game.

There is a strict protocol in Korea for gift-giving. Every Korean knows when they go to a certain event—a wedding or a funeral, a book-warming ceremony or anything in between—what is expected of them in monetary terms, depending on their closeness to those involved in the event and their own financial circumstances. A white envelope with crisp, new bills (never old ones) is in order as a helping hand to those sponsoring the event. It seems that Koreans have a marked, and envious, capacity to keep a mental scorecard of who has given what to whom and on what occasions. There will inevitably come a time when reciprocity requires a similar repayment.

From high to low, a gift is required. The bride's and groom's families provide as substantial presents as possible for the in-laws and their relatives. Insufficient presents from the bride's family may be grounds for divorce; in India, according to the press, it may be grounds for murder. In Seoul, three keys (to the kingdom) were required to be supplied by the bride's family: those for an apartment, a car, and an office for professional practice. If even the poorest student visits a teacher, a single flower at lowest cost is deemed appropriate, for one cannot come empty-handed. If one goes to a home for dinner, or simply to pay a call, a little expression of regard is deemed proper. In itself, and in its innocent form, it seems an admirable custom because it both establishes a mutually determined degree of respect and consideration, while at the same time adhering to social usage that simplifies life.

Americans, on the other hand, have no social protocol in this or in many other aspects of life. Their society is too physically, generationally, and socially mobile, and their backgrounds are too diverse to foster a national set of "rules of engagement." They often struggle to decide what should be given at an American wedding. They sometimes bring a gift of wine or flowers to a dinner party, but sometimes not (a gift should always be brought if the host is Korean). They rarely know when to call someone by their first or last name or title, or how to refer to their spouse to a third party. Sometimes they don't know whether they can drop in unannounced at someone's home or have to call in advance, or invite them to a sumptuous or potluck dinner without being specific. They often do not know how formally to dress when going to an event. They make many mistakes because the rules are unclear, and also vary by region, class, age, and time. The idea that "anything goes" may be attractive on the surface and be considered by some an ingredient of a democratic society, but in reality it leads to more stress, more misunderstanding, and is quite unrelated to either democracy or to social mobility. All one has to do to gauge the prevalent misperceptions and uncertainties is to consider the continuing popularity of books on social protocol by Emily Post or Miss Manners, or look at the newspaper columns to which readers write in for advice. Protocol was established to make behavior easy by making life clearer, but in the United States it is limited to diplomatic circles.

In Korea, gift-giving is a charming custom, but it can lead to abuses of both minor or consequential proportions. I recently got an institutional bill that included a supposedly "voluntary gift" for *chusok,* and another for someone's *hwangap* (60th birthday). I refused to pay them for they were not gifts, but closer to a kind of extortion or tax.

Cross-cultural misunderstandings sometimes arise from misplaced expectations. A Korean professor in the United States, who believed he had established excellent rapport with his American students, was profoundly upset when at Christmas he did not receive any gifts or even cards from his students. He went into a period of self-analysis to determine his inadequacies until someone told him that in a sense the students were protecting him from any possible charges of favoritism by not giving anything.

When is gift-giving appropriate? A timely gift to a teacher in a public school here ensures that a child is noticed in class and given the attention that the student deserves without such a gift. How much that gift is worth, and in what form and manner it is given, is a matter of some concern. In the United States, the old saying, "An apple for the teacher," indicates a token of respect but of no real monetary value and is thus acceptable. Too much in the way of gifts and one is thought of as an "apple-polisher," a term of disrepute. In Korea, a teacher is likely to get a case of apples instead.

Gifts as tokens of respect or appreciation or friendship are delightful. But when do gifts become coercion or corruption—in consideration of dire consequences avoided or future favors expected? We have read in the press of stories of the downfall of powerful people in Korea and elsewhere because of inappropriate gift-giving.

Each culture defines corruption according to its own norms. Each has, of course, some sort of unwritten but socially understood rules evident to its population about how much can be given to whom at what time, under what circumstances, and for what purposes. When, also, are gifts tokens of personal esteem, and when are they institutional lobbying? The U.S. Congress is trying to determine what is acceptable behavior in the acceptance of gifts or hospitality. Any U.S. Executive Branch official who receives a gift of over token value must report it, and turn it over to the government or pay for it. A national security advisor to a president was dismissed for forgetting this rule.

Years ago, when I was negotiating with the U.S. government on behalf of a private organization, I volunteered to pay for my government friend's luncheon hamburger (value about $2.00 in those days).

He refused because we were negotiating, and could not be seen to be indebted to me even for a token. It was an admirable act.

Gifts and hospitality pose special problems in Korea. If gift-giving is ubiquitous, so is hospitality, and in Korea hospitality is associated with food. So accepting the socially required hospitality offered by a Korean may involve nothing more fancy than a hamburger or *naeng myon* (cold noodles—a simple dish) at a major hotel, but one at substantial cost. Yet not to partake in these events is even more inappropriate than accepting. And we all know that in Korea "Dutch treats" are considered rude and virtually barbarian. Similarly, to refuse a gift may be considered a major insult.

According to some academicians, about 22 percent of Korean corporate profits used to go to "voluntary contributions." The Korean press has reported on how the system may be abused. But such giving has implied a sense of protection for those so generous. A refusal to donate "voluntarily" may invite dire consequences. Some churches in the United States used to teach that "it is more blessed to give than receive." On the other hand, gifts in the West sometimes breed suspicions because of unclear motivations. "Beware Greeks bearing gifts" is an expression as a result of the Greek present of the Trojan horse (full of Greek soldiers) to the Trojans, resulting in the destruction of their city.

A culture determines the relationships, if any, between voluntary gifts, coercion, bribes, and corruption. As long as the transactions are internal, the society itself must establish the rules by which it will live, or suffer the consequences of a loss of credibility for an individual, an institution, or even a regime. When such events become international, then foreign rules may apply alongside local ones, and life become far more complex and restricted. Koreagate in the 1970s came about when the prevalent standards of gift-giving in Seoul at that time were transferred to Washington by people who should have understood the social differences.

The rules have partly changed in Korea as a result of internal pressures to weed out corruption. How far these new rules will go, how transparent relationships will be, and how investigative the press will pursue some of these issues are aspects of the Korean scene that will bear watching.

Aristotle was right when he wrote: "To give money away is an easy matter, but to decide to whom to give it, and how large a sum, and

when, and for what purposes, and how, is neither in every man's
power, nor an easy matter. Hence, it is that such excellence is rare and
praiseworthy and noble."

October 1995

On Eating and Globalization

There are three elements of a culture that are slow to change: concepts
of food, power, and sexual relations. Koreans seem most attached to
their own food at home or especially when they go abroad. I used to
know Americans who would look for steak or hamburger when they
went to Paris, but they were in the minority to those who sought a
good, inexpensive French meal, if that is not a contradiction in terms.

There are two kinds of cultures; those that are home food cultures,
and those that are restaurant cultures. In the latter, chefs were a professional class, and well paid. France, Italy, China, Japan are some
examples. Most other societies were those in which the best food was
in the home. Perhaps this is one reason why Koreans are so attached
to their food, as it evokes childhood.

Koreans, more than others, seem to crave their own food. In a city
like Seoul, one of the major metropolises of the world in terms of size
and intellectual sophistication, one that boasts several Western-style
symphony orchestras, a few opera companies, diverse theaters and a
myriad of art galleries featuring all styles, there are very few good
Western restaurants, and those are mostly in the hotels that cater
mainly to international clientele.

Good Western food is unfamiliar, and Koreans seem willing to settle for mediocre foreign fare except in those special places. If one
travels outside Seoul, such food is unpalatable. There, foreign culi-
nary sophistication is a couple of generations removed from Seoul today. This seems because there is little general interest in foreign food
in the provinces. After all, a society that produces *pudae chige* (lit.,
"military unit stew"—cooked with military derived spam-type products in a Korean milieu) is not very interested in the subtleties of
Western gastronomy.

This concentration on Korean food and lack of interest in Western
cuisine is in contrast to the general acceptance of Western imports
and the internationalization of beverages in Korea. Although urbanized Koreans have rediscovered the joys of *soju* and *makkoli,* Kore-

ans have adopted the spectrum of foreign drinks from Coca-Cola to the most sophisticated of liquors, foreign wines at exorbitant prices, and international beers at the many "hofs." Not just any foreign drink will do; it has to be prestigious (although simply to be foreign may give it an aura). Try ordering a Johnny Walker Red Label scotch, the cheaper kind, instead of the more expensive Black, Blue, or Gold labels, or an inferior cognac, and you will find most bars do not carry them. Now Koreans market their own foreign-style liquor and wine products as well, but they are less well received in exalted circles.

But food is different. Chinese or Japanese may wish for rice when they are abroad, but Koreans want more than rice, although that certainly is a prerequisite. Koreans seem to need *kimchi, kochujang* (red pepper paste), *chige* (soup or stew), and *panchan* (side dishes)—the whole satisfying meal.

When we lived in the United States, if Korean guests were coming in from the airport, we would prepare a Korean dinner even if only twenty hours earlier they had left Seoul and eaten two or three airline meals in between. I would comment to my wife that guests should have local food. She would respond that I did not know Koreans, and that all Koreans would prefer to have their own familiar food to settle their stomachs, as they say, when first they arrive on foreign soil. I have learned that she was right.

But why this strong attachment to local foods? Although many Koreans complain that Korean food in Seoul has become homogenized and now seems to partake of a Kyongsang accent, they do not complain when they are abroad. As long as it is Korean, spicy, and filling, it is better than any Western meal. Rice is, of course, required.

But the answer goes beyond rice and national pride. In this period of rising nationalism, there is a rediscovery of the Korean tradition, whether it is folk arts, traditional music, or food and drink. What once were peasant preoccupations have become the province of the sophisticated urbanite. Farmers' dances were once for farmers, *p'ansori* for *kisaeng,* but now they are for everyone. This is a natural and positive phenomenon. But it is not mainly nationalism that encourages Korean cuisine.

Food evokes a special kind of nostalgia that is very powerful, and even more powerful the older one grows. Childhood memories of the tastes and smells of food are enduring. The elderly often long for the cooking of their mothers. In Proust's *Remembrance of Things Past,* the narrator begins that lengthy novel on the recollection from childhood of the taste and smell of a madeleine cookie soaked in chamomile tea, and builds on that experience and several others a theory of literature and art. Nostalgia is closely linked to the emotions, and Koreans and foreigners continue to comment that one of the characteristics of Korean society is the strong overt emotional emphasis, in contrast to the other societies of the region. Food and emotions are closely intertwined, as is language, while the rapid and obvious internationalization of Korean life is more external.

Korean food feeds nostalgia; it is slow to prepare and slow to eat, allowing time to savor the experience, while ordinary Western food tends to be made quickly and gulped down. Foreigners tend to lump Korean food together as hot and spicy, but those who know Korea recognize that it comes in a myriad of tastes and subtleties, distinguishable by region, class, and even family, that the aficionado will immediately identify. But these distinctions seem to lose in translation, as it were.

As Korea globalizes, as more Koreans travel and trade abroad, overseas Korean restaurants are a growth industry. Western fast food is booming in Korea as well, but more among the young who lack nostalgia. But the expansion of fast food restaurants and their easy and simple fare adulterate the better quality Western dishes. If Korea is to globalize, it would benefit from the delights of good, inexpensive, Western food beyond the fast food syndrome. Until that time comes, when your Korean friends or relatives come to visit, be sure to have a proper Korean meal prepared, and then you can modestly say, as all Koreans do, "There is nothing to eat, but eat a lot."

August 1995

4

Landscapes and Aesthetics

On *Aesthetic Continua*

I was studying Korean some weekends ago, but progress was delayed as I looked out my study window at the still somber, pre-spring scene. I am predisposed and partial to landscapes, and this one, while lacking the anticipated verdure of the following month, was still impressive. One peak rose triangularly and majestically with rock outcroppings that seemed ready to slide precipitously, and near one of the peaks the old fourteenth-century Seoul wall snaked around another of the summits. Although I longed for the mountain mists or the purple blush of the spring azaleas, it was a pleasant, if somewhat monochrome, scene.

Until I looked down. At eye level, I was filled with a warmth and tranquility that beauty can bring. As I lowered my gaze, I saw below the tops of haphazardly built apartments and "villas," as they are euphemistically called, traffic backed up on the road through the valley, television antennae, and the general degradation that occurs in Seoul even in affluent neighborhoods.

Landscapes are important to me, in life and in paintings. The cherry tree and the dogwoods of our home in Washington; the Ming pagoda, rice fields, and the river and White Cloud Mountain in Kwangchou; the old Repulse Bay in Hong Kong; the lake in Rangoon, and here the mountains of Seoul—its saving grace.

When I began to read about East Asia, the aesthetic tradition was a major attraction. I was struck by the landscape paintings of the Sung Dynasty—they are still on display in the Boston Museum of Fine Arts where I first became acquainted with them. That had led me to the realization that landscape painting developed in the Chinese cultural sphere at least a thousand years before it began in Europe. In fact, the earliest landscape extant in the world is a Shilla temple floor tile of about the sixth century in the National Museum here, although the tradition must be much older. Nature and man were integrated in a way that was not true in the West until very late in European culture—the rise of the Dutch school of painting and, later, romanticism in art, literature, and music. Nature was first feared and worshiped, and then to be overcome in the West, but in East Asia man and nature were integrated. So one scholar, Professor F. C. S. Northrop, perhaps fifty years ago distinguished what he called the "undifferentiated aesthetic continuum" of East Asian art from the "differentiated aesthetic continuum" of the West. This professional and obscure jargon simply noted how nature and man were integrated into the arts and culture of the East Asian tradition, while they were separated in the West.

I absorbed this with fervor, and thought that I had learned a great truth. I still regard this as an important insight into differing cultural patterns, yet my views have become tempered through experience.

It first started during the Korean War. I was in Japan for a few months as advisor to the U.S. Air Force, and since it was spring, I inquired where the best of the cherry blossoms were likely to be found. Ueno Park in Tokyo was said to be the most accessible and the best in the area. And so I went, and was enthralled. I looked up at the myriad of blossoms in their full splendor, and I was filled with wonder at their beauty. But then I looked down, and there under the blossoms were mounds of trash and garbage where seemingly the whole of the Tokyo population had picnicked and then left their remains strewn over the landscape. I was devastated.

The scene, however, has since been replayed many times in Asia for me. When we were looking for an apartment in Seoul, we were shown one with a lovely mountain view. When we asked the real estate agent about the egregiously ugly city dump that was right below the apartment, she replied, "Look up! Don't look down!"

So lovely homes are juxtaposed next to squalor. Lanes are so narrow fire trucks could never pass. Zoning is absent; green areas intruded upon. Once isolated Buddhist temples have been surrounded with tourist degradation brought on by the greed that the temples were there to illustrate was an illusion—an ephemeral attachment that could only lead to pain. The interior of a home is spotless and the courtyard is swept clean, yet outside the wall filth proliferates, and few seem to care. A river view in a rural, isolated valley that calms and soothes is destroyed by the "love hotels" and food stalls that spring up like, and indeed are, weeds in an otherwise perfect harmony.

So previously local citizens associations, mandated by government, planted flower boxes on some thoroughfares, and villages did the same—to relieve the mind if not solve the problems. Now environmental groups spring up to protect the little that remains unspoiled, reflecting both local needs and international concerns. The rush to development left no place for improving the aesthetic quality of life even if it did increase incomes. Repairing the damage is virtually impossible.

So once entranced with the holistic view of man and nature that was one of the striking contributions of the East Asian tradition to world aesthetics, where the calm and simplicity of a Sung landscape or an Yi Dynasty or Japanese Kano School monochrome draws breaths of admiration and tranquility of mind, that tradition remains only in museums and on the walls of the wealthy. Although the appreciation of nature remains, and can be seen in the streams of people climbing mountains and picnicking on weekends in any verdant spot, the whole grace has been lost, and with it a tradition that was important not only in East Asia, but in the world.

May 1996

On *Pyeo*—Rice

As Arabic has many more words than English for camel, and various Eskimo languages have the same for snow because these are important in those societies, so Korean has different words to describe rice when growing (*pyeo*), husked (*ssal*), and cooked (*pap*). This is the season to think about rice in the fields.

As the monsoon season departs, we look forward to the warm sun of late summer. It is not the "Indian summer" of warmth following the first frost in New England, but it is a time of expectation and anticipation of the ripening of the new rice crop, which brings a special flavor to Korean meals. An old Korean saying indicates that one sends one's daughter-in-law into the fields at this time, but one's daughter in the spring. This illustrates a great deal about family relations in Korea and the daughter-in-law's inferior position, as the still intense heat of the fall sun makes labor more arduous and the skin more likely to blemish than the weaker rays of early spring.

As Korea has urbanized, we sometimes neglect or deprecate the rural scene except when there is a dispute about rice or beef imports and their effects on the Korean farm family. People have escaped from the villages for factory jobs, office wages, and the lure of the city, but urbanization is recent and most city dwellers have rural roots. Perhaps they still remember that there is no more beautiful scene than rice in the spring and in the fall.

Korean poets have written about the beauty of azaleas in the spring—the fabled ones of Yak Mountain. Even in the craggy hills in the north of Seoul one sees splotches of mauve that gladden the eye and the spirit before the trees are fully leafed. In fall we anticipate the changing leaves and fall colors, and perhaps the chrysanthemums in bloom. There will be hordes of people at Mount Sorak for the annual ritual, the "leaf peepers" as they are called in Vermont, and when unification finally comes we can be sure that the Diamond Mountains will be crowded.

But fall and spring have a unity in beauty that lies in rice but in its different hues. As the rice ripens, it turns a rich, dulled gold, a quiet, mature color that rests the eyes and the spirit. It is a deep and subtle tone that in itself is not very impressive. But spread over a valley where a continuous carpet of gold is stretched before one, it is a sight worth traveling to see. Before roads were paved, many of the small country lanes were lined with cosmos in bloom, with their light pastels of purple or pink giving just the touch of youth and life to the maturing saffron of the rice. Korea may be the only country that has produced an art song in honor of the cosmos, whose delicacy contrasts so vividly with the stalwart tones of rice. Added to the scene is the intense clarity of the high, blue sky, still unpolluted, that frames the scene in the sunlight. It is an evocative vista of nostalgia for simpler, if more uncomfortable, times.

The ochre of rice, with its heavier tones, contrasts with vibrant, bright yellow of the spring fields of mustard (rape, *pyongji*) in Cheju. That is a fervent, almost luxuriant, youthful beauty, a sense of vitality set forth against the backdrop of a blue sea that adds contrast. The yellow of the mustard and the blue of the sea is exciting in its dramatic contrast; that of rice and the sky is soothing. Both in their ways are scenes to remember and cherish.

But rice in the spring has another intensity that has special, fresh beauty. There is no lovelier green than that of the young rice plants set out in the fields. They have a vibrancy and tenderness that is in such contrast to the maturity of the fall gold. We all long for the first green of spring, whether in trees or bushes or in the reborn grasses. And the early buds do have a subtlety of lightness and fragility that is appealing. But rice has greater impact, and not just because we anticipate a bumper crop and can anticipate the satisfaction of the cycle of planting and harvesting. Perhaps this effect is not in the single plant. Perhaps, like that of rice in the fall, it is the mass of color, the uniformity of tone, that reinforces this tenderness. We may think poetically of a single violet as expressing this sensitivity, but in the mass we can also see the beauty of delicacy and promises, both planned and fulfilled.

Ralph Waldo Emerson wrote in his diaries, "We are all dying of miscellany." We spend our lives doing the various chores that our responsibilities entail—the myriad tasks that society and our own needs and conscience set forth for us. We seem to have little time, or allow ourselves the time, to step back and consider more fundamental facets of life, like beauty. A. E. Housman in *A Shropshire Lad* wrote that he had few springs left of his allotted "three score years and ten," and so he would in spring seek out the blossoming cherry, the most beautiful of trees, "hung with snow." So, too, however young or old we may be, there is little time left. The wonders of the fall season prompt our thought, even our meditation. We don't have to brave the crowds or climb the mountains to partake in beauty, for it lies in the valleys and roadsides accessible and inviting to us all if we would only look.

September 1995

On Awaiting Disasters

Seoul is a city awaiting disasters. Some will be major and spectacular; others will be private but no less tragic to the families of those involved. When one will occur one cannot readily predict, but the scene is set in so many places that it is highly unlikely that many can be avoided. I am not now writing about faulty building construction, of which no doubt there is a great deal. There has been much on television and in the press since the Sampoong[*] tragedy about cracks in apartments and crumbling streets and infrastructure. I am writing about the urban residential maze into which, when an emergency occurs, neither fire trucks nor ambulances will be able to enter.

The urban maze, the rabbit warrens of houses, both in wealthy and poor areas, is so cramped that access is severely limited. It is a compound problem—in part historical, in part modern, and in part sheer neglect of the elemental rules of passage and transportational civility.

[*] The collapse of a Seoul department store that killed hundreds of people.

In some older areas, where buildings large and small have been piled one next to another and about which little can now be done without major urban renewal, it is like an inherited defective gene, which in time will spawn some tragedy but has been in the body politic for many years. In other contemporary cases of modern construction, it is an infectious disease recently introduced that could easily have been prevented with proper medicine—planning and adherence to elemental rules of safety. In many cases, past and present defects are compounded. In these cases, houses historically have been built so close together that a normal vehicle, let alone a fire engine or an ambulance, can barely enter. And in these areas growing affluence has prompted residents to buy and park vehicles in these alleys so that only the motor scooter is the basic mechanized means of entry. These are like cholesterol-filled arteries that clog circulation.

Much of Seoul in built on hills, and these complicate the problems, because the steep slopes of some lanes essentially preclude vehicles. Even in affluent areas, the sharp degree of rise scrapes the bottoms of cars, or prevents turning except in restricted ways.

All this would be a matter of little concern except to those who choose or are forced to live in this environment. But the problem has broader ramifications. It seems statistically inevitable that some time, in a city that lives on bottled propane gas for cooking, and briquettes for heating in older areas, where electrical wiring is often improperly installed and uninspected, that some misjudgment will take place in a household and a tank will explode, or a kitchen catch on fire, or there will be a short circuit.

I have been told that the fire department is very efficient in dispatching fire engines, and I can testify that emergency ambulances do respond with an alacrity that is admirable. But if they are unable to reach the victims, their efforts are in vain.

Recently there was a fire in a night club in Manila and almost two hundred young people were killed because there was no exit. This situation has occurred in many countries and in many public places. Here, we are not arguing about a single building, but a whole neighborhood where one may be killed in one's own home by simple proximity, not because there is no exit, but because there is no entrance for those who might save lives and property.

I have little doubt that there will be a major disaster sometime and somewhere in Seoul. When it happens, the press will ask what might have been done to prevent it. The answers are obvious to anyone concerned about Seoul citizens.

But the real tragedy may not be the big event that will appear in the papers and on television. What about the little, daily deaths that do not make the newspapers. How many times have ambulances been called to homes of the desperately ill, where minutes are the difference between life and death, but where the ambulance could not reach because someone had arrogantly parked, blocking access without consideration of their neighbors, where lanes were so narrow that it could not pass?

These events don't make news. But we know how they happen. If there are modern zoning regulations concerning the width of streets they may be ignored as householders extend their property little by little into the public way, creating creeping arteriosclerosis of the streets. We have all seen shopkeepers take over public property to increase their display space. And the numbers of vendors, supposedly itinerant but in fact relatively fixed in time and space, are myriad, and not just in the market regions.

Whether egregiously arrogant parking or the virtual theft of public space by incremental additions or by rampantly ignoring whatever regulations exist for safety, we all are a party to the conditions that will result in needless loss.

In the United States, many cities have "fire lanes" that must be kept clear at all times. They may seem a waste, except in the one crisis where one is thankful that such access was mandated. Here, one sees few signs that restrict parking on one side of narrow residential streets. When such signs are violated in my neighborhood near Washington, my neighbors call the police to ticket the illegally parked cars. Here, there are few signs and few regulations, and little enforcement of whatever rules seem to exist. The time to save lives is before the crisis occurs not after, when there is a bemoaning of tragedies that might have been avoided.

June 1996

On "The Beauty Is in the Walking..."

"The beauty is in the walking; we are betrayed by destination." So said the Welsh writer Gwyn Thomas reading from his works on television. On a summer trip to the United States to discuss institutional budgets rather than to cavort on the beach, I took the opportunity one night to catch up on the one Public Broadcasting System (educational television) program to which, aside from news broadcasts, I had become addicted. This was Masterpiece Theatre, which at its best is superb, and at its worst is still better, if set in period clothing, than all American soap operas. The program I watched concerned reminiscences by Gwyn Thomas, and I was struck by this one phrase.

There is more to this comment than simply doubting the old advertisements for ships crossing the Atlantic, which stated that "getting there is half the fun." Indeed, perhaps it is better not to focus on destinations; getting nowhere is, rather, all the fun, and perhaps reaps all the benefits as well.

We have a tendency to concentrate our efforts on ends because they appear clear, distinct, and measurable. Our businesses and governments are now told to be "results oriented," and look to the "bottom line," while increasingly even educational institutions and research institutes are formed around "problem areas" or "themes." All this is very well, insofar as it allows us to focus on issues that relate to improving the human condition in some manner. Too often, however, we inappropriately consider only the destination. We go to university to "become educated" or learn a profession, as if, once one graduates, that is the end of the learning process.

The issue of ends justifying means is a perennial, if rather sophomoric, debate. More likely, over time means meld into ends so that the methods for achieving some aim become inextricably bound, influencing the planned result. Although focusing on achieving some tangible goal is obviously appropriate of certain scientific or technological questions, it is less likely to have relevance to the human condition. We extrapolate from science, and extend the possibility of solutions, or destinations, to areas where in fact there is no destination.

In American terms, and increasingly in Korean terms now that Korea is more affluent, the purported answer to arriving at one's preferred destination is to imply that if one throws enough money at a problem, it is solvable. We have games and need facilities, so we can build stadia with money and time, and even with less time if more money. Spend more money on training and we can break a world record. We end up sending a man to the moon under a crash program, in effect sponsored by competition with the Soviet Union. In Korea, a research institute is formed to solve everything from policies to Korean culture. Would that life were so easily addressed.

The most obvious example these days has been the Olympics, where the destination—medal count for the countries, gold for individuals or teams, and economic solvency for the sponsoring city and the organizers— was pervasive, while the process of healthy competition and sporting spirit seemed lost to these ends. The spirit of sport, of friendly competition, of amateur excellence, has all been subsumed under national or individual glory. Olympic nationalism as a substitute for war among competitive countries may be a step forward, however, even though at times one wonders. But some countries that did poorly in medals agonize over how to reach their destination by winning something, anything.

We tend to designate our destinations too rigidly, and abuse or deny that the process of getting there is perhaps more important. In many instances there can be no destination. Usually we are not, metaphorically speaking, playing golf, where the course is set, the standards established, and the end result can be measured after which we all retire to the nineteenth hole for congratulations and drinks provided by the losers.

Rather, in life we would better concentrate on meandering through the metaphoric meadows, enjoying views, stopping to browse and examine a wild flower, trying to remember the name of a certain tree, or looking for interesting birds and landscapes. We have no explicit destination, although we have dreams and ideals, but we enrich ourselves in this continuing process in a manner both far more productive and holistic than if we were solely engaged in improving our drive or putting.

Each country is on various roads toward destinations stated or implied. In Korea, it is toward democracy, reunification, improved human rights, better economic conditions, improved status of women, and a cleaner environment, just to mention a few areas of concern to a wide swath of the citizenry. But there is no ultimate or real destination in any of these fields. Our concepts of democracy or human rights or the status of the citizenry are ever changing, improving, one hopes, and our concern should be on the process of such change, and not with an end result that may be irrelevant by the time we seem to approach our goals.

We are always moving the goal posts, as Americans say, and setting farther goals, sometimes disconcerting to those with whom we negotiate. In a way this is an indirect recognition of process over product, but it is not sufficient. We need to recognize that process is inherent in the maturation and growth of nations, institutions, as well as people. On the road to democracy or economic well-being, we should not denigrate the importance of the process for the goal. So authoritarian regimes justify themselves for a future subverted by not recognizing that the two are intertwined. The process of democratization and the experience gained by institutionalizing that effort are more important.

Let us compete in sports, politics, or economics, but not solely to reach a single triumphant destination, but to mature in civility and refinement and learn from the process of change.

September 1996

On Visual Pollution

We are all aware of the multiple pollutions against which Korea is fighting. Air, water, land, and noise are the most obvious. They are, of course, potentially damaging to our physical health, and offend our five senses. Most are generated internally, but some infiltrate from abroad. We need to clean them up for the safety of present and future societies. This is extremely difficult in an overcrowded country where demands for housing and mobility and material possessions are expanding faster than normal population increases because of greater wealth, and where diplomacy is required for cross-national problems.

There is also another form of pollution that affects our mental, if not our physical, health. This is visual pollution. It is more severe in urban areas, but the rural regions have not escaped.

The countryside has seen the proliferation of plastic. As one reaches the cusp of a hill and surveys the scene below, whole valleys seem to be seas filled with shimmering foamy waves as the white plastic tents completely covering the vegetable fields undulate in the breeze. The hillsides have not eluded infiltration, as vegetables grow up around plastic sheets that cut weeds and retain moisture. Worse are the jumbled piles of used, dirty, nonbiodegradable plastic lying in heaps along the side of the road, perhaps scattered among the cosmos, or just left in the middle of a hillside.

The countryside has changed visually for the worse with the demise of the thatched roof home with its warm honey earth tones, and perhaps some fiery red peppers drying on the roof with a yellow gourd. New tiled roofs seem to lack depth and maturity. But the villagers may have gained in economics what they have lost in aesthetics through these types of visual pollution. The oriental landscape painters of today would have to employ great selective powers of omission if they were to recreate the ethereal tranquility that their forebears painted.

The major visual pollution is urban, however. There are, of course, beautiful urban moments—an old palace, a traditional house or gate, an ancient tree, an ancestral wall, a mountain park in the midst of jumbled quarters, but Korea has failed the majority of its population—the three-quarters who live in cities. I do not want to consider here the disappointing, bastardized, and standardized architecture of pseudomodern apartments that are inhuman in feeling—monstrosities unimaginatively designed and poorly executed. There is great beauty in Korea, but there are no beautiful cities or towns left.

Here I want to discuss signs. Signs are ubiquitous. Some cover every square outside meter of multistoried buildings. Their jumble creates a visual cacophony that is as unproductive as it is upsetting. Signs are supposed to advertise—they thus are to have some positive economic impact. But the great expenses that are incurred for the production of these signs have little or no positive economic effects—except on the sign makers. So many signs mean that the individuality and identity for which the signs were erected are lost in the welter of other advertising, so that no one benefits.

Signs come in all shapes and forms, covering walls and even windows. Considered individually, few have charm or grace or any attractions that would entice the customer. They rather are repelling. There are few, subtle Korean words—most are foreign words or phrases, often inaccurate or inappropriate in their use, in transliterations and abbreviations that obscure, not edify.

In some countries, cities and towns restrict the number and size of signs, whether they can project over the sidewalk, and if they can be lit or in neon. The concept is to create a planned atmosphere conducive to those types of people who wish to patronize those shops. The result is self-restraint from which everyone benefits. Understatement is the prerequisite of nobility.

Here, unlicensed greed has taken over, and this is true of virtually every urban area in Korea. Subtlety and refinement disappear. Individuality of architecture or neighborhoods is lost. Charm that would attract more customers vanishes. The urban advertising wasteland prevails. How much more attractive Myongdong would be if the signs were artistic, original, and congruent. How much more enticing the back alleys of Taehakno would be if one were not visually offended.

So what can be done? Two simple approaches, drawing on the two growing forces in Korea: local autonomy and civil society. Local administrations need to raise funds to be autonomous from the central government. Let local authorities tax signs over a minimum size, keeping the revenues to help run local government. Graduate the taxes so that a larger size or more than one sign per establishment becomes economically prohibitive.

Second, call on civic organizations to encourage merchants and others who advertise to make their neighborhoods visibly environmentally pleasing through signs reflecting local cohesion not individual mercantilism. The state ordered the formation of *bansanghoe* (local citizens' associations) some years ago. Neighborhood social pressure through citizens' actions, plus discreet indications of potential boycotts of local establishments might do wonders for reform.

Our five senses are constantly bombarded in the cities in which we live. We escape to the mountains to be refreshed, but we need to feel this at home. We would like to end traffic problems, stop polluting streams, and drink safe water. We should make every effort to do so, bearing the expenses. But without new funding we could start with stopping the visual pollution that may not affect our breathing, but does affect our brains.

October 1995

On Perimeters and Peddlers

Perhaps we might formulate some fundamental law, and a corollary axiom, governing the role of perimeters—the edges of geographic control—in open economic systems. It might read: external entrepreneurial activities vary directly as the square of the perimeter's internal diameter. So, the larger the area circumscribed by the perimeter, the greater will be the entrepreneurial feeding frenzy along its borders. The law's axiom might be: such entrepreneurial activity will be conducted in taste diminishing to the same degree as the extent of the entrepreneurial activity grows. Let me explain.

Restrictions on the popular use of large public or private spaces often result in intense efforts to exploit the perimeters of those spaces for entrepreneurial purposes—to capture the assets of those coming in or going out. This is usually done in exceedingly questionable or bad taste. This phenomenon is evident in Korea and the United States as well.

On my first visit to Yellowstone National Park in the off-season when there were few visitors, I was struck by both the number and degradation of the conglomeration of business establishments that seemed squashed together, without planning or zoning, just beyond its northern border. It reminded me of what I had seen around military bases in the United States, where the tawdriness of greed and bad taste were multiplied by the juxtaposition of establishments devoted to the pursuit of the quick dollar. When there are crowds of people either coming in or going out of a restricted area, these phenomena are not unknown.

The problem is apparent in Korea as well. Think of Itaewon, just outside the Yongsan and South Post military compounds. Foreigners who are newcomers to Korea may think of it as an area of increasingly ephemeral shopping bargains, but it once was, and still retains the atmosphere of, the blight of raucous release from imposed restrictions as reflected in businesses of diverse kinds. Even though General Coulter's statue is gone, and with it the aging nymphs, those ladies of the night looking for earthy business who surrounded that stalwart figure at dusk, the scent of degradation is in the air, or so it seems.

Lest we think of this problem as restricted to the military bases and an international combination of loneliness and greed, the overall pattern is ubiquitous. A generation ago, if one went to a famous Buddhist temple, on quiet days and in off seasons the tranquility of the surroundings and the harmony of architecture and nature gave one peace and serenity. A dirt road might lead to the compound, making the temple more difficult of access, but then few Koreans had the means or leisure to travel, even internally. Even if now easily accessible, the essential intent of its founders, whether one or fifty generations ago, seemed to remain: it was a source and site of quiet contemplation.

But things have changed. The temples are there, nature within the park remains unadulterated. But just beyond the perimeters of its borders economic chaos has burst forth. Inns, restaurants, drinking establishments, peddlers, and shops selling the most jejune, sometimes the most monstrous, of mementos, the most garish of towels, proliferate. Buses line up, often keeping their loud, polluting engines running while their passengers shop with the attachment to the transitory world that the temples were built to try to get us to overcome. Pulkuksa's vicinity in Kyongju has become what may be the most popular bus parking lot in Korea.

The same phenomenon is true on the edge of once scenic beaches, and not only in Korea. Think of Waikiki. Sorak-san exhibits the same trend. Haeundae is lost; even a few luxury hotels cannot save it.

In a sense, apartment complexes are quite similar. Just outside, the shops have been constructed with no apparent thought but with considerable expenditures on the signs advertising their wares or establishments in manners that destroy whatever amenities the apartment buildings were trying to create. In my neighborhood, at the bottom of the hill on which myriad villas and extremely expensive houses have been built at great cost, the proliferation of unplanned shops and stalls extending out onto the public way, blocking the pedestrians and the traffic, created largely—it seems—of "grandeur" cars, has built a miniaturized urban chaos in the midst of what otherwise might have been a kind of suburban tranquility.

One cannot necessarily blame the military or the monks, or the builders of apartments, for they cannot control all the activities beyond the scope of their authority. But local officials—those who zone or don't zone—and the local people through their neighborhood organizations should recognize that these activities, whether they occur in the United States or in Korea or anywhere else, destroy what had been an advantage. They could act in unison against them. Once destroyed, recovery of these areas will certainly be difficult and expensive, if indeed it is at all possible.

In Washington, our neighborhood organization fought successfully to keep out a very fashionable department store that would have turned the area into a vast parking lot, and in another case to prevent highway expansion increasing air and noise pollution. The power of people can be effective in preserving the good that remains in spite of unthinking exploitation and greed.

May 1966

On Arcadian and Utopian

When we use the terms "arcadian" and "utopian," we are referring to opposite ends of the temporal spectrum. Arcadian refers to some place that is rural, pastoral, and innocent—a site of peace and simplicity, conjuring up images of the bucolic past. Referring originally to a mountainous section of ancient Greece whose local deity was Pan, the god of shepherds, it became popular by the sixteenth century through a work by Sir Philip Sidney. "Utopian" has come to mean an idealized and imagined future, to mix literary references "the best of all possible worlds," one today with connotations of the impossible. To refer to someone today as "utopian" is to imply that he or she is wooly-headed— not in tune with reality. The word comes from the title of the 1516 novel by Sir Thomas More.

So the word "arcadian" elicits feelings of the idealized past, while "utopian" brings forth concepts of the imagined future. Both are firmly rooted in the Western tradition. Perhaps pastoral peace has its early origins in the biblical Garden of Eden; Shakespeare sets *As You Like It* in the forest of Arden. But it was the rise of romanticism throughout Europe that brought to the fore the concept of the idyllic countryside. So European nobility in the eighteenth and nineteenth centuries tried to recreate arcadia in their extensive gardens. Tom Stoppard, the contemporary British playwright, has a play entitled *Arcadia*. Social evils, on the other hand, gave rise to a wide variety of literature about a better future, of which present science fiction is an offshoot.

The East Asian tradition is somewhat different. The Confucian idealized past is not arcadian—it is instead social, where harmonious human relations existed and states were governed properly. The past was the proper era to be emulated, but it was a past of good governance based on moral examples. Nature was not an important image of that tradition, although the deep involvement in nature, and man as a part of nature, was of course found in poetry, painting, and in Taoism. Being in harmony with nature was considered an essential element of the Taoist tradition. The Japanese and Chinese developed their gardens, as did the Europeans, and they wrote manuals on them (the Koreans had their gardens but did not seem to write original treatises on the subject). In the nineteenth century, many proper English and continental estates had some chinoiserie or japonoiserie gardens or elements adopted from them.

Today, even before globalization began to homogenize the world, the images of utopia and arcadia had begun to merge. Societies east and west are filled with people who want affluence with a certain degree of control over their own destinies, and who have hopes for a better future—a utopian one. Hope, after all, is what the world's middle classes want. It is about a better future for their children. When under the constant pressure of change, people often idealize the past—the physical pleasantness of landscapes bucolic as well as the moral virtues associated with their own images of their imagined arcadia.

The future is at least potentially, if not substantially, under our control, even if the past must remain imagined. The United States, in spite of saving vast areas of arcadia through natural parks, has despoiled much of its land. But it has a great deal of land with at one time a sparse population. Korea is different. It is a physically small country, overly crowded, in which the pressures to achieve a utopian future tend to undercut the arcadian present and future, leaving only the idealized image of the past and a degraded present. Green belts are breached in search of the utopian affluence that is so earnestly desired, Pollution controls seem sporadically enforced, and automobiles multiply seemingly filling all available space for them. The remaining arcadian landscape is strewn with piles of used plastic that destroy the aesthetics even as they may have improved income. The *kalbi* houses and love hotels destroy panoramas of once unique tranquility.

Does Korea have to choose between arcadia and utopia—between bucolic peace and an affluent future? The choices are far more nuanced than that stark dilemma. But every decision on policy or program, every green hectare given over to a needed house or factory, diminishes as well as creates.

At a recent conference on Korea held at Heidelberg University in Germany, a German scholar gave a paper on civil society and the importance of the environmental movement in that context. The environmentalists have become critical social voices, and although they may not think of themselves in arcadian terms, they try to move the society forward toward utopian goals without losing its arcadian present and potential. We should be thankful that they serve to protect the arcadian heritage.

June 2000

On Winter Advent

Winter hardens the soil and leadens the psyche. As frost now becomes pervasive, I seek warmth inside, reluctant to brave the winds off Pukhan Mountain. But I like to recall the first advent of cold some weeks ago, when winter had not become intrusive and the days were still warm although the evenings had turned crisp. I was traveling in the south, and an opportunity arose to pass by Chirisan.

Chirisan is a gentle, harmonious mountain range. It has none of the rocky ruggedness of the Sorak area—it lacks the outcroppings and spectacular vertical transitions—cliffs perpendicular in a visual intensity concentrating the observer's attention, as befits the extension of the Diamond Mountains in the north. It is as high, but the slopes are modulated, the moderated curves sweeping in an almost relaxed manner. The gentler fall technicolor in a way mirrors the contours. It lacks the intensity of the red maples of the Sorak area, or of New England for that matter, and thus may be ignored by the hordes of tourists that make the Sorak experience as arduous as it is gorgeous. The russets, dull reds, and more subdued ocher blend together and dominate the fall—their modesty calms and beckons. Chirisan is extensive, but it is no less inviting.

On the day of the first snow I arrived—a gentle fall gracing the higher elevations and crowning the peaks with a filtered white cap, the trees breaking the snow as if the cap were aged. Below the subdued fall foliage remained untouched. As the morning progressed and as the sun melted the snow on the middle reaches, in the shaded ravines it still sat gently on the pines and on the bamboo, while underneath the russet and burnished gold of low-lying shrubs contrasted with the intensity of the green and the white above.

The earth tones of fall here gave a somber, warm, and inviting—almost dignified—mien to the mountain. It was not the strident, blatant, darkly contrasted but majestical, almost nouveau riche, tone of Sorak, but the considered, quiet landscape equivalent of the Confucian gentleman in his dignified bearing.

There were but few people on the mountain. Among them, as if to illustrate the analogy, were a dozen or so gentlemen of the old Korean school. They could have been a part of an historical Korean television drama, and at first I thought they might well be. But no, they were from a remote area near Sunch'on, viewing the scenery, as did the others of the hardy few on that cool morning. They had the elderly faces lined with dignity and grace one sees in nineteenth-century photographs. Their weathered features were framed with white beards and the traditional Korean horsehair *kat* (hat). Their attire was impeccably Korean—timeless, and they seemed somehow to fit in the landscape, although surely that was my imagination and not their intention.

Down the mountain the surrealistic images of skeletal persimmon trees stripped naked of their leaves with their small globes of brilliant orange brightened the landscape. Hillside orchards of orange balls dangling from spidery limbs presented almost abstract paintings. The orange contrasted with the dark, somber grey of the stonewalls that once were a common Korean rural scene. On the roadside, the cherry trees were turning their dark red, and a few, hardy cosmos sometimes survived, while in back gardens of some farm houses the brilliant yellow of small chrysanthemums invigorated the scene without intruding on its harmony.

Yet you, the reader may maintain, you writer are romanticizing a life of hardship and depravation, one from which there is a seemingly endless migration to escape the very adversities you find so tranquil and charming. There is truth to the charge. I do not have the luxury, a word incorrect in this context, to claim this sentimentalized, filtered heritage and memories of childhood life. I came to Korea late, mature in age if not in mind, absorbing what lessons one might learn from a society old but newly learned, and internalizing the natural beauty, which I have seen wantonly destroyed in the interests of the physical well-being of the individual and the economic advancement of the state. But if rank gives no privilege these days, perhaps emotional adoption does, or at least allows the indulgences that remember gracefulness in an age rapidly losing it. As one stopped and bought dried persimmons, the country candy all the more delicious for its natural flavor, the tastes and sights compounded a feeling that could evoke nostalgia, not for the past, but knowing that the future would allow me the stolen time to reflect on these scenes. If, after all, Wordsworth could reconsider in his "inward eye" the "hosts of golden daffodils" that he made famous almost two hundred years ago, we may be excused for using our meager talents to reflect on such tranquility, artificial as it may be, and bring a sense of harmony and balance to the stresses of contemporary urban life.

November 1995

On Hollyhocks

My fondness for hollyhocks (*chopsi-kkot*, *Althea rosea*) has been short but intense. I always thought of hollyhocks as a flower requiring long vistas for proper viewing. They were so tall and flamboyant that they should be seen from a distance—perhaps over a meadow or a long garden. They were, I thought, mundane, not elegant, and had an old-fashioned air about them. They should not be viewed close-up because they were not exquisite, sensitive, or fine.

Several years ago my attitude changed. My wife visited the painter Claude Monet's home at Giverny in France several summers ago, where one usually goes to view the water lilies that he made so famous in his paintings. While walking through the town outside his garden, she found hollyhocks blooming in profusion. Scattered on the ground were the seeds of the plant, which are both distinctive and large enough so that they cannot escape detection. She picked up some that had fallen and took them home, unintentionally probably ignoring the U.S. Department of Agriculture's strictures on importing such materials.

Rather skeptically, I planted them against a tall fence, and the following spring nothing appeared. I thought I had committed some egregious botanical or horticultural error. Then next year, when all hope had been abandoned, they came up in profusion, some two meters high, and in all their glory. I then recognized in our small suburban garden, from which if we had to earn an agricultural living we would have been called by the agricultural economists "functionally landless," the beauty of the hollyhock both as a background, but as a primary focus as well.

Last summer, under the guise of official business, I drove alone down to Kyongju. Rather than take the highway, I frequented the back roads, taking two days along the tertiary paved narrow ways, and through many that were still unpaved. Some areas in the mountains were so remote that human habitation, even in crowded, urbanized, Korea, was not apparent for many miles. I stopped at the occasional temple, some known and unknown old *sowon*, and generally basked in the rural environments I had so missed after the urban rigors of Seoul.

Throughout this region, I was struck by the hollyhocks. The road shoulders may have been planted in many areas with cosmos, but it was still too early to enjoy their beauty. For me they are forever associated with the gold of the ripe rice, the contrasting colors—the pastels of the cosmos and the burnished yellow of the paddy melding together.

But plantings along roadsides are for public show. Hollyhocks seemed for private pleasure. Almost every house, no matter how poor, and how remote where few outsiders from beyond the village would have reason to visit, had hollyhocks planted along their outer walls, or by the houses themselves. They varied in size—few were the gigantic monoliths of Monet's offspring. Most were shorter, but no less attractive. There were the dark reds, pinks, and whites mixed in a haphazard confusion that only added to their attractiveness. They were hardy and showy, and have a plain but honest mien. The single large flowers bloom vertically along a stalk, contrasting with the horizontal nature of the walls.

The houses had lost their aesthetic appeal. The thatched roofs were gone, many of the old walls had been replaced with ugly, but I suppose more functional, cement blocks. All had television antennae. Sometimes the hollyhocks grew amid the discarded detritus of living—an old tire, torn plastic sheeting. In other places they bloomed aside the large, earthen *kimchi* pots creating a sense of warmth and tranquility. The profusion of hollyhocks softened the appearances of what had become an aesthetic blight, and the care with which they once were planted gave one hope that all sensitivity had not been lost in the search for modernization and relative affluence. It is a common flower in the eye of the public, but one that captures a scene, and exudes a sense of quiet, unobtrusive, friendliness.

Hollyhocks seem to lack cachet in the West, at least in English literature. Perhaps part of the problem is that the word itself is not particularly elegant. I can think of only one, not very popular, western poem in which they are mentioned. Tennessee Williams in a 1946 poem set to music mentions "And hollyhocks grew bright by the door," in "Blue Mountains Ballads," but this depicted a poor rural area. There seems to be no more elegant appeal—no "violet by a mossy stone, half hidden from the eye." No "host of golden daffodils." No "rose by any other name." No "when lilacs last at the dooryard bloomed."

My Korean friends say that there are two poems in which the hollyhock is extolled. One with that simple title (by Chang Hyong-ki, 1934-) is really about nostalgia, not the flower. The other, "Hollyhocks—My Dear" (*chopsi kkot-tangsin*, literally, "Hollyhocks—You," by To Chong-hwan) is a two-volume collection of poems of a decade ago, in which the poet compares his love for his wife to the simple, everlasting beauty of the flower. These poems are said to bring tears to many Korean eyes.

When back in Seoul, the next spring I searched the flower dealers for either seeds or plants to try to recapture the beauty of the countryside in my small, rented plot. It was an arduous struggle, taking me to the outskirts of the city before I found what I wanted.

It is too early to know what will happen to the plants I put in before the frosts were over, or to the seeds I started indoors. I cannot recapture the beauty of the countryside, nor the naturalness of the scene, but the hollyhocks may bring remembrances of beauty past, if they survive my black thumb.

May 1966

On Voids: Visual, Oral, and Aural

Those of us who admire the great tradition of East Asian art of China, Korea, and Japan consider that this genre of painting is one of the world's great accomplishments. One of its essential attributes is the extensive use of space, not as nothingness, but as an integral part of the composition. This is especially true in landscape painting, where the evocative union of nature and man are blended in a harmonious merger of the void and reality. Whether this relates to the influence of Taoism is unclear, but it is true that the Chinese essentially invented landscape painting in a very early period. It did not evolve in the West until the northern Renaissance, while the earliest extant depiction of a landscape may be the Shilla floor tile in the Korean National Museum, not because it was the first but because the materials with which it was made were not ephemeral.

This use of space, an amalgam of man and nature which one author (F.C.S. Northrop) once called the "undifferentiated aesthetic continuum," in contrast to the West where there is a clear demarcation between man and nature at least until the Romantic period, is also apparent in architecture, especially in Japanese structures and to a less obvious degree in Korean homes. The modular aspects of design and the clean and sparse lines seem both harmonious and even restful, compared to the clutter of other architectures.

The importance of space by analogy extends to other realms, but with conflicting impacts. Those who are older may remember the advertisement for an airline that serviced Asia, proclaiming the beauty of the "silence of the Orient," typifying not only aural silence but the silence that seems to come from this amalgam of nature and space. Alas, that seems to have gone. It is difficult to find silence anywhere with overpopulation and urbanization throughout much of Asia. My climbs in the solitude of the mountains behind Seoul in the early morning in the middle of the week were marred by various types of religious chanting reverberating throughout the valleys and destroying the morning calm. On weekends, one may as well be in Myongdong for all the quiet one may find. If one finds a harmonious landscape in Korea with a river, a mountain, and few fields and a forest, the view is likely to be marred by a love hotel or mounds of plastic piled on the ground that had been used for greenhouses or protection against weeds

Some other societies are more extreme. Philippine culture is one that seems to like to fill all voids. The architecture is cluttered and often ostentatiously complex. Silence, institutional or personal, is anathema. In the now ubiquitous Philippine malls, each shop virtually demands to fill your aural space with blatant music blaring in a concatenation of sounds from adjoining stores. One eminent Filipino said that silence is equated with sadness. Perhaps the men's rooms are the only salvation there. One British Member of Parliament recently introduced legislation banning music from public places. Many of us consider "elevator music" the lowest form of musical pabulum because it is designed to annoy the fewest number, but ten shops all playing different rock music at egregiously loud decibels may be even worse. That legislation is unlikely to pass, but the idea, as they say, has resonance, at least in my circles.

But there is a personal Philippine characteristic as well as an institutional one. People have told me that if a foreigner is introverted and quiet, Filipinos tend to worry because one is never sure what he or she is thinking. It is better to have them blurt out whatever is on their minds than to remain silent. Americans have a saying that silence is golden, and that children should be seen and not heard, but those adages seem to have no relevance in some other cultures, or even in the United States any more. If I wanted to find a good speaker for a conference, a Filipino would be ideal because of his or her flair for oratory, far better than most Americans who have a tendency to mumble into their collars. I prefer, however, the *yangban* trait of reticence, where one gets to know someone over time, the growing relationship uncovering more of the personality, like peeling an onion.

A friend told me a story about a younger person to whom he had complained about the loudness of some music. The youth replied that he was annoyed because he was old. This may be true. My college roommate used to say that music was made to be heard, and not listened to. I used to study with background music playing on the radio, but now if I am serious about writing I need silence. It is becoming more difficult to find. Sometimes Marcel Proust's cork-lined bedroom, which he designed for silence and in which he wrote much of the *Remembrance of Things Past,* arguably the greatest novel of the twentieth century, seems more and more needed.

April 2000

On Sex and the Color of Nature

A recent announcement by the American aviation authorities, broadcast on the radio news, warned that pilots should not take the impotency drug Viagra, prescribed for what is euphemistically called "erectile disorder," six hours before they fly because a significant percentage of those that take that male wonder drug cannot distinguish between blue and green for a number of hours. They seem to need to make that distinction to read their flight instruments or to fly safely. That may seem a particularly strange side effect to Westerners unschooled in the ways of science, but this merger of colors is simply a medical manifestation of a concept or a phenomenon that seems old hat to many in East Asia.

The West has finally awakened to something the Chinese, Koreans, and Japanese have known, seemingly forever. That is, blue and green have always been indistinguishable in some circumstances. One does not need a sexual aid to demonstrate that.

The proof lies in the Chinese character *chong* (*ch'ing*, or *qing*, in Chinese, *aoi* in Japanese). It has always meant, according to the dictionary, "the color of nature." That is, it can be blue, green, or both depending on the circumstances. It is a character that is widely used in Chinese poetry, which of course is often about or written in the symbols of nature. Its use is, however, more widespread. There are many Koreans who, when talking about the traffic in Seoul, will mention in translation the "blue" lights, meaning to a Westerner the "green" lights. Although Thai language does not have a single word describing both colors, the Thai often use the terms interchangeably. For example, a "blueprint" in Thai is called a "greenprint." Of course, there are specific words for those colors in Chinese, Korean, and Japanese, but *chong* is the most poetic of terms.

We in the West do sometimes mix our color metaphors. Where I grew up we had the "Blue Hills" of suburban Boston that were, of course, green, and in the eastern United States we have the Blue Ridge Mountains of Virginia. The "bluegrass" area of Kentucky has a particularly vibrant shade of green landscape, and in the northeast of the United States bluegrass is the most popular of lawn seed. The blue-green spectrum of colors changes with the time of day and the intensity of light.

The Chinese also recognize the connection in other circumstances; they say that green comes out of blue, so that a young student can surpass his teacher—the green student becoming more powerful than the scholarly blue, indicating both the closeness of the colors and the student-teacher relationship.

The scientific basis for the relationship of the two colors lies, one must suppose, in their close proximity along the color spectrum. What may be more interesting to the non-scientist is how we view such colors. In Korea, when we think of "celadon" as a color we often describe it as a blue-green. Indeed, it seems to contain both elements with a subtle mixture of light grey that softens the tones. In fact the term "celadon" is sometimes used by Western interior decorators to describe the blue-green of fabrics or wallpaper or paint. The word itself comes from the color of a cape of a character with that name in a seventeenth-century French play by Orfeé, and was picked up in English by the poet Dryden. In Korea these days, celadon is mistakenly used for any valuable ceramics, even white, which loses the poetry of the term.

The Chinese and the Koreans were more accurate—they avoided the seemingly Western need for clear and distinct ideas (and colors), or the dualism that characterizes much of Western thought. The mixture of blue and green into a single character melds both into a whole that captures nature and life far more acutely than either Western term alone in spite of its vagueness. So now when I go to the mountains west of Washington, I shall think about the *Chong* Ridge Mountains of Virginia. And that is what Viagra does for one. But what about Chinese pilots? What do they call the colors of their flight instruments?

November 1998

5

Education, Language, and Media

On Elites and Universities

The Korea government, according to the local press, is determined to break up the heavy concentration of university professors who have graduated from the university in which they eventually are hired to teach. After a five-year transition period, universities were supposed to have no more that 40 percent of their faculty as alumni of that university. Right now, 96 percent of the Seoul National University (SNU) faculty attended SNU, while 80 percent of the Yonsei and 60 percent of the Korea University faculty did the same with their institution. The Ministry of Education also wants to eliminate bribery and favoritism, and foster transparency, in hiring practices.

There is no question that the elite groups in Korea are either ratified or entered through attendance at one of the major universities in Seoul. Look, for example, at the incoming class in the foreign service, or the appointment of ambassadors or other chiefs of mission: the vast majority have been from SNU, and even more specifically from the College of Law.[*] This is also true of those who pass the civil service examination, and of course the major corporations have recruited from this very talented pool of students from top universities. If you want to get married, a graduate of one of the major schools is a catch. The elite structure of society is thus reinforced and ratified through the attendance at one of these schools. It is the Korean equivalent of the British "Oxbridge" (Oxford and Cambridge) or the U.S. Ivy League schools of a generation ago.

The stress on education is so encompassing in Korean society it needs no discussion here, nor does the role of the premier universities in social and intellectual affirmation. A graduate of one of the major schools, when introduced, causes the appropriate eyebrow to be raised in recognition and additional respect. As a result of getting the best education possible in Korea at one of these schools, it is no wonder that in the recruitment of faculty for that school emphasis should be placed on graduates. There is also a kind of intellectual and social coziness in the faculty relationships, because then everyone knows

---

[*] By March 2002, of the thirteen potential candidates in the presidential elections of December 2002, 70 percent were from Seoul National University.

everyone else, and thus the sense of hierarchy and status can easily be understood and maintained.

One of the negative factors that becomes apparent is the development of a sense of arrogance toward those outside of the prized institution, and, as we all know, academic rivalries within an institution can be both tedious and devastating. After all, academics are paid to be articulate, and they may be so in furthering their own particularistic goals and interests and denigrating others. Henry Kissinger is said to have remarked that academic politics was remarkable because never had so many fought over so little.

More intriguing to the outsider, however, is the continuing role of the government in all of this. If the state wishes to reform a state-sponsored and supported institution, such as SNU, that is an issue that can be debated based on the wisdom of the particular reform proposed. But the Ministry of Education is attempting to reform all institutions, public and private, as seventeen universities in the country are said to have over 40 percent of their faculty recruited from their alumni. Now the question used to be: how private was private education in Korea? In the old, authoritarian days, the answer was: very little. The government virtually controlled the complete process of education, and could, and did, cause the firing of staff or presidents or students it did not like. It set the fees and numbers of students down to department size. As one former president of a private university in Seoul said, there were no private universities in Korea.

But we are now supposed to be in a different age. In economics, the government says it should not control businesses and the market, and that the relationship between the state and business should be far more distant than it once was. That is what banking reform is all about; that was what caused many of the economic problems, or so the IMF indicated. So why is the government setting quotas of alumni to be hired as faculty in private universities? What right has the state to so intervene? Does this not indicate that the predilection of the state to control civil society (and surely private universities should in theory be counted as part of that nongovernmental group) is alive and well and living in Seoul?

Korea has traditionally, as well as in modern times, been a society in which the distance between the government and civil society has been very close; that is, the state has viewed, in a good Confucian manner, its right—even its duty—to intervene in all aspects of life for the betterment of society. Moreover, in general people have accepted such intervention far more readily than in many Western countries. In spite of what some Korean academicians argue, civil society in the sense of those institutions truly independent of the state did not flourish until after 1987, although a few may have existed but were noncontroversial.

But the evidence here clearly indicates that in spite of the development and success of democratic procedures in politics, the invisible academic hand is still encased in the iron glove of the state and its bureaucracy. If the state intervenes here, cannot it intervene anywhere? Will not the state continue intervening in business? Will the people accept such interventions? Where are the reforms that have been promised?

September 1998

On Corporal Punishment in Schools

A few years ago, while driving on a secondary road through a rather backwater area of southern Korea, I passed a middle school early in the morning. In the yard between the school and the road there were a large number of students whom I thought were doing early morning calisthenics. But no, a number of male students were lying prone on the ground as if they were doing push-ups. But this was no physical exercise class. They were being whipped by someone I assume was a teacher. Other students were lined up watching, presumably to learn the lesson of proper behavior.[*] I did not stop, and thus have no idea of the purported offence(s) that may have been committed. But I was appalled. My initial reaction was that I had come upon a scene out of some Asian version of a Dickens novel—a nineteenth-century phenomenon.

The recent decision by the Constitutional Court allowing corporal punishment of students as "rightful" conduct is disquieting. It is more than the "pedagogic failures"' that the *Korea Times* editorial of January 30 indicated, although it is certainly that as well. Its implications are far-reaching, beyond those of a particular student crime or misdemeanor, or even of the whole genre of student relations. The ramifica-

---

[*] Sometimes students are warned in advance that they will be punished and then wear extra clothing to soften the blows, if not the humiliation.

tions extend to the whole question of violence in Korean society, and even of teacher-student relationships and concepts of learning. That caning or whipping occurs in other societies today, such as Singapore, simply indicates the continuation of what I regard as an archaic practice.

As an American, I am certainly aware of the amount of violence in American society, and it is shameful to have to admit that it is a major problem that we have not adequately addressed. It is no solace to claim, as some do, that this is a product of the frontier and the early history of settling the country. Certainly violence in and out of American schools affects teaching and the whole social fabric, and must be stopped. How is the question, but more violence is unlikely to work.

Some will say that I have no right to question practices in other societies. Yet the issue is of profound importance, and in the spirit of positive criticism I would like to raise points connected with how such actions, and the essential approval of such actions by the highest court in Korea, will have an adverse effect on Korean society in and beyond the classroom.

Violence is endemic in Korean society, although most of it is submerged under a Confucian facade of proper and formal relationships and behavior. It need not result in death to make it any the less ominous. And it is not just students or men. There is an overwhelming pattern of physical abuse against women, as any one of the number of Korean nongovernmental organizations that deal with this issue will attest. Some statistics show that one-third of Korean women are so treated. Torture has been an element, even if unofficial and unstated, of the Korean police and intelligence systems. This has been extensively reported in the past and has been the precipitating cause of demonstrations against various administrations. Physical abuse of men in the army is prevalent. Even in overseas factories and against foreign workers, Korean managers often physically abuse their local employees, as the press in a number of countries such as Indonesia, Vietnam, and China has commented. We know that similar abuses do take place in Korean factories in Korea. As a result of all these activities, the reputation of Korea as a "tough" country is widespread.

How do all of these factors relate to corporal punishment in the schools? If students have been physically abused, even for causes that the authorities consider "righteous," the pattern becomes ingrained. Students in turn abuse younger students. After one graduates, these violent tendencies are likely to continue under other circumstances and against those in subordinate or weaker positions, such as wives, employees, and the young. The precedent set by the Constitutional Court is deleterious to both the substance of what Korea hopes to attain, and the external image Korea hopes to reach.

What effect, do you suppose, corporal punishment has on the student-teacher relationship? Does it lead to a better understanding between them, to better intellectual inquiry, or to the development of innovative and inquiring minds? As in an answer to an examination question, none of the above.

Respect for knowledge, for free inquiry, for the spirit of civility to which these concepts are related is lost if the relationship is one of fear. No one claims that a student and a teacher are always equal, but there is a mutuality of respect that is required if education is to accomplish its goals. There is, or should be, equality as human beings. There are other ways to enforce civility in and out of the classroom, for such civility is necessary for an atmosphere in which learning can take place. There are major problems in Korean classrooms: the class size is far too large for effective teaching and real student counseling is lacking.

This is not simply a matter of what is legal. Rather, it is a matter beyond legality—what does a society hope to achieve for its children, and what future does a society want for itself. Korean authorities should consider the broad implications of this decision.

February 2000

On Questioning Authority

Dignity and authority go together in most societies. In Korea, they seem to be so closely connected that they sometimes subvert the very institutional processes with which they are associated. This is true in education, as in other fields. If a student fails a final examination with—as we all know—dire consequences for that person's future, he or she would normally be afraid to approach the professor to determine the cause and attempt to improve by finding out why the failure occurred, and perhaps plead reconsideration. That would be questioning authority. A good student follows the judgment of the teacher as a good son does as the father dictates. A student, or a junior in position, should never appear smarter than the teacher or a superior.

Instead, the usual practice would be for the student's parents to talk with the teacher to find out why. But teachers often used to refuse to discuss the issue with anyone, including parents, claiming that it is beneath the teacher's dignity to do so. The teacher's word is law, and no discussion could change the professor's view. A reversal of opinion would be regarded as a personal betrayal, as well as the subversion of the teacher's colleagues and the school itself. This is an example of the "imperial professor," indicating that the essence of education in that instance was lost—that hierarchy and authority take precedence over dialogue and the search for knowledge and improvement. One hopes this is an image from the past.

What is this authority that denies discourse? The dignity that is associated with authority is important in Korea—more important than in many Western societies, it seems. As we say in the United States, it goes with the job, assuming the position is high enough. In the West, or at least in English, "dignity" (from the Latin for "worthy") includes a variety of attributes, from intrinsic worth, excellence, and high status to stateliness and decorum. There seem to be many more expressions in Korean indicating dignity in its many aspects. One of these, *Chonum*, in Korean has these attributes plus the added implication of sanctity, and if the word is used in connection with the authority of a teacher (in contrast with that of a prophet), then it is powerful indeed. Respect is demanded, and subordinates (in this case, students) act out their roles on the surface, but what goes on in their minds may be quite different. One could argue that dignity and authority are really about power— who has it and why.

True, dignity is implicit in the Korean social structure. It is related to rank and age and social status, and in its moral sense, when combined with these other attributes, it can be both a noble and potent concept.

When, however, it is used to deny discourse and avoid the free exchange of ideas and understanding, the concept is prostituted. Education is critical to virtually every family in Korea; its worth has been accepted to such a degree that it has been recognized as a prime component of the remarkable growth Korea has achieved. The denigration of the essence of education, which is that free interchange of ideas regardless of status, age, or dignity, subverts progress. In a number of other societies, questioning and criticizing are not easy, but as long as the manner in which this is done is appropriate to the occasion, it is normally accepted. There are few intellectual untouchables.

We often see officials in Korea assume a public dignified mien, reflecting their authority, when they attain a certain bureaucratic rank. If they are secure in their role, they may believe that the external face mirrors their internal strengths. If they are insecure, they may feel that this outward manifestation of authority provides inward support for that concept. To some foreigners, a person whose outward behavior reflects high status would be called pompous, while one who assumed that demeanor without reason would be called a poseur, one who adopts an outward stance to mislead the audience. That is in a sense the personal equivalent of a Potemkin Village. We would like to see an outward manifestation of dignity and authority mirror an inward concept in a moral and intellectual sense.

Some Westerners consider that "face," the outward manifestation of dignity, is an Asian concept. That seems based on multiple mistakes. First, what is Asia? In addition to the fact that there is no single Asian culture, but rather multiple and disparate cultures in Asia, which in itself is simply a term of geographic convenience and not an analytical construct, most societies, including those in the West, have an equivalent concept. But Koreans are especially careful to keep dignity and try not to destroy it. One reporter wrote a critical article about a high government official, and the editor, without the reporter's knowledge, changed the focus to that of the "government," to avoid, he said, hurting the dignity and saving the face of the individual.

Years ago, in the worst period of human rights under the Yushin Constitution, to criticize the head of state (or any head of state for that matter) was a crime, for the dignity of the individual was related to the question of his political legitimacy.

One hopes that no professor, however hoary with age and however high his or her status, however widely admired or published, would refuse to discuss intelligently the opinions, mistakes, or strengths of any student, or indeed him or herself, for without such discourse there can be no growth, no dialogue, no democracy. Education represents endless possibilities, not stifling conformity or a single mold.

Does this academic problem mirror other issues in the political sphere? If so, the implications are profound for the deepening of the

democratic process, for an "imperial" government is even more deleterious than an "imperial" educational system.

February 1997

On Unintellectual Property Rights

There is a great international furor over the stealing of designs and
commercial plagiarism, which allows companies overseas to imitate
with minimal overhead the products that other industries have produced at far greater costs. Asian states have the entrepreneurial and
technological skills to do this well, so attention has been focused on
these countries, including Korea. The situation is said to be improved
here, as Korea adheres to many of the international copyright conventions and practices.

The East Asia tradition in a sense discouraged the individuality associated with ownership of art or authorship of literature. They say
that in the West, imitation is the sincerest form of flattery, but in East
Asia it is also the institutionalized form of learning. So junior artists
apprenticed to some master will not only copy his style, but his signature. This is not unknown in the West; there are many Renaissance
and other paintings attributed to "the school of...so-and-so." One
learns calligraphy by imitation. One is not attempting to confuse or
deceive—one is trying to learn from the most authoritative available
source. It is art rather than artifice.

Although modern Korean academicians are scrupulous in their
footnoting, others seem less inclined to recognize the sources of some
of their ideas or the work of others. We have had in recent years some
prominent American figures who seem to have conveniently forgotten where they read certain passages that then crept into their own
works, but the readership is wide and vocal, and even the most eminent, perhaps especially the most eminent, could not hope to escape
detection and public censure. In Korea, many seem to evade exposure
because some of these concepts originated in foreign languages, so no
one is supposed to be aware of the source.

But there is also another form of exploitation of property rights
within Korea. I do not know whether there is sexual harassment in academia here, although there certainly has been in the United States, but
there is evidently something we might call "intellectual harassment."

It seems that often senior professors ask those more junior both by age and status, but not limited to research assistants, to undertake research or write papers, which are then appropriated and presented to various journals or given at international meetings. Although some consider such research a collective effort, this in the modern world does not stand up to scrutiny.

But the junior staff have no options, and cannot refuse the misappropriation of their hard work, nor can they publicly complain. The elite group is small, and social ostracism would follow should even a word be mentioned in some informal drinking party. The senior professor is exploiting the deference that he or she expects from junior staff both by reason of position and age.

As a foreigner outside of the social system, I sometimes hear rumors without names and innuendo without data. I sympathize with those so maltreated. Once I was plagiarized. I had written a volume on Burma, and it contained what I thought was an elegantly phrased paragraph on the place of rice in Burmese culture. I gave the manuscript to an eminent professor for his comments, and he in turn passed it to a research assistant, who then proceeded to publish an article that contained that single paragraph—its individuality and polish so apparent to me that there was no mistaking the authorship. I quietly complained, but there was no point in pursuing it further as the purported author soon vanished from the field.

The misappropriation of the work of others more junior illustrates the problem of both hierarchy and power in Korean elite society. Because the professor is so revered in Korean society and the model for many, and because education is so consummately important, the actions are more heinous.

This is also often a misuse of the public trust. The Korean government provides massive funding to university professors for research in all fields. If the money is not used by those for whom it was intended, or is misappropriated through its product being wrongly attributed, then this is a type of embezzlement of public funds.

We call for transparency in government, and we want to see campaigns to clean up corruption move ahead and succeed. In a field such as education, where virtually the whole population mobilizes to achieve success and spends inordinate treasure and time to do so, educational transparency would seem to be a critical concern.

A supervisor in an organization, or a professor in a university, has an obligation to help more junior staff become professionally visible, and give them opportunities to achieve enhanced status and respect.

October 1996

On Meddling in the Media

The Fourth Estate in Korea has had a difficult past and even a problematic present. It has been subjected over the past forty or so years with various levels of harassments, purges, and constraints, effectively limiting its watchdog role and even circumscribing its autonomy, albeit more recently through indirect and sometimes personal means in the past decade. It is not as if the press as a group of disparate elements does not have its internal problems. Some individuals and institutions have demonstrated little regard for responsible reporting. Truth has often been viewed subjectively, according to the whims and predilections of reporters, editors, or publishers. Sources are sometimes not verified, and facts not checked. Yet in spite of these shortcomings or those of the press in any country, a free press is critical to the vitality of a modern society and good governance.

Each society develops the necessary controls on untrammeled freedoms and license. Slander, libel, extortion, defamation, blackmail, and other deleterious actions are effectively limited by law. Korea has an array of such legislation. Now the courts are far more autonomous than they ever have been in Korean history; they have been known to rule against the state. People now feel that recourse to the judicial system is not something to be avoided and by which one loses "face," but rather one essential element of a just society.

What, then, was the Korean legislature doing last year when it attempted to pass legislation limiting what was said to be "unfair" reporting on election campaigns. After the press complained, the National Assembly thought better of it. But on February 8 of this year it passed similar legislation. This was not a matter of partisan politics, with one or another party in favor of it, but rather a general reaction by legislators to what they must have thought were threats to their efficacy. A related issue is why the Korean press did not report on it for a considerable lapse of time. The watchdogs were not guarding their own premises.

Now President Kim Dae Jung has stepped in and wants to be assured that nothing unconstitutional is in the new legislation. The older constitutions of Korea before 1987 allowed the state to intervene and limit the articulated freedoms incorporated in those documents for some public good, although it was the administration, not the people, who defined what that "good" was. But the 1987 constitution changed that, and eliminated such qualifying language, making such freedoms far more absolute (although no freedom is completely absolute). There are, as noted above, other means by which the irresponsible in the media can be held accountable.

There are three worrisome aspects to this continuing, and still unresolved, issue. The first is that of the self-serving attitude of the National Assembly in protecting their own rears without considering the constitutionality of what they had proposed. The second is that the media was not alert enough, or perhaps it was too intimidated, so as not to report on it in a timely manner. The third is less obvious, more basic, and thus more disquieting. That is, there is the strong and continuing predilection of those in power to intervene in civil society in a wide range of fields. No matter how much economists, political scientists, and sociologists discuss the need for there to be a considerable distance between the state and civil society, including markets, academic inquiry, and the media, the proclivity to try to control continues to reemerge, and often virulently so.

The press has established mechanisms for self-inquiry and standards for responsible reporting. It has the means to police itself. There are also elements of civil society, nongovernmental organizations, outside of the press that monitor press performance. There are in addition numerous schools of journalism at various universities that teach about the media and appropriate standards of reporting, objectivity, and responsibility. Why, then, should the state feel the need to intervene? Korea has become, as is so evident, a democratizing country, and the positive evolution of governance is so apparent that one must wonder what underlies this kind of regression into control. Korea has a right to proclaim its positive changes—the growth of free elections, the retirement of military government without untoward incident, and the capacity to deal with a dire economic crisis.

But old attitudes die hard, and self-policing of a profession is difficult when one is connected to an elite through pervasive personal ties.

Yet a vital press is essential to Korea, and however unpleasant any particular disclosure or incident may be, and however slow redress may be (and if slow it should be speeded up), it is a very small price to pay for the need for a press that is both professionally responsible and acts in its role as the modern equivalent of the "Imperial Censorate," which tells the court and others in power what is wrong. If they do not perform with this freedom, much will be lost.

March 2000

On Newspaper Endorsements

As any presidential campaign in Korea nears and excitement becomes more frenzied and complex, one turns to the Korean press to inquire how they report the news related to the campaign, and what stands they or their columnists may take on the parties, the candidates, and the issues. There has developed an interesting phenomenon: Korean newspapers rarely, if ever, endorse editorially any candidate for office. The propensities of individual columnists may be inferred from their writings, and that of the papers themselves by the inclusion of columnists or academicians writing columns. But the papers editorially are usually more circumspect, however critical they may be of any administration.

This is in stark contrast to the United States and other democratic societies. In any political campaign in the United States, and at any level of government, as the elections near many citizens await the announcement of the local press on which candidate they will endorse for office and for what reasons. These positions then become national, and even international, news. Very often one can, of course, predict which party most closely adheres to the proclivities of the local papers, but in a close race there are often some surprises. In many cases, the nationally circulated press will not endorse a single party, but will pick individual candidates from between or among the parties for support, or sometimes support an independent candidate. Occasionally they will proclaim a plague on all political houses. Television in the United States does not take overt political stances, which may relate to licensing regulations.

Speculation on the reasons for the Korean press to eschew endorsements comes naturally to mind. Of course, there is no inherent reason why the press should have to support editorially any candidate or party, but either the absence of such endorsements or their presence prompt inquiry.

Endorsements may come for two reasons, one altruistic and the other cynical. The paper may feel that it a public duty to support a candidate that it feels is in the public's interest either nationally or locally. That is, of course, the desirable interpretation. But to those cynically inclined, a paper may also support a candidate who will service the special interests in which the newspaper may be involved.

Explanations for a lack of endorsement in this liberalized political era in Korea must also be essayed. Criticizing the government in the Yushin period was illegal, and at other times it could lead to closure of the press or intimidation, or withdrawal of government advertising, which in those days was a major source of newspaper revenue. Three possible reasons come to mind for current practices. The first is that there is no interest in the race. This is highly improbable in Korea, where politics may be the second most popular indoor sport, the first involving gender relations. The second is that the outcome is predetermined, and that any endorsement would have no practical effect. This was true for much of the history of the Korean republics until 1987, but is certainly no longer the case. The third issue is more disconcerting. This is, that if one endorsed the losing party, one's influence, perhaps one's future, might be in jeopardy.

All this is to say that politics in Korea is a zero-sum game. Koreans have said that to back publicly in editorials the wrong party would be suicidal. Although this is obviously hyperbole, there may be an important kernel of truth to the charge. Those in power may become vindictive against an organization that is perceived to be the enemy. The loyal opposition as a concept is an oxymoron in Korean politics.

Now, it is true that in other countries those in power have railed against the opposition press, and in extreme cases "enemy" correspondents and press representatives were sometimes banned from certain officially sponsored events. In the past, the White House even cancelled the subscriptions to some papers that the leadership felt were too extremely negative against the administration. But these actions seem to sit badly with the American people. Americans seem to want newspapers to take a stand, and to explain why such a stand is in the national or local interest. Although there seem to have been no studies on the issue, it is likely that an American newspaper would lose readership if it neglected editorially to face the issues and the elections in a forthright manner. These endorsements occur toward the close of the campaign, allowing the newspapers to claim that they have studied the candidates and their platforms and so can make better judgments, whatever their political predilection might have been.

We have learned worldwide, as Americans say, that politics make strange bedfellows. This is evident in Korea in the campaign alignments that sometimes defy any logic except that of attempting to achieve power. Koreans have a saying about sleeping in the same bed but having different dreams. The common denominator of politics is power. Whether it is the highest or lowest denominator is an open question. But the press seems to try to keep out of the public bed with politicians. The real question, however, may be whether this serves the public's interests.

October 1997

On Memory and Memorization

Not long ago I was trying to find my way to a friend's house in Seoul. He had sent me a map, so that I was able to maneuver through the maze of unnamed and unnumbered streets—a problem we all know so well. That is, of course, not quite accurate, for one can find the general area, but within that subdistrict (the *tong*) the houses are numbered but not for the convenience of those trying to find someone's house, but for those who administer the area, since they are numbered in the order built. To get to someone's house requires that one is either given a map or one has been there before, so one memorizes the route and the turnings and the gate or other features that will be helpful in future trips.

I have always admired those who have photographic memories, who can absorb masses of material easily. Koreans have prodigious memories. This has many advantages, although many studies of the Korean educational system have asserted that the concentration on memory and rote learning is detrimental to individual and creative thought and innovation. Certainly the concentration on the examination process produces a single focus of purpose that induces repeating back at the examiners what specifically one has learned in class and in the authorized textbooks. Other learning and knowledge are irrelevant for immediate purposes. So to do well on Korean examinations requires great feats of memory as well as intelligence—one without the other will not be successful. Now the government is trying to change the system to allow for less rote learning and more analytical thought, and this is welcome. Whether this will be successful is a separate issue.

The problem is common in East Asia. Complaints about Japanese and Chinese education have focused on the same issue. When I was studying in China many years ago, I was impressed that so many Chinese students studying English literature could easily memorize a page of complex poetry for an examination, even if much of it was not really understood. American students would have taken forever to learn such material even if it were required. My own problems with memory (especially Korean vocabulary) reminds me that Montaigne wrote four hundred years ago that he was a man of some little reading but of no retention. I feel as he did, but without his talent.

Memory is important, and while the vagaries of English spelling and irregular French verbs are legion, anyone who has seriously attempted to learn Chinese characters knows that there is no substitute for memory. Although there are often logical elements to some characters in terms of both meaning and sound, they do not displace the need for concentration and memorization. It seems a never-ending process. There is a rather obscure novel in which a very old Chinese gentleman, in his declining years, just finished learning the 39,999th Chinese character of the apocryphal 40,000, and as he memorized the last one, he died.

Some societies have long and complex oral histories recorded in epics and tales that have been retold for hundred or thousands of years. Where the written record was not important or not developed, these myths and history, and whole cultures, would be lost without prodigious memories, and we all would have been the losers. Homer was oral history, and the storyteller was an important figure in many societies. The Victorian pseudo-Chinese tales by Ernst Bramah of Kai Lung, the itinerant storyteller, are a fictional account of an earlier era and are still a delight. In the contemporary period, the Indonesian dissident novelist Toer, who recently won the Magsaysay Award for literature, was jailed for years without paper or pen. He told his tales to other inmates, who memorized them and later wrote them down.

We all have developed our own mnemonic devices that help us memorize a name, a place, a date, a formula, or a telephone number or a zip code. There were elaborate constructions made to help the memorization process before Western printing was very common, and one could rely on reference works. Matteo Ricci was said to have impressed the Chinese in the sixteenth century with his systems of memorization. I used to use the commercial Chinese telegraphic code numbers for characters to help remember telephone numbers.

Today, most Americans don't want to memorize, and students will complain that there is no need to memorize even the multiplication tables because one can always look up what one wants or use a calculator. So few want to learn to spell, a talent I have never developed, alas. The days when as middle school students we had to memorize a 24-line poem every week or so and recite it before the class are gone. Now, I still recall lines of what I was forced to memorize, and in retrospect my teachers were generally quite balanced in their choices, more than I was when I had my pick of poems. I can still recall, from a later era, the first few lines of the *Classic of Filial Piety,* part of which I had to memorize when I studied classical Chinese.

Western popular music is full of references to memories, and their sweetness, for, as the song goes, when one becomes too old to dream one has memories. So the great new fear for many these days is not only cancer and its insidious internal decay, but Alzheimer's disease. As one gets it one loses the memory that one even has the disease, and the basic bearings of mental life on which all else depends are slowly and inexorably diminished. The burdens placed on those who must care for the sick are perhaps even greater than for those with cancer, for the burdens are often prolonged and must often be undertaken by family, not professional care institutions. So a danger for caregivers is that the immediate memory of decline and senility will replace the fond memories of youth, vigor, and maturity.

Let us celebrate memory, and even some memorization, but not at the expense of individuality, creativity, innovation, and even eccentricity. They are not necessarily antithetical. Now where did I put my glasses?

August 1996

On the Press and the State in a Mode of Confrontation

Societies with a strong Confucian background, like Korea, are still governed on the model of the patriarchal family, with the leader acting as the father. In spite of the democratic processes, he rules less by law than by the moral authority of his position. Thus he and his administration consider that they have a right, indeed an obligation, to intercede into what other societies would consider private realms, including attitudes and expressions of opinion. This Confucian-style leadership thus has had a strong tendency toward orthodoxy, and there are historical reasons why the Korean presidency has long been called "imperial." Any opposition is not easily countenanced; compliance on critical policies is expected. Opposition is anathema and tolerated only under the duress of modern public and international scrutiny, and then reluctantly.

One exception to this rule of orthodoxy in traditional times was the Imperial Censorate, which was the institutionalized moral conscience of the society, and whose members had access to the king, and could not be dismissed. They told the leader what was proper and appropriate, and what was beyond the Confucian social pale. The leader had to listen, although often he ignored their admonitions.

In modern societies, we no longer have an Imperial Censorate, but we do have a press that performs a similar function. It tells a leader or an administration what is wrong, and in a sense represents the social norms to those in power who tend to become isolated from their own publics. In contemporary Asia, an aloof leader could become even more remote from his own people if the press does not act as a modern equivalent of the Censorate, and if there are no other internal avenues of dissent that can reach him. The tendency toward orthodoxy and state control is an important element of the political culture, which although changing, retains important vestiges of the past.

The Korean administration of President Kim Dae Jung is in confrontation with much of the press in Korea. Much of that confrontation stems from disagreements over the pace and conditions of engagement with North Korea, which has become the hallmark of this administration's policies and President Kim's administration. Although there is general approval of increasing reconciliation with the North, there has been extensive criticism of costs, speed, and lack of reciprocal measures from the North. As the most important pillar of the present government's policies, criticism of it is of special concern to its leadership, as it could undermine the process.

The administration believes that there should be no impediments to its policies. So in August 2000, many South Korean publishers agreed not to be critical of the North. The administration in Seoul has tried to silence the North's most vocal critic—defector Hwang Jang-yop. And now the tax evasion and personal indictments brought against the media, heavily weighted against the administration's leading critical papers, are seen as obvious and heavy-handed attempts to introduce orthodoxy on this important policy issue.

Orthodoxy runs counter to the spirit of democracy and its effective functioning. However unpleasant the press may be, however lacking in professional standards, however tax laws may have been evaded, the tax evasion and personal charges brought by this administration at this time and in the unprecedented magnitude will only result in reducing the credibility of the administration, its popularity, and in further undercutting the policies that it is pursuing. It is, thus, self-defeating.

The Chosun Ilbo, July 2001

On the Korean Press and Orthodoxy

The Korean administration of President Kim Dae Jung is in confrontation with much of the press in Korea. On the basis of charges of illegally avoiding taxes, the government has set fines of almost $400 million on twenty-three of the major media institutions. It has also fined sixteen selected individuals $23 million for irregular business transactions and indicted some for tax evasion. The heaviest burdens have fallen on those papers most vigorous in criticism of the regime and its policies. Naturally, the opposition Grand National Party, which will be competing against the government's candidate in the presidential election of December 2002, is protesting and demanding a legislative investigation, which Kim Dae Jung's Millennium Democratic Party, vigorously opposes.

Charges are hurled by both camps; the opposition claims the government is attempting to stifle press freedom, guaranteed under the Constitution of 1987, while the government states that the press is not above the law, and should be granted no special exemptions from their tax obligations. A senior member of the policy committee of President Kim's party was quoted in the English-language press as saying that paying taxes was more important than freedom of speech. The press under each administration in Korea has been under direct attack by dictators, and indirect intimidation and influence in more open times. But this occasion seems unique in the financial magnitude of the charges. The impression created at this time is that the government of Kim Dae Jung, that fighter for democracy and Nobel Peace Prize laureate whose election signified the maturation of democracy in Korea, has opted to stifle or intimidate its critics. Even if this is inaccurate, observers of Korea, noting the previous rapid drop in Kim Dae Jung's popularity, will interpret this action as an attempt by a regime in trouble to regain their dominant position.

Even if the charges against the presses are in whole or part true and that some or all have been involved in tax evasion, and even though the press has also often been less than accurate and scrupulous in some of its reporting, the magnitude of the fines in this period of economic hardship is enough to force the closure of some papers, if they are actually imposed, and are out of proportion with all reasonable attempts to deal equitably with the fourth estate. This effort to impose "law" on the media will in fact further undercut the credibility of the Kim Dae Jung government. Whatever may be the facts of the case, the government will lose credibility in the long run, for the action will be interpreted as self-serving.

The leadership of Confucian societies has had a strong tendency toward orthodoxy, and the Korean presidency has long been called "imperial." An opposition is not easily countenanced. Whether Imperial, Republican, or Communist China, or Korea in any of its political incarnations, the state leadership, governing on the analogy of the moral authority of the father in a Confucian family, expected compliance with its official views. Opposition is anathema and tolerated only under the duress of modern public and international scrutiny.

One exception in traditional times was the Imperial Censorate, the institutionalized moral conscience of the society, which had access to the king or emperor and could not be dismissed. It told the leader what was proper and appropriate and what was beyond the Confucian social pale. The leader had to listen, although often he ignored their admonitions.

In modern societies, we no longer have an Imperial Censorate, but we do have a press that performs a similar function. It tells a leader or an administration what is wrong, and in a sense represents the social norms to those in power who tend to become isolated from their own publics. In contemporary Asia, a leader could become more remote from his own people if the press does not act as a modern censorate, and if there are no other internal avenues of dissent that can reach him. The tendency toward orthodoxy and state control is an important element of the political culture, which although changing, retains important vestiges of the past.

Kim Dae Jung cannot again run for the presidency, and there will be new elections in December 2002. Whatever chance his party may have had to win next time, this action undercuts its prospects in the practical political arena. More importantly, it is another detour on the long road toward a mature democracy.

International Herald Tribune, July 2001

On Academics as a Contact Sport

Many authorities of all political persuasions in Washington believe that there is little in the way of a comprehensive American policy for Asia. We seem to stumble through a crisis, and may take advantage of, or miss, an opportunity. There are, however, many, many individuals who have academic and practical experience on virtually every aspect of Asia within the metropolitan area. Yet we do not seem to use them well or to organize to consider seriously Asia more coherently. Yet we meet all the time.

There seem to be almost a myriad of conferences, meetings, workshops, lectures, or seminars on Asia in Washington in any month. And this is beyond the normal academic teaching and courses offered at each of the many universities in the area. On Korea alone there are probably six or eight such events monthly, and those are only the ones about which I am aware; there are surely others as well. How do we deal with such multitudes of intellectual feasts, or perhaps gluts? Our absorptive capacities, intellectual as well as gastronomic, are quite limited. Although the United States is trying to stop the proliferation of weapons of mass destruction, we are compounding the proliferation of mass ennui, which some would characterize as mass destruction of our psyches as well as our available time since it is questionable of what remains of "redeeming social value," as the courts have considered in judging pornography, after such meetings have concluded.

We are in an age of technology whereby we can easily hold conference calls on the telephone. The more modern of us may be able to have television conferencing—we see that on the nightly news shows where several discussants may be anywhere in the country or the world. The only obstacles are egregiously different time zones that prompt one person to talk at a civilized hour while another may be trying desperately to keep awake at 3 A.M. Calling Korea from Washington and expecting both persons on the line to be in their offices is virtually impossible. Faxes keep us informed, and e-mail keeps us in touch and harassed, perhaps too much and too quickly.

But somehow all of these techniques are not satisfying. There seems to be a psychological need for academic contact—for face-to-face discussions. And so we have the proliferation of meetings. It is true we often circulate papers before a gathering and hope that participants will read them before the meeting, so that the speaker will not have the tedious task of reading a paper that is difficult to follow, for while the difference between spoken and academic English is not as great as between classical and modern Chinese, it sometimes appears to be as dissimilar because of the obtuse jargon of the academic trade—to prove that one is part of the in-group. Thorstein Veblen wrote a prescient study at the beginning of this century called *The Theory of the Leisure Class*, demonstrating that societies often find means to validate status through showing that leisure is available. Perhaps academic papers and meetings do just that. They might be called the leisure of the theoried class.

So academic conferences demonstrate that academia is a contact sport. We feel the need to get together. We want the chance to talk with colleagues, or even adversaries. Writing acrid reviews of their latest tome is not sufficient. We want face-to-face confrontations, and the opportunity to make criticism public. And we like to meet old friends and colleagues, air rumors, and even exchange a few ideas, thereby enlightening all. But there are dangers even in academia, where intellectual property rights are sometimes disregarded. Many years ago, the parodist song writer Tom Lehrer wrote, "plagiarize, plagiarize, plagiarize, but be sure to call it research."

So academic meetings continue, and the amount of the gross national product is affected by their numbers, frequent flier miles are accumulated, bar owners become wealthy, and the hotel industry might collapse without such gatherings.

I believe in dialogue at the governmental level, and even in academia. Mixing the two is more of a problem because those in government often come to such meetings to proselytize for their policies rather than engage in dialogue. Such venues look good when reported in the press, but there has been little in exchange of ideas that could improve policies.

We need to meet, but meetings should lead to action—to resolution, if possible, of issues, or at least clarification of problems. Perhaps we need a meeting to discuss this issue?

May 1999

On Education and Professors

In the early 1960s, my wife used to say that Korean professors had little money and great prestige, while American professors had little money and little prestige. But that situation has changed. In Korea in the 1990s, Korean professors had both money and prestige while American professors still had little money and little prestige. In terms of status, it was, and still is, far better to be a professor in Korea than in the United States.

The American academic community is currently in considerable disarray, even though, if considered as an industry, it is one of the things that Americans do quite well. Foreign automobile or steel manufactures may make major inroads on American products, but American universities continue their prestige and preeminence. But pay levels are still below the private sector, and tenure is becoming increasingly difficult for the younger members of the profession because the financing of universities has become more difficult. Yet publishing is still the name of the academic game. For those academicians involved in contemporary events, by the time that an appropriate university press or respected journal engages in the required peer review and gets around to publishing, years may have elapsed and the world changed so markedly that all the work undertaken may be completely passé. Of course, the classicists or theorists might say that it serves them, the modernists, right, because their disciplines are more reportorial than academic, and thus not completely respectable. I cannot agree, but in a sense, American professors publish too much, often inundating the disciplinary literature with minutia that few need and have marginal utility in contributing to new knowledge. After all, professors are at least as egotistical as anyone else in wanting to see their names in print, perhaps more so, and since they are paid to be articulate, egoism is channeled into print as well as the classroom.

But Korean professors, according to the Korean press, have been living in a kind of paradise that may be coming to an end. They are now well paid, respected, and have tenure. But things are changing, they say. Korean professors do not publish adequately, according to the Ministry of Education, although why they should be concerned about professors in private universities is a separate matter, inexplicable outside Korea. The Ministry says they need to be evaluated by impartial judges to review their publications to determine how good they are. They are also under siege because of charges of intellectual cronyism by staffing universities with their own graduates, which the Ministry of Education seems determined to change. And there now are few new jobs at prestigious universities in Seoul because the intellectual cohort of professors is relatively young, and positions are simply not available. So they migrate to the provinces or to the research institutes attached to various ministries and other bureaucratic entities, public and private, which employ many, and no doubt are the better for that.

If we go back a bit in time, there was a period in the old, bad, authoritarian days when the government started to award research grants to university staff on an almost wholesale, noncompetitive basis. Ostensibly, these were to encourage scholarship and improve university life. In fact, many were designed as supplementary income to professors, the primary purpose of which was as a reward or inducement to prevent their students from demonstrating. Of course, these often-generous grants did sometimes result in good research, or, in the arts, good works or performances, but their motivation seems primarily to have been directed toward academic tranquility, not quality. They had an added incentive to the state by not increasing base salaries on which retirement was calculated.

Anecdotally, it is said there are more Ph.D.s in Seoul than in any other city in the world. This may not be statistically true, but it certainly often seems that way. They have social prestige, can gain more prestigious marriages, and generally are part of the Korean elite. Overall, they have been a force for modernization, and they contribute to the progress of the society. They too feel the need to publish, which they do with alacrity and often at their own expense. Whether the research produced in Korea is up to professional standards is best left to the judgment of the readership of the volumes or articles, whether in Korean or foreign languages, by peers who will establish, enhance, or destroy the reputation of those publishing. The question that might be asked is why the Ministry of Education, which to date has not been exemplary in its innovation in educational reform, believes that it can supervise such review, even of public institutions, and why it feels it appropriate to manage private universities better than they can themselves.

December 1999

On Romanizations

According to the *Korea Times*, on July 4th a new romanization system officially went into effect in Korea. Although the government will begin to use it immediately, it will be introduced over time into a variety aspects of Korean life. The article speculated that a new round of contentious debate will ensue, and no doubt that is correct. I leave it to others who have written eloquently on the problems of romanization in Korea and the issue of for whom such systems are devised—Koreans or foreigners. I will concentrate here on other matters.

Any romanization system of another script is a crutch for foreigners. The central idea is to eliminate the need for it on the part of any serious student. For foreigners in only superficial touch with those societies that have different scripts, some form of internationally acceptable romanization is required, if only to mail letters. Local people romanize their own script only when attempting to communicate with outsiders. So the purpose of romanization essentially is to communicate effectively and efficiently with the outside world.

I am no stranger to the problems of romanization in a number of languages, including Korean. In a much earlier incarnation when I was studying Chinese, I was exposed in the space of three months to three completely different systems of Chinese romanization: the standard Wade-Giles system, which dictionaries of that time used and that had numbers for tones, a Yale University system that indicated tones with diacritical markings, and a Harvard University system that incorporated tonal indicators into spelling. This was a maze through which it was very difficult to navigate, and one was constantly confused; I sometimes unconsciously combined different elements from all three on tests, much to my, and my teachers', consternation. My problems were complicated because, while studying Burmese, other romanization systems were used for Burmese, adding further to my confusion.

I studied Chinese in a period long before the *pinyin* romanization system came in under the People's Republic and one then had to learn that together with a whole set of new, simplified characters. There are many problems with the official Chinese romanization system, but that is a different issue. What struck me as singular was the uniformity and immediacy of the response in the use of the new, imposed system on the mainland. Not only did such romanization seem mandated for all uses, public and private, although one expects that kind of senseless uniformity under a totalitarian system, but foreigners immediately adopted the new system without much murmuring. I never understood why such a uniform and prompt response was necessary.

I was struck by the news report on Korea that although the state will move immediately to use the new system, the article indicated that the current systems on proper names of people, companies, and associations can continue "for the time being, until a standard format is developed for implementation." The Minister of Culture and Tourism strongly urged the immediate adoption of the new system for all.

There has been a long, unpleasant debate about romanization systems in Korea, and an earlier, mandated, official system was finally abandoned when it was not well received. But even then I do not remember that the use of the new system was required in private matters. So this new effort, which seems a prelude to a concerted government push to mandate certain spellings for personal use and civil society, is a singular intrusion into the lives of the citizenry. If the *Korea Times* article is correct, then will a family have to change its name from Yee to Yi (or visa versa)? And what about Lee, Li, Rhee, not to mention Lho and No and Rho? And what do we do about Choi and Choy? If change is required, then I suppose one can have some solace in knowing that this is only a spelling change, and not, as under the Japanese colonial administration, a change from Korean to Japanese names. But only a modicum of solace.

The explanation seems to be that uniformity would help globalization, competitiveness, and efficiency. That is far-fetched. If the United Kingdom suffered economically under globalization for a period, it was not because there were many Mr. Smiths, and also Mr. Smythes. International businesses have higher levels of intelligence and can adjust.

In a number of articles I have commented that in Korea there has been a major stress on orthodoxy of thought and ideology traditionally and in the contemporary period, and this in spite of free and fair elections under democratic processes. This view has caused considerable debate. Uniformity is a good thing when we want to feel secure in buying some advertised, mass-produced product, and predictability is necessary for an effective and vibrant private sector economic system to work. But uniformity is not necessarily a desirable trait in all matters, and to even consider requiring the private sector to conform to even the best and most enlightened of academic pronouncements on the most effective romanization system is to usurp individuality in the cause of pointless and nameless conformity. It is one thing to devise standard spellings in Korean for Korean words. It is also important that a government be ably to convey its views in some standardized system so there is no ambiguity. It is quite another to force this on society as a whole.

No doubt in this modern Korea where debates may freely range there will be many who will comment far more learnedly than I on the adequacy or lack thereof of the new system. My concern here is on the intrusion of the state into the private lives of its citizens.

July 2000

On Informational Arbitrage

In the entertaining and important volume *The Lexus and the Olive Tree,* Thomas Friedman coined the expression "information arbitrage" to describe one of the phenomena associated with globalization and the tension between that process and keeping one's cultural and social roots. The former is exemplified by the Lexus, and the latter by the olive tree.

Arbitrage is the buying and selling of the same commodity and earning income through the process. International brokers today do this with alacrity through exchange or interest rate investments, but the process can by extension apply to other activities. One of these is the incessant expansion of information that becomes readily, almost instantaneously, available. The volume of such data may overwhelm us; it has changed the way we live whether or not we appreciate it.

In reflecting on the Korea scene, there seems to be a number of informational arbitrage systems in operation. Some may relate to money, and although others may not directly produce income, there is value added to the process. That value-added in one sense relates to convenience and thus the saving of time, and in another, more important, case it relates to added credibility.

I subscribe to several free services and have access to a number of web sites on the Internet that enable me to gain a great deal of concentrated information about Korea in one such service, Burma in another, and on other topics through different systems. These services organize and compile information on countries and issues, and on a daily basis allow one to get aggregated doses of data (or sometimes speculation) on what is going on related to those societies or questions. These services compile stories from a variety of sources and package them together. So in a few keystrokes and a couple of dozen seconds I can keep up to date on what is going on. It would otherwise require considerable time and energy to have such access, but they provide the material to me without any real effort on my part. This is not always a pleasant experience, depending on the material and how harassed I might feel at that time, but it makes one more efficient. Now, if one does not become involved in having such data in almost real time, one feels an outcast in this era of instant communications. So in a sense I benefit from this process—one type of informational arbitrage.

The second instance of arbitrage relates to Korean society as a whole, and to the press in particular. It is not surprising that Korea, which is dependent on the external world for its economic well-being as a major manufacturing state and for its security, should be concerned with what is reported on Korea abroad and how such developments affect its external economic and diplomatic relations. After all, if one is to attract investment and have good trading relationships, how others view Korea becomes important.

But that importance is not simply over information originating in Korea. What foreign sources write about Korea has a far greater influence within Korea than it probably has abroad. And there seems to be a greater informational value-added attached to what some foreigner writes about Korea than what is reported in the local press and media. So if an influential paper picks up a story about Korea, one can be sure in the freer Korean society we now witness that it will be reported on in the Korean press, and indeed treated more seriously than if the genesis was some local source. This is not a desirable phenomenon because it undervalues local initiatives and gives greater credibility to sources that may be no better than local ones, and which are probably less well informed. But if one wants to get the attention of any Korean government about any particular problem, arrange that it be reported abroad, and you can be sure that the issue will be seriously considered at relatively high levels in Seoul.

This, of course, is not only true about Korea. If a mid-level U.S. government official wants to suggest policy changes in some field in his or her own agency, it is far more expeditious to have some congressman raise the issue to one's own agency than to try to buck from inside a recalcitrant bureaucracy that is reluctant to make more work for itself. Because it comes from outside and from a source that is important to any executive branch agency, due attention is given. That too is value-added arbitrage.

There are not only the questions of greater impact or improved credibility, even if one or both are erroneous. Such foreign reporting encourages the publication of information that local sources might have wanted suppressed or at least downplayed, or that other elements of the press might feel it politically inexpedient to publish, even today. The fact that the *New York Times* first published the massacre during the Korean War at No Gun Ri prompted serious consideration of the issue within Korea itself, and only after which did the Korean press air it. In a sense, then, the external reporting on the same issue gave added value. The Korean press was engaged in a type of informational arbitrage.

Arbitrage—informational, intellectual, or otherwise—will continue. It can be a useful process, but organizations either in government or media should be able to make their own assessments of the importance of information, and not only rely on foreign sources.

April 2000

6

Korean Politics

On Alternating Currents of Concern

Although the poet W. H. Auden wrote of a different age of anxiety, we live in alternating eras and foci of anxiety in Korean-American relations. But perhaps a less extreme term might be used; as the United States has changed the characterization of North Korea from that of a "rogue state" to a "state of concern," we might consider the present state of peninsular-U.S. relations as one of concern. The Korean-American relationship, thankfully, is closer under President Kim Dae Jung than it was under President Kim Young Sam. This profoundly important alliance is in the national interests of both states. Yet it has been hounded by disputes and disagreements even as it has been continuously and closely linked by mutual advantage. These divergences are prompted by normal differences in interpretations of the national interests of each state as well as by the increasing nationalism on the peninsula and in Asia.

In half a dozen years we have seen a complete shift in the locus of these concerns. The metamorphosis in this critical bilateral concern is a result of North Korean actions related to South Korean-U.S. relations, which may have been unintentional even as they have been significant.

In 1994 the United States recognized that its worldwide nuclear nonproliferation policy was threatened by North Korea and that security in Northeast Asia might be seriously jeopardized. The United States was considering what steps it might take, including aggressive action, to prevent this happening, when Jimmy Carter stepped in, negotiated with Kim Il Sung, and effectively defused the crisis. The result was the Agreed Framework, which is still in effect today. But one of the requirements of those talks was direct, exclusive, and bilateral negotiations between North Korea and the United States, with the explicit exclusion of South Korea at the insistence of the North.

Although the United States promised to keep the South Korean authorities intimately informed about these discussions, there was a sense of great anxiety in Seoul about the danger that the United States would abandon the South in favor of some sort of bilateral deal with

Note: This article is included to demonstrate the volatile nature of the Korean-American relationship that shifted following the first, and then the second, Bush-Kim summits.

North Korea— securing the equivalent of a "trophy wife" and desert-
ing its old ally. The continuous U.S. reassurances to the South Korean
government did little to assuage these concerns. The tension was exacerbated by the poor personal relations between the presidents of
both states.

Then that situation reversed. The warming of North-South relations as a result of the successful June Pyongyang summit has meant
that the principal actors on the peninsular stage have changed. No
longer was the United States at the center of the drama.* It then became a completely Korean play, with the United States in the position
of only a supporting player. As the social scientists would say, South
Korea has changed from a "dependent variable" to an "independent
variable"; South Korea has metamorphosed from being acted upon to
becoming a causal factor in the changing peninsular relationships.

In a real sense, for the first time since 1945, the United States was
not the primary principal on the peninsula. This came as the United
States had evolved into the world's only superpower, and thus this
subordinate role seemed even less anticipated than it might have been
a decade or two earlier. This was an unusual position for the United
States in the world, let alone on the peninsula, and there were some in
Washington who felt a great sense of unease in this new role. President Kim Dae Jung and the Korean people were in the forefront of negotiations on the future of the peninsula, as indeed they should be. As
the United States promised to keep the South Koreans informed about
North Korean negotiations in 1994, so the South Koreans then assured the United States that they will do the same thing.

As President Kim Dae Jung has engaged in his Sunshine Policy to
warm North Korea, perhaps Chairman Kim Jong Il had formulated
his own "Sunshine Policy" toward the South. In 1994, the determination of North Korea to avoid talking directly with the South on nuclear matters was widely interpreted as a means to drive a wedge between, or split, the South Korean-U.S. relationship. That period, by
analogy, was a North Korean hard line or "Storm Policy." But the
summit and related events and negotiations have become the North's
Sunshine Policy toward the South. To continue the 1994 analogy, the

---

* This has changed with the Bush administration following the
Bush-Kim Dae Jung summit in Washington in March 2001.

North today may be attempting to drive a wedge between the South and the United States—not on the part of the government, perhaps, but among a significant portion of the South Korean people by appearing cooperative. It is well to remember that 10 percent of the South's population originated in North Korea.

If relations between North and South have so warmed and the threat of war seems even more remote, so the argument by many South Korean people goes, why does South Korea need the United States? Would it not be better to ignore the United States and get on with improving North-South relations without U.S. involvement and troop presence? Even if President Kim and Chairman Kim have agreed that this troop presence (whatever its size, composition, and location) is not an immediate issue,* a new problem has developed—how to deal with this question in South Korea.

The transformation of the Republic of Korea into a pluralistic state where the government in a democratic manner must take into account the views of its citizenry means that somehow the Korean administration must effectively explain to the Korean people the nature of the South Korean-U.S. relationship and its importance to the Republic. The need for popular support generated through the leadership's explanations to the people is the price of democracy. Of course, North Korea need not explain anything to its people but simply offer official dicta.

But the United States for its part at this time must be sensitive to the changing situation and its new backseat role. This will not be easy for a superpower that has continuously been the center of the action related to the peninsula, and the danger of arrogance that often accompanies power. This delicate approach to the new situation on the peninsula should be reflected in negotiations on SOFA, defense arrangements, as well as in trade or other bilateral matters. The policy issues are far broader than the technicalities in such arrangements. A new American administration of whatever party should be prepared to understand the delicacy of the situation, the importance of the Korean-American alliance, but also the rise of anti-Americanism in the

---

* Although president Kim had indicated that Chairman Kim Jong Il had agreed that U.S. troops might remain, in later statements the North Koreans called for their removal.

South and the potential for its exponential increase as a result of U.S. missteps or mistakes. Peninsular affairs should be a primary concern of any new U.S. foreign policy formulations.

September 2000

On Political Legitimacy

How does a society determine that its government is proper and appropriate, and thus accepted? What elements go into this formation of attitudes about a regime or even a nation? How does all of this change over time? These are some of the issues associated with the question of political legitimacy—a question that has been transformed over the years of independent Korea. Economics now has become a vital factor.

Political legitimacy is essentially the moral basis for a government to issue laws and commands, and for the populace to accept that these are binding and appropriate, and that they should be followed. So political legitimacy is not based on the punitive power of the state to enforce its will, nor is it solely a matter of popularity, although this is closely related to legitimacy. After all, President Kim Young Sam had legitimacy as a freely elected (although minority) president, but that did not make him popular in the last years of his presidency. These attitudes toward legitimacy are usually not directly articulated, but are a subconscious stream that affects the sense of the common good. Political legitimacy is not a constant, however, and evolves over time, rising and falling depending on events and attitudes.

Legitimacy is usually associated with regimes—individual governments—but it may also be associated with nations. Colonial powers often arbitrarily, individually or in rivalry with other colonial powers, created artificial boundaries that divided ethnic, linguistic, or religious groups, creating minorities in dispute with central authori-

Note: This was written after the financial crisis of later 1997 and before the summit in Pyongyang of June 2000 that changed the equation. That summit became a decisive moment in President Kim's political life, and improving relations with North Korea became the most important element in his legitimacy, except for the fact that as a lifelong dissident, he was elected to office in December 1997. The lack of reciprocity on the part of North Korea, however, has undercut President Kim's opening to the North, and this was further eroded by President Bush's antipathy toward northern engagement.

ties, and spurring questions about the very existence of a unified country. Korea is fortunate that this is not the case; it is unique in essentially being a homogenous society, no matter how much people may complain about provincial regionalism—it is regionalism within the broad consensus of "we-Koreans." Of course, it has been true that the both South Korea and North Korea have in the past decried the legitimacy of the other state, and of the regimes that controlled that state.

Political legitimacy is considered to be based on four broad principles: shared norms and values between those governing and those governed; conformity of the government to the established rules of the governing game; the proper use of power; and the efficacy of the administration. Within this configuration, there are a number of elements that may be part of the equation. These include the roles of nationalism, religion, ethnicity, economic effectiveness, ideology, status, procedures by which authority is established (elections, heredity, etc.), even international recognition or support, and ironically the perceived illegitimacy of previous governments.

The Korean case offers many instances illustrating the importance of the issue of legitimacy, and indicates shifting aspects of this important question. Ethnicity, as we have noted, has not been relevant. Religion has not been a factor of critical importance—presidents or leaders have been Protestants, Catholics, and Buddhists, and they have all been accepted by the population.

As in many countries evolving out of the colonial experience, nationalism was an early important element in the legitimacy of both rulers and regimes in a wide spectrum of countries. Sukarno in Indonesia, Nehru in India, U Nu in Burma, Ho Chi-Minh in Vietnam are all examples out of many. In Korea, it was Syngman Rhee who could claim nationalistic credentials in his search for legitimacy. As a staunch anti-Japanese fighter, he emerged as the leader (with U.S. assistance) in contending with others who shared an anticolonial past. This, of course, was also the original claim to power of Kim Il Sung.

The Second Republic represented a shift, where there was less emphasis on the nationalistic element. Heritage played a role; both Yun Po Sun, the president, and Chang Myon, the prime minister, had heritages and backgrounds that placed them in an appropriate social position to assume leadership according to the traditional patterns of Korean society. But essentially the regime's legitimacy, while it lasted, was based on the illegitimacy of the closing years of the Syngman Rhee period, which it replaced.

Park Chung Hee's coup of 1961 overthrew the traditional aspects of legitimacy. Having been in the Japanese Army, he could not claim nationalistic credentials. He was from a poor, rural, non-*yangban* (gentry), family. The military then was not considered a prestigious career path. Because of earlier involvement in a communist-inspired uprising, he was suspect to the United States, which at that time was an important, if secondary, element of legitimacy. Thus his search for legitimacy came through the economic channel, and his stress on this element ensured his place in Korean history, in spite of his suppression of most of the elemental civil and political rights.

Chun Doo Hwan's rule was in many respects similar, because of the heritage from the previous military government and the coup of December 12, 1979. But President Roh Tae Woo, in spite of his military career, was different, for once again the procedural elements of legitimacy came to the fore, and even though he had been a critical actor in repressive governments, his popular election as a minority president ensured his legitimacy. Thus, the nature of the procedural element of legitimacy (that is, elections) began to play an increasingly vital and necessary role in the process. This, of course, has continued under presidents Kim Young Sam and Kim Dae Jung.

An important factor in legitimacy since formation of the Republic has been ideological, as one of the established norms of the society. This has been the anticommunist stance of each government (with varying degrees of intensity depending on the external environment and internal political alliances). This element has receded in importance, although any government in South Korea must be, and appear to be, extremely vigilant toward North Korea.

For the moment, the legitimacy does not focus on nationalism (for all Koreans are now nationalistic), nor status, nor external approvals. Procedural criteria (elections) are established, and it is highly improbable that they could be set aside. But the issue now is economic efficacy. Syngman Rhee paid little attention to it, as long as U.S. aid flowed in. Chang Myon had too little time—the issue there was social chaos into which society seemed to be headed. Since Park Chung Hee, with an iron hand and who essentially established economics as a critical area of legitimacy, it has played an increasingly important role.

President Kim Young Sam's legitimacy eroded not so much through economic malaise (until the end, when he became essentially irrelevant), but through corruption scandals and political factors. President Kim Dae Jung is faced with a different problem. He has impeccable procedural political legitimacy, which gives him an opportunity to deal with the economic crisis—an opportunity that could turn into trauma and undercut his legitimacy over time if the economy does not improve. Although he cannot be accused of being a party to the crisis, he must show resolve and determination in coping effectively with the issues in what the Korean people feel is a fair and balanced manner—the suffering that is being imposed on the populace must be perceived to be equitable. That is a very difficult task. So his long-range legitimacy will not only depend on the method of his assuming power, but how he governs, and, most importantly it seems, how he manages the economy. For the moment, then, economics has assumed a more important role in the political legitimacy equation than other factors; it seems in command of politics.

July 1998

On Power and Proportional Representation

Much has been written about the process of democratization in Korea. Progress is apparent, and overall there is little doubt that a long distance has already been traversed. Korea is now admired by many countries, and not only for its economic accomplishments, but for the peaceful changes of government, and its ability quietly to move the military back to the barracks. Korea can be proud of its many achievements in this regard. But no process is completely smooth, and no such arduous road void of potholes.

Yet of all the aspects of democratization, the one issue that remains central to the implementation of democratic governance is the liberalization of concepts of power. It is important to have democratic institutions and procedures in place and functioning, and Korea has all such elements operational from a broad electorate and fair elections, a vigorous National Assembly, a somewhat more autonomous judiciary, an articulate civil society, to heightened press freedom and greater pluralism. I have called Korea a "procedural democracy," because the forms are followed, but the democratic spirit is sometimes lacking. How those institutions function is a product of how power is conceived.

Although Korea has modernized in so many aspects of its life and economy, in many ways it is markedly traditional when it comes to the issue of power. Power is viewed as highly personalized. This is not only true in government, but also in business, academia, and in the nonprofit field. Personalization of power and the concept that it is limited means that sharing it is losing it. This makes reaching compromises and delegating authority far more difficult than if power were considered infinite and sharing it was not a zero-sum game. As one Korean scholar said, "Korea operates on Western hardware and Confucian software"; the institutional components are all international, but power and authority still consist of strong insular traditions. Related to this concept is the use of information as an element of such power, and thus transparency is seen as a weakness.

Political parties are the best illustration of the problem of power, where parties are founded or realigned to serve the purposes of their leaders with the object simply to get or retain power. Few parties have distinguishable programs or continuity, or train younger leaders. A contributory factor has been the prevention of the formation of left-wing parties, but the problem is far more basic.

The recent debate over the question of proportional representation in the National Assembly (that is, the extra number of seats from a national constituency to which a party is entitled is based on the percentage of votes a party wins) is a case in point.

The original idea behind the proportional representation system seems to have been to ensure that the losing party (which theoretically could receive 49 percent of each seat and still have no representation) should be adequately represented in the Assembly. This concept is quite reasonable, but the way it operates causes problems.

The argument against the present system of a total of 75 seats[*] allotted to all parties on this basis is now a major issue of debate in the National Assembly. The question seems to focus on corruption; that is, do parties receive enormous funds from party members who wish to have a proportional seat in the legislature, and do individuals pay more for a "safe" seat—one they think is assured because of the relative popularity of their party?

As an outside observer of the scene, one has no verifiable knowledge or data on this issue, although the generic charge seems credible. Until

---

[*] This was later changed to forty-six seats.

there is evidence presented in court, this must remain speculation, although the possibility of such activity must be closely scrutinized.

But another aspect of this issue seems ignored in the press. It relates not to money, but to this question of power. The ability of the head of a party or some influential figure to choose proportional representatives for the National Assembly in reality further personalizes and centralizes power within the party structure. Whoever chooses such individuals, even if no money changes hands or perhaps especially if no money is forthcoming, creates a bond of obligation that is not easily overcome or severed. So the method of choosing proportional representatives, if not the system inherently, further consolidates power in the hands of any political leader and broadens the entourages around such leaders, thus furthering the personalization of power and factionalism in Korean society.

Although this may seem to be highly abstract, in fact it has highly practical implications for good governance and the nation as a whole. Local autonomy will widen the democratic basis of party politics over time as locally elected officials will not be beholden to the centralized party leaders for support, but to their electorate. Thus, centralized party control will be reduced. If the debate on proportional representation could be widened to discuss all attributes of the question, and a more democratic means found to choose such proportional leaders, this would help the democratic process.

October 1996

On Confrontation and Emotions

Koreans seem both emotional and confrontational to many foreign observers, and there seems to be a close correlation between the two. Expressing our emotions to a third party is a type of confrontation, even when it involves love. Watching Korean television reinforces this feeling, and even in the most benign of circumstances, emotions seem fully expressed. Most Korean dramas are heartrending experiences. And indeed Koreans in social science surveys do rate themselves as highly emotional—three times more than the Japanese and seven times more than the Chinese. The Chinese reverse the statistics, considering themselves much more emotional than the Koreans and the Japanese, while the Japanese consider the Koreans three times more emotional than they are, and that the Chinese are least emotional. Although social scientists would immediately qualify, even question, these generalizations, self-perceptions are important means to understanding societies.

There are many societies that go to extreme lengths to eschew confrontations or publicly expressed negative feelings of any sort. Elaborate linguistic and body language techniques have been developed so that confrontations are avoided among members of the same social, ethnic, or linguistic group. Linguistic circumlocutions are developed. Third parties are introduced, so anger can be vented on another person not present, or even on a nearby animal. Direct insults and threats are elaborately masked according to rules established, so that everyone involved knows what is going on, but there is no need for blood revenge or violence, which is what confrontation might bring. This is true in traditional Thailand or Java, for example.

The United States, on the other hand, is a confrontational society —as our "in your face" expression indicates. We value plain speaking and the whole fabric of our society is built around confrontation. So we want to know what people really mean, and we want it to be direct and explicit. We have no use for subtle hints and delicate body language. We say in the vernacular, "Let it (emotions) all hang out," and "talk turkey." The English language is exact and clear-cut. Even in love we want explicit expressions of feeling, not hints or surrogate indicators, as the social scientists say. We have seen this in recent sexual harassment rules established by one American university, where sexual intentions and consent have to be explicated. If this were to happen in Korea, the population would probably be reduced.

This confrontational approach is perhaps an element of a society that prides itself on its diversity and egalitarian nature, however much the latter may be fictional in practice. The United States is too diverse and people come from too many different cultures to have clear, established and understandable but unarticulated subtle rules for everyone. It may be more important to avoid mistakes by being blunt than to guess at the cultural context in which another person operates. Explicitness thus becomes the lowest common cultural denominator. But because we expect such straight talk, when we deal with other societies we may misunderstand and miss the nonverbal nuances that are equally valid means of expression, and indeed more interesting. This often increases problems in diplomatic negotiations.

Confrontation is also expressed in our legal system; in civil cases we confront each other through the courts. In nonconfrontational societies, there is more room for compromise and negotiation. That is why the American legal system may not be suited in many ways for export abroad. The Korean legal system in such cases provides ample opportunity and favors out-of-court settlements.

How confrontational is Korean society? That is, how confrontational are Koreans among themselves? Dealing with foreigners is a completely different issue. Very often foreigners are told yes, when no is implied, or Koreans sometimes avoid answering even urgent letters, because to disagree or refuse would be impolite and, in effect, confrontational. But foreigners have stories of Koreans who get angry in public, fight among themselves, get drunk, and generally act without decorum or civility.

Whatever may have been true of the Korean upper classes in a more traditional era, today confrontations seem everywhere. It is not only in Tongdaemun market, but in the streets and in more elite shops. Driving is a series of endless confrontations that, one hopes, avoid the actual clashes of matter and involve only emotional wills. There are even the aesthetic disharmonies of urban life, with the endlessly repeated and grating signs and advertisements; that is a form of confrontation. Negotiating a contract is usually a form of confrontation, when earlier the word of the parties involved would have been sufficient.

Emotions run high in Korean drama and television. Crying must be the most called-for response required of actors and actresses. Love is also clearly expressed on Korean television, even though kissing seems forbidden, and sex is implied but rarely stated.

Expressing emotions is now supposed to be good—it cleanses the psyche, and American men are now taught that they should not be ashamed to show their feelings, whether joy or sadness.

The self-perception of Koreans as emotional does seem accurate, and because Americans are also emotional, especially as contrasted to the phlegmatic British, perhaps this in itself is an unconscious bond between the two cultures.

January 1997

On "Heathens Though They May Be..."

The early Western travelers, missionaries, and colonialists generally tended to judge non-Western cultures by two interrelated Western standards: whether they were technologically or mechanically advanced, and whether they were Christian. These attributes were correlated in Western eyes, for to them these were the two attributes of "civilization." Of course, an exception might be made for the wonderful crafts of China or India, but because they were not Christian they were automatically inferior in some way. Social values, such a group harmony and sharing, nonviolence, etc., that today we may treasure among the most technologically simple societies rarely entered into the judgmental equation.

Those who remained in foreign lands over prolonged periods sometimes developed a degree of respect for aspects of local cultures. Often there was a kind of grudging admiration for some social trait or virtue, of course as perceived through Western lenses. Whether it was an economically simple society or one highly urbanized and socially differentiated, Westerner residents sometimes would find something of value. Those Westerners, referring to a people among whom they lived for a considerable period, might preface a complimentary but stereotypical response, with, "Heathens though they may be, the X people are...(kind to strangers, love their mothers, respect their elders, write good poetry, etc)."

These left-handed compliments are now recognized for what they were—highly condescending remarks that passed at the time as "liberal" views of foreigners. To those a hundred years ago or more (or perhaps even less), these statements were evidence of the sensitivity of the speaker and indeed of the listener, for both could share in the virtue of Christian charity toward the "natives." It was then an accomplishment to find something socially good in many of the cultures that were not part of a highly sophisticated tradition of written intellectual life, like those of China and India whose contributions had been recognized by the Western intelligentsia for at least two hundred years. Of course, those Westerners who came to such countries were generally not of the intelligentsia.

We have thankfully long passed the stage of those types of remarks that cheapen the compliment. "Heathen" is not a word in fashion, and people today are much more sensitive to many cultural nuances. Cultural liberalism is a virtual necessity in today's interpenetrated and interdependent world, in spite of the Archie Bunkers of U.S. television fame. But if these remarks are no longer made, the underlying attitudes sometimes linger in more subtle but still uncomfortable ways. This is perhaps more true among the older population than among youth, whose culture is more international.

The "them" versus "us" syndrome has moved beyond the gross to the insinuated. But it is still there. We may no longer (one hopes) hear the expression, "Damned clever, these Chinese," as a reluctantly backhanded compliment to a people whose civilization predates that of the West and whose cultural and other accomplishments are as historically undeniable as they are admirable. Yet the attitudes sometimes remain, even if the words are not spoken.

Too often in Korea these residual prejudices still occur. They are sometimes subtly evoked in the complaints aired in the English-language press in letters to the editor, or in columns that occasionally appear. These attitudes may lie dormant like an undetected virus, only to erupt into a recognizable affliction when prompted by extraneous factors. An unpleasant incident, a seemingly unprovoked insult, a crime, or even a particularly insensitive remark by a prominent person can release a cascade of prejudice transcending the original problem.

How does one learn about a society relatively unknown? We explore books that generalize from our individual experiences. The foreign nonspecialist in Korean affairs who is seeking to find written material that will be a guide to understanding a country like Korea is hard-pressed to find works that combine objectivity with sensitivity and avoid what we might call the "heathen though they may be" syndrome. Cornelius Osgood, the anthropologist who wrote the first English-language study of a Korean village (on Kangwha Island), could say in the early 1950s that there was no country in the world as important as Korea about which so little was known in foreign languages. This is not quite true today. There are a plethora of economic studies, and now good translations of Korean classical and contemporary literature, but in certain fields we still find gaps. Where is the single, nonacademic volume that one might recommend to the intelligent but generalist reader of English that will materially help understanding of Korean society? Where is a study that is neither classical history nor economics nor sociology but combines in a cohesive manner the best of the academic disciplines in a nonacademic setting? Where is the volume that is void of cant, of superficial generalizations, of propagandistic content, of idealized myths, that neither writes down to the reader nor engages in arcane disciplinary linguistic jargon?

Potential writers of such a work encounter obscured roadblocks —an unrecognized prejudice, a foreign-imposed value system, a tendency to engage in gross generalizations (like this one, I confess), and simplistic stereotypes. Yet those who are the most qualified to write such works, such as Korean or foreign academicians, are little rewarded should they venture into quasi-popular literature. They do not gain tenure from such efforts, are often derided by their colleagues for abandoning their academic elitism, and are accused of inappropriately making money.

We are still searching for the (wholly) literary grail that will explain Korea to foreigners—one that is literate yet accessible, accurate yet understanding, and nuanced without being obscure. We have such works for some other cultures. Where is our Korean Virgil who will lead us through unknown lands?

April 1997

On "Let Me Count the Ways"

Those of us immersed in Korea are used to seeing Koreans refer to themselves in the press with great and understandable pride in terms of numbers. It is not so much counting how much I love you, but rather you (the broad, outside world) counting how much you love me (Korea). So, Korea at one point was the tenth-largest trading country in the world, the twelfth-largest economy, and the fifth-largest market for U.S. exports (the fourth for agricultural products), and has the fifth largest car industry in the world. It has the fourth- or fifth-largest army. Its literacy rate is one of the tops in the world, and Korean children rank very high internationally in their scholastic achievements. And on and on. All of these numbers give reassurance to a population risen from colonialism and the ashes of war to heights very few, Korean or foreign, deemed possible a generation or so ago.

But now come different sorts of numbers, some negative ones that disappoint and undercut the advances made. Is Seoul the second- or third-worst polluted major city in the world? Does it have the highest automobile death rate per car or per kilometer or per person? What about certain cancers? As they say, who's counting? We know the numbers are bad.

Now we have another number to contend with—the fourth-most stressful country for foreigners. The articles I have seen have not specified much beyond the bald assertion that foreigners regard Korea, after Vietnam, India, and China, as the most difficult country in which to do business or live or both. Switzerland is the world's least stressful of those listed, Australia is high, and Singapore is the best in Asia.

Is this a fair assessment? How do we define what is stressful? Traffic and the ability to get around physically are no doubt bad, but Seoul holds no candle in Asia to Bangkok or Manila or perhaps even Jakarta, and beyond Asia, to Cairo.

What makes Korea difficult? Is it language? Certainly foreigners recognize that learning Korean is difficult, but there are probably more speakers of English per capita in Korea than in Japan, and the Arabic, Hebrew, or Chinese scripts are far more difficult than Korean. Perhaps it is the complexity of living, which many foreigners and Koreans returned from abroad, find difficult. Take shopping for necessities; it is essential but most often inconvenient. Both Koreans and foreigners alike would consider it difficult because of the problem of finding a accessible place to shop in which goods are displayed for the convenience of the shopper not the owner, and to which one can walk or in which one can park (unless of course there is a driver, which is very nice but growing less possible except for high officials and businessmen).

If one is in business, then perhaps it is the very talented bureaucracy, which can make life hell if they want, simply because they are so talented. Korea hires the best and the brightest to staff their government, and they say there is enough discretionary authority built into government that individuals can reinterpret policies coming from the top. Perhaps it is the opaqueness of regulations, or perhaps the penumbral areas in which officials make their own policies according to their whims. Some would argue that it is growing nationalism, in which Koreans really do not want to deal with foreigners, and especially Americans even as they rely on the United States for security protection and must export to maintain their living standards. Americans have been the big brother too long, and with that role has often gone attitudes of superiority that no one would like. Some Koreans and foreigners alike claim that modern Korea has become rude—in the market or on the street, or to anyone not part of one's established social set. If true, that could increase stress, although I find people in Hong Kong or New York far more rude than those in Korea.

There is an internal tension in Korea in which foreigners often find themselves caught. Although my personal experiences have been universally pleasant, the foreign businessman may be forgiven for his confusion if he says that Korea has a national policy of globalization, which is designed to make Korea a more active participant on the world economic and cultural scene, and nationalism, which unconsciously attempts to filter out foreigners and foreign thinking and influence. The press is filled with consternation about the import of foreign luxury goods, which may indeed be a problem, but I see no complaints about Hyundai Grandeur cars or locally produced luxuries.

The tendency for foreigners, based on their own societal experience, is to insist that these conflicting concepts in states or individuals be resolved or rationalized in some way. They often have problems in entertaining at the same time varying positions that they determine to be inherently antithetical. Yet this insistence on consistency in itself may be a cultural trait. Why do we demand uniformity? Is this a virtue? Emerson, in his essay on "Self-Reliance," wrote that a foolish consistency was the hobgoblin of little minds.

The noted Korean writer O-Young Lee many years ago wrote the story of two Koreans who were arguing and were watched by two other Koreans. The first person arguing, Mr. A, turned to Mr. C, an observer, and said that he was right, and Mr. C agreed. Then the second person arguing, Mr. B, said to Mr. C that he was right, and Mr. C agreed as well. Then observer Mr. D turned to Mr. C and asked how both could be right. Mr. C replied that he too was right.

So views that appear to be in conflict, such as globalization and nationalism, may never have to be resolved because the concept that there is such conflict, and that such differences are psychologically disturbing, is culturally determined. A reader might complain that logic does not allow this to happen, but the reply might well be that logic, indeed, is a part of culture and is affected by the same patterns, and that you, too, are right.

August 1996

On Ritual Retribution

A political ritual has developed in Korea. It is a ritual because it has all such characteristics: it is a predictable and seasonal occurrence and is supposed to produce some efficacious result. It is not a force of nature, like a solar eclipse, but is a man-made and potentially alterable phenomenon. Its very continuity says something about the society. Rituals are regarded as necessary, whether they be sacrifices to a particular local or extra-local deity or to service a social need, or simply to provide assurance to those involved.

These rituals are political purges. These occur whether under democratic or authoritarian leadership. Each administration that has come to power under whatever circumstances—by revolution, coup, or election—has engaged in a ritual purge of some who were associated with the previous administration. Now, these purges are not the murderous events of a Stalinist period. Nor are those dismissed usually exiled to remote corners of the state, such as to Cheju Island during the Chosun Dynasty, or abroad. And although some are jailed or just simply dismissed, most will find their way back into the good graces of the society in a later stage of that or some succeeding administration, for they all have very good personal connections with factions or individuals of whatever political stripe.

In other societies, the changing of the political guard cannot be called a purge, because those that came in with an administration are expected to leave before or with its exit. These are the political appointees, and although I think that in the United States there are too many, their departure is predictable and occurs normally without rancor. They have no trouble finding alternative, and often more lucrative, employment.

In Korea there is not only a changing of the guard, but an opening of the jails and an especially busy season for the prosecutor's office. It had become fashionable to arrest the very wealthy (after the fall of Syngman Rhee or the coup of Park Chung Hee) for what amounts to egregious wealth or profits related to presumed corruption. For suitable donations to less-than-transparent entities, these charges seem to evanesce quietly. After the Chun Doo Hwan coup, there were the intellectual purges of the media, claiming that they were corrupt, and although some may have been, it was an ideological purge of the middle and the left by the right-wing.

In Korea under the Kim Dae Jung administration, we have seen a modest purge of two key individuals engaged in previous economic policy not based on any charges of corruption or illegal activities, but rather on poor judgment—charged in this case as dereliction of duty. That the previous regime turned out to be economically incompetent in the fall of 1987 is evident. That it, during the same period, tried to deny the failing economic situation by criticizing the reporting in the international press was egregiously silly, as anyone who has dealt with the international media would certainly have attested. Bad judgment is simply that—but it is not a crime. To try the critical figures in court smacks of something more profoundly disturbing.

These individuals were recently found innocent, but that they were brought to trial leads to two conclusions. The first, and a salutary one, is that the courts are far less influenced by political considerations than in the past. That is the good news, and however one feels about the outcome of this case, and there were public protests about this decision, this is an important and positive development. The bad news is that this seems to be in the pattern of the ritual purges of the past.

What is the function of a purge? Obviously to cleanse, to purify the present in the light of the past, and to make the present and future either appear to be, or be, better, or both. To do this one assigns individual responsibility. It is common knowledge that in Korea when there is a problem, someone must take responsibility and resign. The fact that a new administration is anxious to make its mark and improve on the previous one means there is always something wrong with what went on before. A train wreck forces the resignation of the minister of transportation. In the past, a *gunsu* (county chief, previously appointed) would be forced to resign or be reassigned if there were a forest fire caused by lightening and he had put up the required signs warning against fires. Although this may be better than the American system in which few actually take responsibility for anything (remember that President Harry Truman, disturbed by this, had a sign on his desk that said "The buck stops here"), it has become a ritual as well.

The ritual purge is related to the resignation syndrome, and both to the personalism that is profoundly important in Korean politics. Those associated with the previous leaders normally must be dismissed. Since loyalty is personal, these individuals will be presumed to be disloyal. There is thus some "objective" excuse for a purge beyond any personal animosities that may have existed between the critical individuals involved.

But the real issue is how to overcome this seeming need for purges. This is not a product of a single individual or administration, but of a political culture in which politics is a zero-sum game with someone forced to lose, and lose more than simply a position. Politics is not a game for "gentlemen" (*kunja*) in the Confucian sense, nor is it a parliamentary debating society. It is more potentially devastating. Society must begin to require politicians to accept a new, more inclusive, role, and not seek to conduct vengeful campaigns against those who came before unless there are clear grounds for criminal action. Someone has to break this cycle of political bulimia.

October 1999

On Ideology and Orthodoxy

The student demonstrations of August 1996 and their aftermath are a most important and immediate topic of concern and conversation in Seoul. The press rightly bemoans their confrontation with the riot police, the loss of the life of a young policeman, the injuries sustained by those on both sides, and the wanton destruction of property. It is only natural that in the aftermath of these violent events and arrests, the worst in Korea in some years, recriminations of responsibility and suggestions for preventing future such occurrences are heard from all levels.

These ritualistic demonstrations have lost their meaning. They are evidently not supported by any significant segment of the public, and seem anachronistic holdovers from periods when the government was considered illegitimate by some large segment of the populace, and when the students as incipient literati—the conscience of the nation—could hold up the banner of morality and righteousness. Those days are long gone. If some students had wished to demonstrate against certain policies of the government, there were more effective ways to do so. They were remarkably naive in their expectations, and all they accomplished was to diminish their causes in the eyes of the populace.

Yet no matter how far apart the students—at least the hard-core leaders—and the government may be, they share some common characteristics. There seems to be in Korean society a need for uniformity of views. Both sides seem to require orthodoxy of opinion and a core ideology. This, of course, is nothing new in Korean (or world) history. In the Yi Dynasty, factional disputes arose over the "correct" interpretation of the orthodoxy prescribed by neo-Confucian thinkers, and it was the threat of unorthodox thinking that was deemed to be destructive of the whole social order that led to the exclusion of Western ideas and the martyrdom of many Catholics.

If the materials collected by the police have meaning, we can see this orthodoxy on the part of the student leaders. Anachronistic materials inculcating the failed obsessions of the North Korean regime and its requirement of almost religious veneration of Kim Il Sung and his supposed invention of *juche* (self-reliance, autonomy) ideology were used to persuade young students of the nationalistic worth of the North. These young followers, often lost in the new experience of university life, anonymous to the university administration, and often alone for the first time, sought solace and friendship among those who befriended them—often the ideologically tightly knit study organizations managed by a small coterie of doctrinaire fanatics.

One can understand the students' concerns, even when one disagrees. Some have said it is not only the nationalism of the North that is appealing, for the essence of *juche* is nationalism, but the increasing conspicuous displays of wealth and income disparities in the South, and the jejune equation of poverty in the North with purity. They are said to applaud the anti-Japanese activities of Kim Il Sung, and oppose the United States presence here. Illegal North Korean radio is said to be persuasive to these groups.

The student's actions are sad. They were violently demonstrating against a government that was duly elected in a fair election and which is perhaps the most legitimate government the state has seen, at least since 1960. Whatever its policies and however effective it may have been are quite different matters. The violence that erupted, and the obvious planning that went into these demonstrations, indicate that this was not a matter simply of protesting for a more effective government or specific policies, but against that government itself.

On the other hand, the government calls for the ideological "purification" of the students, their remorsefulness over having evil thoughts, and the need for a new ideology to replace their erroneous thinking. The government exhorts the professors to influence the attitudes of their students, and claims that the professors have failed to live up to their responsibilities as mentors of the young. Is this realistic or even appropriate? Life is not an examination, where students will regurgitate at teachers the required answers on the test pages. Although the role of teachers and professors in Korea is far more influential than in most of the West, the government does not recognize that although there may have to be intellectual obedience to pass an examination and get into university or receive good grades, alas even today, yet the extracurricular, mentoring role of most professors has diminished over time. They cannot perform the tasks that the state has set forth for them. In the Park Chung Hee period, the government used to give "research" allowances as bonuses to professors who were able to keep their students from demonstrating against the government. This was a prime professorial responsibility of professors and university presidents, who were dismissed from even private schools if they could not perform as the state wished. The system didn't work.

The search for a new ideology on the part of the government is the search for a new orthodoxy. And that is not what democracy is about. Any democratic government, even one at war, as South Korea technically still is, has many means and laws by which to prevent violence and undue disruption of the lives of its citizens. It does not need a new orthodoxy. Its strength, in contrast to the North, is in its pluralism and diversity of views, freely but nonviolently, expressed. The call for a return to the Korean traditional values of the Confucian canon is all very well, but that does not require such orthodoxy. The contrast might be between a North ossified in a kind of intellectual rigor mortis, and a South vibrant with the peaceful competition of ideas and values, not only in economics. Who would want the northern formula under such circumstances?

September 1996

On Hard and Soft Power

Several months ago, Singapore Senior Minister Lee Kuan Yew gave a speech in Beijing in which he distinguished between what he called hard and soft power. Hard power is simply economic and military strength—the usual attributes of what we think of as national power. Soft power is a new concept. The senior minister, with whom I am often in disagreement on conceptual issues such as values, rights, and democracy, said that a state has soft power when other states attempt to emulate it. He went on to note that China could achieve hard power in thirty years.

Soft power, by implication in his speech, although he did not say so, resided in the West, and specifically in the United States, which for all its faults is still a society that has enormous impact over the world simply because other peoples want to copy many of its attributes.

China today does not have soft power. Except for Burma/Myanmar and Vietnam, there are few countries that would like to copy its combination of autocratic state control and economic liberalization and growth, its marginalization of minority group power at the national level, and its attempted silencing of dissidents. If it does not yet have hard power, it is a hard state in a number of ways on the road to becoming a hard power, at least regionally.

It was not always thus. China was until several centuries ago the Middle Kingdom, as it called itself. It was the one that from its center radiated throughout Asia power, both hard and soft, at various periods, the one that other countries, such as Korea, tried to emulate in many ways. It welcomed world trade and world travelers, used foreigners in pursuit of its own goals, and absorbed conquerors into its own system as long as they played by Chinese rules. It exported products, but more importantly it exported its culture. It was truly a world center. As the Ch'ing Emperor Ch'ien Lung told the British envoy at the end of the eighteenth century, you foreigners need China; we do not need you barbarians.

To have soft power does not mean that other societies want to copy all your institutions or social or cultural patterns. But it does suggest that there are things in that society that are deemed by others to have some important transnational worth. More than specific institutions and beyond styles of living or consumption, although both may figure in the amorphous equation, it is basically in attitudes toward how power is conceived and used, and the role of the state in society.

Vaclav Havel, then president of Czechoslovakia, told a joint session of the U.S. Congress that the United States had been a beacon of freedom for oppressed peoples during the Cold War. That is a prime example of soft power. Although many would denigrate the copying of much of American popular culture, interpersonal relations, patterns of consumption, and even individualism, the fact that these forces can exist relatively autonomous of the state and its interference is an attribute of that more basic admiration.

What about Korea and hard and soft power? Korea's economic growth has been phenomenal and its local military capacities substantial. The Republic of Korea, alone or unified, is well on its way to achieving some aspects of hard power in economic terms. Although its military capabilities are formidable on the peninsula, it cannot yet project its force beyond its land base. There are plans, however, for Korea to acquire sea and air power, including an aircraft carrier and air superiority within one thousand kilometers of the peninsula, that would give it regional power of significant magnitude in a decade or so. To build such a force, if indeed those plans are pursued, would likely set off a regional arms race that would have the most serious repercussions.

More important to me in immediate terms is Korea's potential for soft power. There are stirrings in that direction that need encouragement. Developing states turn to Korea as a model of economic development. Even though this may be a simplistic approach, because what Korea accomplished was done under unique internal circumstances and in a favorable external environment, it is a beginning.

A second phase may be underway. That is the reduction, and one hopes eventual elimination, of the corruption that has been rampant. Worldwide coverage of Korea's retribution of past leaders for their illegal activities has given Korea a fillip in this direction, whatever immediate shame it may cause. If this continues, and does so without partisanship and favor and if the root causes are expunged with justice and fairness, then Korea will be highly regarded in international circles. Other nations will turn to Korea for advice—the beginnings of soft power.

There are other aspects of soft power, however, both good for Korea in terms of international prestige but also internally desirable. These include greater freedoms internally in the press and in the privacy of individual life, in the fairness of enforcement of appropriate laws that encourage civility of living in an overcrowded state, in the improved status of elements of the population, such as women, and in protection of the already fragile, partly destroyed, environment.

Korea has been ambivalent. It has been rightly proud of its many accomplishments, but often self-conscious about its perceived shortcomings. The state has engaged in extensive public relations campaigns to convince the world of the image that Korea would like to portray externally. This can only at best be marginally successful. In this information age, data will out, even or perhaps most evidently, unpleasant data; and official rose-colored glasses becloud the eyes not of those viewing Korea from outside, but those in Korea who attempt to influence those viewing in.

Continued reform and the graciousness that we associate with traditional Korean etiquette toward those respected transferred to a national level and applied abroad will project soft power in a manner that will redound to Korea's long-term goals. When we talk about globalization, we should be considering both its hard and soft power components.

December 1996

On Reforms from Below

Since Korean independence, there have been only three occasions when there have been substantive political reforms—progress toward a liberalized polity. At each of these times, these changes have been either forced by or mandated from below—from the people. At those times, the government had been reluctant to make major concessions in the way power was allocated and the administration carried out. Rather than lead, the government followed. Only after a clear signal was sent by the people did change occur at the apex of power.

The first of these occasions was the Student Revolution of April 19, 1960, which forced into exile the autocratic president Syngman Rhee and initiated a period of reform after over a generation of pent-up demand for liberalization. That period, alas, was so turbulent that it became unmanageable, as pressures from a variety of groups made demands that could not be realized. The result was the military coup of Park Chung Hee of May 16, 1961, which did not usher in reform but repression, even as it began to produce economic growth.

The second occasion was the spring 1987 incipient peoples' revolution that grew in intensity, eventually forcing the government of (former general) Chun Doo Hwan and his designated successor (former general) Roh Tae Woo to issue the June 29, 1987 liberalization decree that established once again the direct election of the president, the freedom of the press, and the reinstatement of the civil rights of Kim Dae Jung. Here again, it was pressures in the streets that brought about change. The government may have wished to appear magnanimous, but the people demanded change; the administration could not have continued its set course without chaos evolving.

The third event was the election of December 18, 1997. Here it was not demonstrations in the streets, but an election, probably the fairest and most transparent of any presidential election in Korean history. It was the people who had once again mandated change; all political parties were intent on distancing themselves from a government that had the lowest popularity in the recent history of polling.

Each time the role of foreign influence was not inconsequential, even if it may have been inadvertent. There seems little doubt that the financial crisis and the bailout of the International Monetary Fund were instrumental (although clearly not the only or even the primary factor, as a general malaise had earlier set in) in Kim Dae Jung's victory.* It thoroughly discredited a government already on the edge of moral collapse. The need for the bailout, intensified by the administration's early refusal to admit the problem for a period when to outside specialists it was evident, and its lack of transparency in reporting its foreign debt, all heightened frustration. It also undercut the political legitimacy of the regime, for economic efficacy has become increasingly important (as the polls have noted) as a hallmark of regime validity. It was further exacerbated by the state's inept, inappropriate, and futile attempt to stifle foreign press criticism of the dire economic straits into which Korea had inadvertently strayed.

In each of the previous instances as well, foreign influence was important. In 1987, with the specter of the potential cancellation of the Seoul Olympics in 1988 should demonstrations continue and become uncontrolled, and with the United States in a rare public statement warning against the use of the military in suppressing what had clearly become a popular revolution, the administration's options were severely curtailed. And it was also the United States that advocated to Rhee his 1960 exile in which he finally died, although, to be balanced, his rule was perpetuated by U.S. support as the specter of a resurgent and belligerent North Korea posed a danger perceived as greater than internal autocracy.

---

* The government party split and Kim Dae Jung entered into a critical alliance with the conservative Kim Chong Pil to win the provinces in which he held considerable political power.

The December 1997 election is a milestone, not only for Korea but in Asia. It is the first transfer of power in Korean history between political parties (not factions of the same party) as the result of an election, but it is also one of the few times in Asia that this has ever occurred. Only in India, Sri Lanka, the Philippines, and most recently in Japan* has this happened, and in each country there have been severe political problems. This transfer, in the midst of a national crisis, is even more profoundly important because it indicates an element of political maturity, even of political grace, that one hopes will continue. As much as the economic debacle is considered by many Koreans to be a national shame, the election should be considered as a national triumph in the face of adversity.

IMF conditionality will be painful, and there are those who argue that broadly the IMF has been insensitive to the internal political problems of a variety of countries, including Korea. Yet the reforms that they advocate, and to which Korea has agreed, are in general those that other organizations have championed for years, and to many of which the Korean government had previously acquiesced, but its reform rhetoric was far in excess of actuality; change proceeded at a glacial pace. Progress has thus been forced, its pace increased.

The people, who have mandated change, will be asked to bear a major burden of economic recovery. Korea's previous success was largely built on the backs of its workers, who for years were denied the rights allocated to other groups and to workers in many other societies. Solving the economic problems will in part be determined by how the people in this democratizing society will view the equity of this burden. The government should not underestimate the issue. An October poll indicated that the majority of people thought that growing income disparities between the rich and the poor were the most important internal problem facing Korea. The new government, if it wants to succeed, would do well to ensure that the problems facing Korea are perceived by the people as ordeals equitably endured. The new government has moved in its first acts to heal open wounds and bind the state together. This is progress, but the success of the govern-

---

* Thailand, as well, since this was written.

ment will in large part be determined by its ability to provide moral and transparent leadership to address burdens mutually shared.

October 1997

On Gregory Henderson—An Appreciation

We are all in Gregory Henderson's intellectual debt, whether we recognize it or not. Yet he was foreign intellectual public enemy #1 to South Korean authoritarian regimes for a couple of decades. He was also the leading foreign theorist on the nature of Korean society. His book, *Korea· The Politics of the Vortex*, published in 1968 by Harvard University Press, was the first major contribution in English to theories of the Korean social and political system. He was an art critic of singular proportions. He was, and remains, the most literate and stylistic writer on Korea in English.

On October 16, 1998, the tenth anniversary of his untimely death by accident as he was pruning a tree from the roof of his garage outside Boston, Massachusetts, Korean friends and admirers held a memorial ceremony for him in Seoul. Some two dozen people came, all Koreans mostly of the older generation except for a couple of old-time resident foreigners who knew him in Korea and respected his work. The president of the Republic sent flowers and a personal note.

What was all this about? Why should people in Korea spontaneously organize an event in honor of his memory? Why did the Korean government in the past treat him as a pariah? And why were his ideas so important?

Gregory theorized on how Korean society was organized and the forces that wrought political and social life by pulling Koreans into the vortex of centralized power. He was an intellectual pioneer; as such, he may have overstressed some elements, and Korea has in part changed in the three decades since his major work was published. But some Koreans denigrated his study because it was politically correct, even politically required in Korea, to do so, and some because foreigners were not supposed to know so much about Korea. Yet for any foreigner attempting seriously to understand the dynamics of Korean society, it still is essential reading. And yet, because of political pressures, for a generation no one was willing to translate or publish this work in Korea; it remains the one essential book by a foreigner on

Korea that has not been translated into Korean.* Ironically, the Japanese translation has sold well.

Gregory was passionate in his defense of human rights. An intellectual, he fought for intellectual freedom, and this alienated him from authoritarian Korean regimes. Trained in classical studies, he was a modern liberal in his views of history. Although he was a Boston *yangban,* he was concerned about the common man. His upper-class status was a Korean strength, however, for he knew and was concerned about lineages, and wrote about Korean ones. Yet in official egalitarian American circles, it was a weakness. He was a member of an elite New England family of distinguished heritage related to one of the presidents of Harvard University. He rarely let you forget it, and he did not suffer fools gladly. This grated on American classlessness. But he was an important member of the American Embassy in Seoul, at various times in political and cultural affairs. In 1963, he was unceremoniously expelled from Korea by the American ambassador, who perhaps reflected in his impatience the discrepancies in their class origins, for indiscreetly talking to a Korean reporter friend off the record about a potential Korean election. His remarks found their way into the press. His foreign service career with the U.S. government disastrously deteriorated and he was dismissed before he was eligible for a pension. This professional and emotional catastrophe became his salvation, allowing him to pursue his intellectual bent and writing in Boston, teaching part time at Harvard, and writing on a variety of Korean subjects. We are in his debt, for his trauma gave us so much.

In his day, the Korean elite was small, and Gregory knew everyone. A cultured man, not simply a cultural officer, he frequented concerts and art galleries. At concerts, he would often sit in the first rows of the preferred first balcony, and on entering turn his large frame back toward the audience and acknowledge with discreet waves—almost as if blessing—all his multitude of friends. It is said that he wrote a classified embassy report in which he catalogued the provincial elites; for embassy officials who traveled in the provinces this was required reading. Only Gregory could have written it.

But it was his unfailing advocacy of the rights of ordinary Koreans that resulted in a campaign, official but surreptitious, of vilification

---

*   Since this essay was written a translation has been published.

that was an attempt to destroy him. He was in essence exiled from Korea. His interest in and collection of Korean ceramics was used in an attempt to silence him. Yet he did this not as a merchant or speculator, but as a literate specialist who wrote the catalogue to his own collection, later donated to Harvard. Almost as late as his death did this crusade continue.

At his memorial service at Harvard University in November 1988, after liberalization, the Korean consul general (later foreign minister) spoke—a quiet reflection of a change in official attitudes. The printed program aptly quoted Shelley (*Adonais,* XL):

> He has outsoared the shadow of our night;
> Envy and calumny and hate and pain,
> And that unrest which men miscall delight,
> Can touch him not and torture not again;
> From the contagion of the world's slow stain.

Those of us who knew him will not forget him, and it was fitting that those here concerned with human freedom and intellectual inquiry and exploration remembered his death and celebrated his accomplishments.

November 1998

On Scandals and Civil Society

The recent political and financial scandals have shaken Korean society. They will have a profound effect on the political processes for at least the next two years, and perhaps far into the future. The present turmoil graphically illustrates many societal problems, but if we examine some of them from a different, more fundamental, perspective than who specifically gave or received how much from or to whom for what purposes, we may have a clearer understanding of the issues, and some of their possible solutions. This perspective is a recurring theme in contemporary Korean academic literature—it is the issue of "civil society."

One of the important characteristics of a democracy is the effective functioning of "civil society," by which we mean those institutions separate from the government that act as avenues to develop and make effective plural centers of power, thus mitigating the concentration of authority in any one, or set of, government institutions. These organizations act as watchdogs, and can represent a very broad range of economic, social, cultural, religious, and political interests. They can either be the conscience of society as a whole, and thus be positive forces for the nation, or they may be captives of specialized interests detrimental to the commonweal. As a whole, however, they are a force vital for the functioning of a democracy.

Korean scholars have debated how the concept of civil society applies to Korea; indeed, some doubt that it existed at all in the past. There have been many academic meetings and volumes on this topic. However one views the issue in the Korean context, it seems necessary to develop new understanding and definitions that will be applicable to the Korean scene and clarify some basic issues. This current scandal illustrates the problem.

In the West, civil society is defined to include not only the civic organizations and pressure groups, such as those concerned with social welfare activities, neighborhood problems, women's rights, religion, or the environment, but also the business sector, many financial institutions, and the media.

In Korea, the financial scandals and the public's response have demonstrated several important lessons that policy-makers should consider in the future. First, they have shown that public opinion, as organized by the civic associations that have demonstrated for justice at this time, is vigorous and can effectively be expressed through civic groups banding together to voice their discontent. This is a healthy democratic sign.

When we consider Korean businesses, especially the *chaebol*, our conclusions will be different. The large business private sector was created, fostered, used, and controlled by the state for national purposes. That does not mean there was a unanimity of views among them, or that competition abroad and elements of a market economy did not exist, or that there have not been disputes about state-business relationships. But overall the relationship has been so close that the term "private sector," if it is to have cross-cultural meaning, has to be used with great discretion because of these differences.[*]

Many scholars have argued that the *chaebol* in Korea have been in effect outside of civil society, and have been in very close symbiotic relationships with the government. This has been obvious for two decades. That large conglomerates gave enormous financial contribu-

---

[*]   At least until the financial crisis of 1997 and its aftermath.

tions to the government either directly or through individuals or the government party, legally or extralegally, should therefore come as no surprise. That they also gave to the opposition is simply a sign of prudent management—to ensure support from potential leaders and groups and avoid adversarial relationships. Whether these were "voluntary" contributions or in expectation of specific favors is something on which an outsider should not comment. If we consider the *chaebol* as indirectly linked to the state, then the contributions are essentially inherent in the system; consider them as simply an informal but necessary tax on doing business in Korea. In this light, the ubiquitous nature of the donations are understandable, if regrettable.

In a similar vein, one should look at financial institutions. They were more stringently controlled in 1961 by General, later President, Park Chung Hee, and somewhat freed of more obvious government control in the 1980s. Their control of credit was an essential element in the government's policy of rapid industrialization and exports. But everyone knows that banks were, in effect, indirectly controlled by the state, which could influence their leadership, force them into bankruptcy, and certainly affect their policies. This heritage is one reason why Korea has been reluctant to open the financial sector to foreign investment. The expansion of banks in Korea has meant intense competition in attracting deposits, which have made these newer institutions even more vulnerable to temptations. The banking sector was directly involved in the operation of the scandals by receiving almost incalculable amounts into various bank accounts as if, according to statements in the press, these were routine activities. And in a sense they were. President Kim Young Sam's reform of enforcing "real-name" bank accounts was a major step forward, but did not prevent the collusion of parking, thus laundering, funds in accounts of actual, cooperative persons. Thus, financial institutions have been included within the wide web of government influence and policies.

Some Korean scholars also believe that the media, which is the critical element of ensuring government transparency, should also have been excluded from civil society. Historically, the media have been under government control or extreme governmental pressure, although this direct pressure is now said to be absent. Now, many of the leading papers and media organizations are owned by the *chaebol*, and thus may be charged with being less than objective under circumstances of stress where businesses are concerned. The government authorization of expansion of newspaper pages produced massive increases in advertising, mostly from the *chaebol*, which has made the press more dependent than ever on businesses, and thus more vulnerable to such pressures. The press has been reporting on the scandals with great vigor, but their objectivity in treatment of the conglomerates and other issues in the scandals has yet to be demonstrated. Some Koreans believe that the influence of the newspapers has grown so rapidly that the press does not know how to use their expanded role.

For the future of Korean pluralism, and for the deepening of the democratization process, these concerns should be addressed through regulations severely limiting donations of businesses to political parties, requiring all banks to report large deposits or withdrawals to the Board of Audit, and to encourage the independence of the media in its watchdog roles. Limits on election spending need strict enforcement, although some claim that the present law restricts spending too severely, and thus invites abuse. Some say that the election law allows more chances to speak, and fewer chances to spend money.

The lessons from the United States are important to Korea, although they are negative—how not to go about dealing with political donations. The United States has to date failed to regulate adequately political donations because of loopholes in previous legislation and because of a Congress reluctant to deprive itself of such funds.

In Korea, the egregious use of funds must be curbed for the future of the democratic political processes in the state. Whether the materialism of the affluent elements of Korean society reflects politics, or politics reflects this society, or both influence each other, is a matter of conjecture, but the results are the same. The equation of wealth with power, and power with wealth, is nothing new. But when it undercuts the legitimacy of an administration and affects those in, or who aspire to, the highest offices, it creates cynicism about politics, about political leadership, and about the future of the country. One rarely sees a poor politician. The society would do well to relook at itself, and make strenuous efforts to reform for its own sake. This is especially important in a society where democratic deepening is still in process.

One should not only personalize the problem, although focusing on individuals makes the issues more concrete. But we may lose sight

of generalized lessons as a result. Individuals may be guilty, minimally of indiscretions or moral lapses or criminal activities, but these
dramatic events should not obscure the structural problems so strik-
ingly evident as a result of this scandal.

Korea needs to develop both the legislation and the enforcement
encouraging the separation of power among the governmental appa-
ratus, the courts, and as this tragedy demonstrates, among the elements of a newly conceived civil society that will ensure that these
events cannot reoccur.

November 1995

On Korean Nationalism and Cultural Intrusions

Korea is unique. It is the only country in Asia, perhaps the world,
without significant minority groups. This has become a distinct advantage when mobilizing popular opinion for political purposes, or
organizing for economic growth. Even if regionalism seems too severe today, in international comparative perspective it is a minor
factor.

Consider that there are no minorities who control the economy and
have leading entrepreneurial roles, such as the overseas Chinese in
Southeast Asia, and no minorities so low on the socioeconomic ladder that they inhibit equity of income distribution and create social
cleavages—such as a caste system.

Korea is thus blessed. But this blessing comes at a price—both ad-
vantageous and disadvantageous to Korea. There is little question
that the cultural and linguistic unity of Korea has been a critical factor
in the survival of Korea as a distinct entity when surrounded by countries far more powerful and populous, and at one time or another all
with imperialistic designs on the peninsula. *Uri*-ism, or "we-ism," is
an important element of Korean cultural survival, and has thus been a
positive force in Korean history. As *The Economist* noted, "The nation-state is the politics of the first person plural." No matter how
plagued with factionalism traditional Korean history may have
seemed, and no matter how splintered political parties are today,
when national crises occur, Koreans generally band together against
the common enemy. It is a frequent attribute of many groups, but in
Korea it may have been more important than in most. It is a positive
aspect of Korean life.

Cultural homogeneity, however, lends itself to a kind of intense nationalism that may be positive in crises, but can on other occasions be negative, even jingoistic or xenophobic. The rise of nationalism in Korea is both apparent and rapid, and is in evidence everywhere. Its positive attributes include far greater appreciation of things Korean.

Nationalism is a product of both negative and positive forces, and the era in which we now live. The colonial subjugation, the humiliation of foreign military occupation, poor economic and social conditions all influenced Korean society to reassert its identity and obliterate past misfortunes. The rediscovery of traditional Korean arts and crafts ("aesthetic nationalism"), some denigrated because they were not *yangban* in origin, is a welcome product of nationalism and cultural pride. The creation of a separate Ministry of Culture and the publication of many works on Korean culture for foreign consumption are not isolated phenomena, but are part of this milieu.

When we compare the interest in the traditional arts, crafts, and music with that of a generation ago, the conclusions are startling, and positive. There is more traditional music publicly performed and more students. Before, if it were not a *yangban* art, such as traditional painting, calligraphy, or literature, it was considered inappropriate for serious consideration. The study of *p'ansori* singing was for the demimondaine, not proper society; farmer or masked dances were for commoners. This, thankfully, is long gone, and we are experiencing the growth of *minjung* (mass) art, which is a reflection of nationalism. So we see a flowering of interest in traditional things Korean, and even Korean artists in a Western medium, as the modern art museum in Kyongju notes, are reverting to traditional themes. Ethnomusicology as a proper field of study was a very late development in Korea.

In North Korea, the essence of *juche* is simply nationalism, and that is its appeal to youth. Although the reality in North Korea has been markedly different from the ideology, it effectively has declared an end to Japanese or Russian influence, and decried the *sadaejuui*—reliance on traditional or modern China, and the United States. History, mythic or otherwise, becomes an element of nationalism. It is no accident that the North has declared that it found Tan'gun's tomb in Pyongyang. What better way to claim primacy in Korean history and nationalism.

But "globalization" as a national policy today and nationalism may be in tension. How a society maintains its cultural integrity while allowing in foreign influences is subject to much dispute. How can a society be multicultural and still maintain its core values?

Multiculturalism is not new in East Asia, and globalization is not simply a current political slogan. Whatever one may think of these concepts in contemporary Korea, they have been a reality in East Asia for at least 150 years. Their past and present effects are still debated; they excite passionate responses, both nationally and individually. They have taken different forms in each country, have had a variety of positive and negative impacts, and have been called by different names. Yet both are ubiquitous. Globalization is extending one's culture abroad, and allowing in foreign cultural influences. In effect, it is minimally an intrusion on both cultures, and in its extreme form an assault on the established orders. It is, however, neither a product nor an end result, and is never complete or finished, but is rather a ceaseless process of tension, accommodation, and reformulation that has been the basis for both growth and decay in all fields since the earliest records kept by man. No major culture has been isolated for long.

Multiculturalism, or the import of elements of a non-indigenous culture, has often, but sometimes not accurately, been defined as "Westernization" in this region. In some cases it has been called "Americanization," and thus in a nationalistic context feeds anti-Americanism. In essence, globalization (*segyehwa*), whether as reality or a political slogan, is not only an attempt to enable Korea to compete effectively in the world economic order, but is far more broad: "Segyehwa entails a sweeping transformation of society," according to a publication of the Ministry of Information. The implications for Korea, whether successfully implemented or not, are profound.

In effect, then, the patterns of nationalism and globalization in their undiluted forms generally are, minimally, in tension, and may be perceived to be in direct, sometimes strident, conflict—an unsettling intrusion into the established social order and an influence undermining accepted authority and norms. Korea is obviously studiously attempting to avoid this inherently destabilizing effect.

Two forces have heightened the growth of the tension between what we might call indigenous and external cultures, or nationalism and globalization. First, the vast increase in global communications, travel, and economic interdependence has speeded the impact of foreign cultural influences. Instant contacts, whether of concepts that certain states might regard as subversive or inimical to their interests, cannot be completely excluded, and broader cultural influences easily cross borders. The Korean government may ban a Michael Jackson concert, but these influences (which I do not condone) cannot be completely eliminated. We think of trade and investment in terms of commodities, but clearly these move many more people accompanying both than heretofore, and there is significant, even profound, importance to trade in people—migration, overseas employment, military alliances and bases, labor flows that affect the economies and even the societies of the senders and receivers. Since there are well over a million Koreans in the United States, a large percentage of families in Korea have American cultural contacts and relationships. Note the program "L.A. Arirang" on Korean television. Tourism, encouraged by most states for foreign exchange and prestige, brings in its wake foreign cultural influences, many of which we may deplore. So today Korea considers whether it should control or stop the inflow of Japanese "mass" culture, and the debate is featured prominently in the press. And what is "mass"? A Kurosawa movie? Or is it art? And if stopped or allowed, should it be this year or next or when? And how does all this relate to free trade and joining the OECD? If the United States presses Korea to import cars or movies or mass culture or luxury items, should not the same criteria apply to Korean cars and materials in Japan and Japanese items to Korea? There are no real answers to this 150-year-old debate—no Cartesian clear and distinct ideas to solve the dilemma. But to a foreign observer, Korean culture has exhibited remarkable resiliency and power to have survived so long, and whatever inadvertent assaults on it are made by foreign influences, what culturally will evolve in Korea will distinctly reflect this society and its values, and that what we know as Korean culture will persevere in some form acceptable to most of the Korean people.

Modern nationalism in East Asia, about which so much has been written, has grown concurrently with the rise of international contacts. Nationalism is, of course, an element of culture, and may be considered as a form of culture elevated to state level. It appeals to the indigenous patterns of thought and practice, and is critical to the formation of a self-identity that allows a culture to survive. Korea could not have endured as a separate entity in the face of its powerful, encroaching neighbors without this strong sense of what we might call *uri*-ism, or we-ism—we Koreans. In the modern age, it has a very strong emotional pull on much of a society. It may be virulent or benign, or both at the same time.

The second force is the discontinuity between a state and a culture, or when a single culture does not encompass a country. This is different from multiculturalism, which implies importation of one or more cultures. The Korean peninsula is unique in Asia. It is the only area where the territory of the state (under unification) or two contemporary states have a single culture. Thus, in the two Koreas today each state is truly a nation with generally accepted or tolerated articulated national goals because there are essentially no minority groups in the society. Whatever regional differences exist socially or linguistically (thus, whatever subcultures there evidently are based on regional affiliation, for example), they are in comparative terms marginal no matter how important they may be on the local scene today. This overall cultural uniformity gave Korea a developmental advantage because it allowed for easy political or economic mobilization. This gives Korea a very strong, and often negative, reaction to foreign cultural imports which then are seen as subverting the "Korean race" (*Hanminjok*), in itself a concept rarely used for a linguistic and ethnic group in Europe.

All the other Asian countries are composed of multiethnic societies in which peoples may view themselves for certain purposes as, let us say, Malaysians or Sri Lankans, but in other instances they may primarily consider themselves as Malays, Chinese, Muslims, Tamils, Singhalese, etc. Japan closely approximates this equation of state and society, although it has perhaps 1 percent of its population composed of minorities.

Second, the end of the Cold War has intensified the rise of linguistic, religious, tribal, and ethnic (that is, cultural) tensions as overarching security needs have disappeared and the strategic glue that held multiethnic states together has withered away, instead of the Marxist prediction of the withering away of the state itself. The most obvious example is the former Yugoslavia; the disintegration of the former Soviet Union is another. So forces held in check by national needs are now erupting in negative ways. There have also been positive results; attempts to rediscover the cultural roots of social groups have become apparent.

This rapidity of change and the loosening of much that has been traditionally regarded as valuable often has resulted in an increase in frustration, anxiety, and insecurity as customary and comfortable patterns of social life and interchange are eroded and often lost. This has sometimes had the effect of producing an intense antiforeign reaction bordering on xenophobia, and a return of what is safe and secure and known. In the United States, these have sometimes been called "family values." Islamic fundamentalism, the growth of the Christian right-wing and militia groups in the United States, and the development of what has been called "new religions" or sometimes "cults" are products of these forces, and are more easily understandable within this broad context. They provide emotional security—often absolutist—within an acceptable social context in the face of unknowable and often terrifying change. One may speculate that at least one of the causes for the spectacular rise in Christianity in Korea over the past generation has been a need to ease the insecurity of rapid social and intellectual dislocation.

The forces of nationalistic culture and globalization in East Asia have often been viewed simplistically as separate and always in tension. Although there is often considerable and obvious stress between influences that appear to be diametrically opposed, this opinion sometimes misinterprets or ignores the accommodations between the new and old that has resulted in the strengthening of both.

Over forty years ago, when I started studying East Asian history and culture, we were taught that a society that retained Confucian values could never be "modern" and could not develop economically. Confucianism, these eminent Asian authorities said, after all, was backward-looking, seeking to reestablish a golden age, not future oriented. It supported the status quo, and demeaned technology and commerce. The hubris of Western scholars then has been superseded by the reality now that in some manner Confucianism rather than just retaining the old and retarding the new, has adapted to innovation, and that its stress on meritocracy, education, and self-efficacy have helped lead those states emerging in the "post-Confucian" era to be world leaders in economic development. Singapore, as a result, has explicitly introduced Confucian teachings into its school curriculum.

The emerging nationalism in East Asia has become a major force in each of the states concerned.

Korean nationalism has grown, spread, and deepened. In *Minjok Kaejoron* (On reconstruction of the nation), Yi Kwangsu, now reviled for advocating accommodation with the Japanese, in 1922 still advocated the creation of a spiritual and cultural Korean core. Today, even as globalization is declared in the South and as North Korea allows in foreign investment and more foreigners, nationalism in both states mushrooms. This growth is a natural phenomenon, and is especially prevalent among youth. It has an obvious and easy target —the United States, partly a result of its overpowering past role in the South, partly because of mistakes made, partly because of the convenience of the mark, and partly because the foreign influences seen as deleterious seem to stem from that country.

Anti-Americanism in Korea is a product of Korean history. It had to happen because the new generation seeks a more independent and assertive Korea. In short, anti-Americanism in South Korea is a kind of symbol of Korean nationalism calling for Koreanization of answers to Korean problems.

Culture is used by states for their own purposes—for prestige, for profit, for propaganda, in foreign policy, and for political legitimacy. I remember years ago in London seeing a Soviet folk ballet in which everyone smiled and danced vigorously, while an obviously leftist English women in front of me turned to her 12-year-old son and said, "See how happy everyone is in the People's Republic!" No government wants to be too closely identified with a foreign power and a foreign culture. Yet multiculturalism is a natural byproduct of this continuing process. But most states, which use the cultural processes, want to control both their indigenous forms and foreign importations. The degree to which this is prevalent in East Asia may be greater, both because of the histories of the strong state in the economic development processes in this region and, I would argue, because of the Confucian predilection to treat the state as the father, and the people as children who must be benevolently regulated and controlled for their own good. The Korean state has regarded culture as an important and inherent attribute of state power and control.

So states try to control many facets of life—from pornography (which is culturally defined—kissing in the cinema in some countries is not allowed) to literature regarded as subversive. The controls, usually only minimally effective under current technology, are in a sense a snapshot of perceived values at a single point of time—values that may change markedly in the matter of a few years. Karl Marx, for example, can be read in South Korea today, when a few years ago his books were banned. In the West, consider the Catholic Index of proscribed books, and the fact that a classic such as James Joyce's *Ulysses* was banned for import into the United States for many years. Such practices become anachronistic rapidly, and are ineffective.

But states do not speak in unanimous voices, so who decides for the state, under what standards, and to what ends? These issues are rarely debated. Perhaps the more fundamental question is who watches the watchers, and to whom are the watchers accountable? It is easy if, as in a theocracy, they claim to be only accountable to God. But even concepts of religion vary; Catholicism in Korea is not that of Ireland, and neither of yesterday, and Indonesian Islam is not the same as in Iran or Algeria.

January 1996

On Censorship

I grew up in Boston, where at that time the banning of books because of so-deemed salacious material was a constant feature. This was ridiculed throughout the country as all it accomplished was to improve sales elsewhere. Those books today are considered so tame as to be boring. I also knew a man who inherited a considerable sum of money because his father was the lawyer who fought and won the legal case to bring James Joyce's *Ulysses* into the United States, where it had been banned since publication in France, and from which thereafter he received a royalty on every copy sold.

Censorship is degrading. It assumes that adults are not responsible to decide what they should read or watch. It sets up a hierarchy—not so much of values but more of elites—elites who often are not subject to the same imposed constraints as the populace. The practice is essentially antithetical to democracy.

I was recently reminded of this by two events. I watched a Korean television program on the life of the popular singer Yi Mi-ja, whose songs were banned in the bad old days because they were said to be too sad and were Japanese copied or inspired. The program showed her singing the banned songs in the Blue House, where it was said that Park Chung Hee really liked them. How archaic all this seems today. How silly the censors.

I was enthusiastically reading Salmon Rushdie's new novel *The Moor's Last Sigh* not too long ago when an Indian noticed me, and told me that he had to read that book because it was banned in Bombay. It seems it bitterly satirizes the leader of local government in that city.

A few years ago I was in Jakarta when President Suharto had ordered all *International Herald Tribune* articles on papers circulated in Indonesia reporting on the corruption in his immediate family inked out by hand. A leading intellectual in Jakarta told me that this was foolish because all it did was to give business to the xerox machine owners, of whom there were many. This was, of course, familiar to me, for in Park Chung Hee's days articles on North Korea in the international press were so treated.

Korea continues to have selective censorship, although the days when Marxist literature was banned but widely circulated and when one could not perform music from the Soviet Union are long gone. Japanese movies and "mass culture" are prohibited entry. President Kim Young Sam prevented a concert by Michael Jackson, not counted as one of my heros, but I would not deny him or others that opportunity. Movies are cut for sexual explicitness, and dramas cut or banned for the same reason. The government has great freedom under the National Security Law to interpret antistate activities in essentially any manner it chooses.

Korea is not, of course, alone. There are many "big brothers" in the world watching and attempting to limit knowledge. The Vatican Index of proscribed books went on for centuries, while today we abhor the sentence of death passed by Iran on Salmon Rushdie for his novel *Satanic Verses*. Chin Shih Huang Ti burned books in China in 221 B.C. Hitler did the same. Humans seem to have a penchant for control of knowledge and information, both of which are power.

Censorship can be accomplished in many ways, and banning books or films or art is just the most blatant form. Dictating the content is another; the U.S. National Endowment for the Arts now puts pressure for preventing "outrageous" art that offends certain members of Congress to be funded with federal funds. Patrons of art, institutional or individual, have throughout history attempted to control content with little lasting effects.

Governments censor not only imports, but any material it generates by classifying it. If it can be considered a "national security" issue, no matter how far-fetched the connection, classification takes it out of the realm of publication and locks up access, except to a relative few. I attended a meeting years ago when some responsible USAID officials suggested classifying a piece of federally funded academic research on another Asian country because it was unacceptable to policy at that time. Cooler heads prevailed, because the authors would have published it anyway and all the government would have done would be to appear foolish.

When I was in USAID, I had some personal experience in attempted censorship. A speculative article I had written for an academic journal on "Burma after General Ne Win" caused an outcry from one quarter because it was considered "embarrassing" to the U.S. government. The State Department lawyers upheld my right to publish under the First Amendment—the right to free speech—embarrassment was not considered a just cause for censorship.

We all know that there are few absolute freedoms. The right to shout falsely "fire" in a crowded theatre is often given as one cardinal example. The protection of children is another. So we rate films for their suitability for children. But the banning of epithets considered nonpolitically correct on college campuses, for example, is sensitivity run rampant. Taking *Huckleberry Finn* out of school libraries in the United States is another. There are many examples of the modern equivalents of "bowdlerism," named after the eighteenth-century writer who edited Shakespeare because he felt that contemporary eyes and ears were too sensitive for so earthy a writer.

Confucian residual attitudes seem to affect how Koreans regard interference into the private lives of individuals. On the analogy of the state as father, they seem more willing to see government play the role of controlling materials circulated for public consumption. There seems less interest in questioning the premise that, in fact, the government knows best than in some other states.

China recently indicated that it was going to control economic information circulating in the state, and Internet users have to be registered. Thus the state has assumed the role of the ultimate economic, political, and social arbiter, which will slow both economic development and political liberalization, but will, I feel sure, ultimately fail. How to ensure the free flow of information required for a modern society and for a globalized economic order is a problem that all states will grapple with while trying to insulate themselves from what they regard as pernicious and politically threatening, thus "subversive," material.

We should ask ourselves: who appoints the censors, and what are their special qualifications? Thus, who censors the censors? What recourse have we should we disagree with their conclusions? How transparent are their operations?

Censorship is analogous to the prevention of developing antibodies and an immune system. Too much intellectual or physical protection does not allow us to sort out truths or develop resistance to disease. A.E. Housman was right. In a poem beginning "Terence, this is stupid stuff," he cited the case of Mythridates, the legendary Middle Eastern monarch, who, when assassins were attempting to poison him, took small doses of the very poison and thus built up immunity. He outlived his would-be assassins. As Housman tells it, "Mithridates, He died old." There is a lesson for us here.

April 1996

On Individual and Collective Rights

There is a major debate in world circles whether human rights should be considered as individual or collective. Many argue that such rights are universal, as reflected in the UN "Universal Declaration of Human Rights," and are based on the concept of the individual as the central focus.

Some Asian governments, including Burma, Indonesia, and Singapore, regard this concept as a Western intrusion—a kind of cultural colonialism—forced on Asian societies with long and proud traditional values of their own that are different from the Western experience. They have also argued that economic rights must take precedence over political rights—you must have enough to eat before you vote. Many, however, suggest that these states take this position to justify policies that are generally regarded as repressive of free political expression. Other groups argue that there is ample evidence for democracy and human rights within the various Asian traditions, and thus rights are not the sole legacy of Western influence or imperialism.

Patterns of individualism or collectivity are not limited to rights —they reflect broad social forces. Many have observed that in Korea most activities are performed for the group—marriages are often familial alliances; group solidarity in business, school, or other social settings is the norm. In the West, the individual is more the focus of activity.

The concept of individual rights has the advantage of being clear-cut, since the individual is the basic human unit. Collective values, whatever their ideal form, raise the problem of the size of the collectivity—is it the family, clan, neighborhood, region, village, ethnic, religious group, or class? How also do we create priorities between political and economic rights, and can one exist without the other for any extended period?

Some would say that it is up to each society to determine the internal issue of rights, and that rights should not be the overarching criterion of foreign policy. Rather, they might continue, trade and business should be separate from concerns over rights. If a regime has a poor (in the universalist conception) record on human rights, should such regimes be ostracized (South Africa during apartheid) or should there be "constructive engagement," that is, continuing normal trade and investment while quietly advocating an improvement in the rights record? The current example is Burma (Myanmar), where ASEAN had called for constructive engagement while the United States had called for ostracism.

Now, a variety of countries have built into their foreign aid programs human rights considerations. These include the United States, the European Union, and Japan, among others. In some instances, donors are less than absolute in considering whether a potential recipient's human rights violations warrant cutting off or withholding foreign aid. The national interests of the donors, however defined, take precedence over rights through rationalization of constructive engagement or other criteria.

What has happened, at least in the case of the United States, is that each country seems to be treated differently depending on how the importance of that relationship is perceived. The United States will discuss nuclear nonproliferation with North Korea, whose human rights record is arguably the worst in the world, and it has provided most-favored-nation status to China, whose concern about human rights is questionable at best. But since it has no national interest in Myanmar, it can have the courage of its human rights convictions.

As part of the human rights equation, we often call for the "rule of law" as if that could be legislated and would itself solve the problems. But law is codification of society's political and power norms at some point in time, and thus is reflective, and not formative, of political and social values. Aung San Suu Kyi was under house arrest for about six years "under law." Criminals may be executed for certain crimes in various U.S. states under law (in contrast to much of Europe). In Korea, a man who is said to be the world's longest held political prisoner (a dubious distinction for the *Guinness Book of Records*) "under law" was pardoned after over forty-three years in jail for being a spy and not recanting his communist ideals. Three men were released in Indonesia after thirty years in jail. Law in many societies is simply codified power.

There is, however, another element in the rights equation. The West, in keeping with its individualistic approach, has often centered its attention on individual human rights—the personalization of rights—in manners that sometimes seem to downplay human rights in general or in the abstract. So we concentrate our emotions on an individual to try to convince governments to free him or her, while we relegate to second priority the mass problem.

This concentration on the individual has been very productive in other cases. Amnesty International has built an important network of tracking and influencing human rights by concentrating on the individual in the hope that it would have both individual and collective effects. It has become the premier organization in the world on this issue.

In a sense, seeking to assist the individual through public or private organizations conforms to the Western emphasis on the sanctity—the religious derivation—of individual rights in that tradition. But it seems that in foreign policy we have often relegated the society as a whole to second place as we concentrate on the individual in a variety of states.

It may be more emotionally rewarding for Westerners to concentrate on the individual, for we can feel deeply their poignant plight and we can identify with those incarcerated. But it is also necessary to advance beyond the individual to the general, and not lose sight of the needs beyond the individual case, no matter how it excites our natural sympathy and plays on our emotions.

Although Asian states sometimes use collective rights as a subterfuge to prevent reform or progress, Western states use individual cases to neglect the more general need. We need to balance the needs and appeal of the individual and the collective.

October 1995

On Living in Delicate Times

Some time ago I sent an article to a Korean-language newspaper related to the Korean internal political situation and U.S. relations. Although that paper had printed many of my previous pieces, the reply from the editor was that this was a "delicate time" and that such an article could, or perhaps should, not be printed, at least in Korean with the wide circulation that such pieces normally get.

In a sense that editor was correct, although his decision may be disputed. We do seem to be entering a period of delicacy in Korea. When that happens, people become circumspect in publicly stating their views, and a sense of concern becomes evident. A state of delicacy becomes a state of anxiety, although let us hope it does not extend into the dimensions of an Audenesque age. Even in democratic periods in Korea in which the state does not directly control the media, the press engages in a degree of self-censorship; responsible media people know the limits beyond which they might fall into the abyss of scorn or retribution.

Any analysis that purports to be balanced or objective of an event or a relationship is bound to excite negative reactions among some significant portion of the articulate public. The opposition press is under attack from the government on tax evasion charges, resulting even in a tragic suicide in one of the principal families concerned. The government is under attack from the opposition— and any opposition party will in Korea normally attack the sitting government for whatever they do—and from both labor and business because of economic restructuring problems and the fragile state of the economy. There have been too many examples or corruption.

Korea clearly has problems with the United States. Seoul is not pleased because the U.S. missile defense plans (whether theater or national) cause problems for Korea with China and Russia, but cannot be too vocally critical without creating additional difficulties. The warm relations with Japan that President Kim had skillfully established have become undone because of the Japanese textbook controversy and the resulting nationalistic Korean reaction. Relations with North Korea, never warm in spite of the euphoria immediately after the South-North summit, have perceptibly cooled after the Kim-Bush summit, and have not recovered even after the completion of the U.S. policy review that calls for continuing dialogue with the North, although on a broader base including conventional forces. The President's popularity has declined markedly over the past six months or so. Now, politicians are already jockeying for position related to the forthcoming presidential election of December 2002, and the present administration is viewed by many as already transitory. One added degree of uncertainty is what North Korea might think about all of these events, and the virtually breathless anticipation in the administration on whether Kim Jong Il will visit Seoul, and if so, when.

All of these forces have created concerns and uncertainties that have affected the body politic as a whole. Although democratic procedures and institutions are not in question, they are being tested throughout the society. The spirit of compromise, so essential to the democratic spirit and for navigating through the shoals of political partisanship, seems still to be lacking. Although politicians on all sides may consider that confrontation is the key to success, it may more likely be the avenue to disaster.

This should, by all objective standards, be a period of satisfaction. The dire conditions of the financial crisis of 1997 are essentially over, even if restructuring continues at a slow pace. Tensions on the peninsula are down. The fact of having elected a dissident as president is a positive attribute of the deepening of democracy. Whatever Koreans may feel, the Nobel Peace Prize was an honor to the Korean people as a whole. This patently does not reflect Korean opinion.

True, unemployment is still larger than it should be, and the social safety net needs broadening. Corruption continues to be charged, and no doubt there is widespread tax evasion—after all, it is a society that essentially deals in cash and for which there are few receipts. In spite of all of these and other remaining problems, many shared by a variety of countries, it is sad to observe the malaise in which Korea now finds itself.

To extricate itself requires the understanding by both the government and the opposition that there are more important issues than positive or negative orthodoxy, that diverse opinions are a societal strength, and that it is possible to disagree and maintain civility in the national interests. Let us offer up incense to the local deities that those in the public realm will recognize these potential attributes of good governance.

July 2001

7

Korean-American Relations

On Negotiating

Negotiations are usually discussed only in terms of the content of the subjects under dispute. Rarely do we weigh the style and manner in which negotiations are carried out (the shape of the table in the Vietnam War negotiations was a notable exception), nor do we often consider what happens after we may have "won" or "lost" that round in the discussions, debates, or even verbal battles.

Negotiating means compromise—an amount of give-and-take. Setting rigid or unrealistic demands creates costs even if one wins. "Unconditional surrender" is a political slogan, not a negotiating tactic. The Koreans have a saying, "A cornered mouse bites a cat's nose." If you force the issue, there well may be retaliation that could be unpleasant.

Negotiations should be as cost-free as possible, even though we know that to negotiate means to give up something to gain something else. Even in war, the greatest victory involves the fewest losses, while a Pyrrhic victory, as we know, is one so expensive to the victor that he is virtually vanquished even though he may titularly be the victor. Pyrrhus, who defeated the Romans, understood this.

The great Chinese general Chu-ko Liang, in the classic Chinese novel *Romance of the Three Kingdoms*, said that when he surrounded a city, he always left one gate unguarded so the enemy could escape. He wanted the city at least cost.

There is a moral here. When negotiating with either a friend or an adversary, it is wise to offer the other party one open gate—a way out that allows a graceful retreat or exit. Such a gesture does not diminish the prospects for success, but may make the aftershocks far less acute. This kind of "face" and "face-saving" is virtually universal.

"Face" also involves the issue of whether negotiations are held in public or private. Secluded discussions may be burning, but the fire is limited. Private face may be lost, but public face is maintained. When negotiations become public, then it is very difficult with today's technology and political systems, and even in dictatorships, to keep politics out of consideration. Going public in a sense is a last resort and may obstruct reaching agreement.

In the 1950s and 1960s, the United States would constantly negotiate with the Korean government over a variety of economic stabilization measures, some of which would be unpopular for the people or difficult for the government, and the United States would link such policies to the level of U.S. economic aid. These sometimes acerbic discussions were all held in private. The Koreans knew that the Americans had to provide such assistance eventually because the security of the peninsula was more important than any economic factor. The only leverage the United States had was to threaten to go public with the dispute, which would in those days undercut the legitimacy of the unpopular government. Today, if those events occurred, with the diminished influence of the United States and the rise of Korean nationalism, it might make the government more popular to be seen standing up to the Americans.

Although there are no more negotiations on money supply or revenue policies, there are on a variety of trade and market opening issues. From an American perspective, Korean market openings have been slow, sporadic, and reluctantly undertaken, with Korea's positive rhetoric about liberalization outstripping the reality. But from a Korean vantage point, the openings have been real and extensive, and have contributed to the current account deficit that is of such immediate Korean concern.

We are in a different world from the days of U.S. aid when all funds flowed toward Korea. If we were to examine nontrade movement of funds, Korea is probably a net supplier of monies to the United States. Korean tourists, the education of Korean children, and the operations of Korean foundations in the United States may have reversed the previous trend. Perhaps now Korea invests more in the United States than the Americans do in Korea. In the 1960s, a well-known Korean wrote in *Foreign Affairs* that Korea was accused of having a "mendicant mentality," always asking from and dependent on the United States. He argued that there was a mutuality of interests that better characterized the relationship. In the 1990s, as Korea provided funding for Korean studies overseas, and as the United States wanted Korean assistance in other parts of the world, it seemed that the United States had the mendicant attitude and was always asking for Korean assistance.

Yet U.S. pressures on Korea have now become far more public than they once were. This is understandable in a democracy. But it makes these negotiations subject to political influence and local politics, and thus far more difficult. This is especially true at a time when

Korean nationalistic sentiment is high, and anti-American feeling has significantly increased in many Korean circles.

Now this is even more important. Korea is entering a period of extreme political stress: the Hanbo[*] and other scandals, the declining popularity of the [Kim Young Sam] administration, and the presidential campaign that will increase in intensity and heighten emotions within and among the parties for the remainder of this year. There is evident public frustration with all of these happenings. When combined with the uncertainties in North Korea, then sensitivities are strengthened.

Some eminent Koreans have suggested that the United States should declare a moratorium on public criticisms of the Korean government concerning trade and market-opening issues during this difficult period. They argue that such remarks will fuel further anti Americanism and could be used in the political campaigns to the detriment of good Korean-American relations.

Some Americans have countered that as Korea is now a member of the OECD and the World Trade Organization, and as a major world economic actor, it should be prepared to play by the international rules of the game, and thus such pressures are appropriate.

The problem for the United States, even should diplomats recognize this sensitivity, seems more complex. The Korean government speaks with one voice on most issues; the U.S. government speaks not with forked but with multiple tongues. Each element of the U.S. administration has its own agenda and own reward system for actions undertaken or withheld. Sometimes there seems to be less coordination than might be desirable. So Korean officials have complained in the past that it was difficult to determine with whom they were negotiating because there were a variety of powerful institutional actors (State, Treasury, Commerce, Agriculture departments, etc.), and each member of the Congress also had individual views, and often they have been contradictory.

Both sides should indeed understand that these are trying times. What happens after specific negotiations may have important impacts on broad relationships. For the good of long-term bilateral rela-

---

[*] A steel company that was accused of securing illegal loans from the government and then went bankrupt.

tions, the rhetoric would best be low and private. Each side would do well to remember *Romance of the Three Kingdoms*: consider leaving one gate open, so that face and grace may be preserved.

May 1997

On Politics and Old and New Wives

The Koreans have an expression *jo kang ji chuh*, meaning a wife who has been through difficult times and stood by her husband. To discard her would be considered the height of immorality.

Americans have a despicable pattern of obtaining what is called "trophy wives." Wealthy Americans sometimes discard their older wives who have been with them through poverty and hard times and while the husband has been struggling to succeed, and then they try to find some younger and more attractive woman to take her place after they have become established. This is both morally and socially repugnant.

Koreans have a similar problem, but it is a bit more humane. Korean men may not replace such a wife, but supplement her by supporting another woman on the side. It is a sort of trophy mistress or concubine rather than a trophy wife. Both cultures share in some manner this deplorable habit.

This expression is now current in some Seoul circles as depicting the relationship of the Republic of Korea with the United States. Koreans charge that the United States is abandoning their old time partner, South Korea, who has been together with the Americans through very trying times, in favor of a younger and more glamorous consort, North Korea.

Note: The issues presented here were serious in the Kim Young Sam administration. During that of Kim Dae Jung, the Sunshine Policy shifted the emphasis, but then under the Bush administration dealing with North Korea, and thus support given to South Korean policy, was downplayed. The essential issue is not whether the United States or Korea is taking the lead on the peninsula, but rather the volatile nature of the South Korean-U.S. relationship that has been illustrated continuously over time, and is likely to cause problems for both sides in the future.

The moral implications of this in Korean society are highly significant, and to imply that anyone would consider such a move is to cast great opprobrium on that person. To accuse the United States of such an act is a very serious affair because of its moral implications. One does not, of course, hear this in official circles, but rather in the coffee shops and at cocktail parties around town.

To Americans, the charge is patently absurd. The relationship with South Korea is not only formally tied through the defense treaty of 1953, but far more importantly there is a marriage through a wide variety of other, more intimate, relationships that could only be severed under the most unlikely circumstances. Trade and investment going both ways are important. There are almost 2 million South Koreans now resident in the United States. Many of the Korean elite received graduate training there, and many of the institutions in Korea have been influenced by the American model. We need not even mention the influence of American pop culture (for good or evil) on Korean society. Over a million American men have served in Korea in both war and peace, and over 30,000 died here. Although these ties are not irrevocable, they are deep and are likely to endure.

It is certainly true that there are immediate disputes with the United States, whether they be of a trade-and-investment nature, the opening of markets, the Status of Forces Agreement, under which U.S. troops are bound when dealing with the Korean civilian community, and on a wide variety of other problems when one side or another makes some offensive or insensitive statement, or when internal politics takes precedence over foreign policy.

Most important these days is the issue of nuclear nonproliferation and North Korea, and the related problems of whether to supply food aid to prevent starvation in the North or the collapse of the North Korean regime. These are matters of high import, and ones on which different emphases may be argued. Some in Seoul feel that Washington is paying more attention to the North, and that its priorities have shifted away from Seoul. Washington officials seem to believe that South Korean policies shift depending on the internal political wind in Seoul, from hard to soft line and back again, and that the South Korean government sometimes does not take into account its own longer-range interests in dealing with the North. But both Seoul and Washington want the South and North to talk directly with each other.

That there are disputes and differences of interest in any such close relationship, or marriage, is normal, because the shorter-term national interests, as perceived by each government, may differ even if there is a longer-term mutuality of need. The official political rhetoric on each side will paper over these disputes, for there is a feeling among some that even to mention them in public is to increase the tensions they evoke.

In fact, it may be better to air the differences, not only among responsible officials who are well aware of the problems, but among the public in both societies. In democracies, any administration cannot be too divorced from educated public opinion, and this is true not only for domestic policies but in foreign policy as well. If this happens, and government does not adequately explain its foreign policies and they remain unpopular, the regime will suffer at the next election.

It thus behooves every administration to make their case to their people, and confirm their concerns, if they are accurate, or assuage their anxieties if they are not. We see very little of this on both sides of the ocean. Although American presidents have sometimes said the appropriate words in public statements, and they are vigorously reported, there seems a lack of continuity and discontinuous attention at the highest levels. In Korea, it seems that presidents do not directly discuss foreign policies and relationships with their own people with any degree of regularity.

The anxieties in Seoul are palpable, and should be addressed. Americans believe them to be wrong, but that does not make them disappear. There is a growing distrust of the United States that both sides should openly consider. If this does not happen, drift may make the problems more acute in the years ahead.

March 1997

On a Tale of Two Memorials

Memorials are by definition designed to spur memory, but their symbolic subtext is usually to encourage nationalism. They are normally heroic in scope, often extolling the leaders of the state and their victories. Western countries are full of bombastic statuary of men on horseback. In modern states, the almost Mussolini- or Stalinistic-style massive, false, larger-than-life, heroic seems common—Jakarta is full of these Sukarno-era monuments, as was Saigon before it became Ho Chi Minh City, to mention two examples. Monuments may be personalized or abstracted or both. The Washington Monument in the District of Columbia is the abstracted personification of a man—but so abstracted that the man is virtually forgotten—most people probably think of it as a city memorial. The Lincoln or Jefferson memorials are more successful, combining personalism and architecture. The Arc de Triomphe in Paris glorifies the state as a whole and its victories. As the Arc was based on a Roman model, so the Arc in Vientiane, Laos, and the Korean Independence Arch in Seoul are based on Paris. Those who win write history, as they say, and to commemorate history as they view it they put up statuary and memorials.

Memorials normally evoke the past. In 1958 when I first visited Bangkok, shortly after one of Thailand's numerous coups that overturned the constitution, I was taken around the city by a member of the royal family who said, as we passed an impressive monument, "This is the monument to the constitution, and as you know we only put up monuments to dead things." When any kind of memorial or monument glorifies the present, it is often subject to almost instantaneous reevaluation. Postage stamps are a kind of memorial, and Imelda Marcos may have been the only sitting First Lady in the world who was on a stamp—one so large that ironically it left little room for an address on a postcard. It was even more evanescent than the regime.

As war has become less glamorous, as suffering has increased with the technology of death and the tacit inclusion of civilian populations in direct torment, and as victories become more ambiguous, so have memorials changed. The Vietnam War Memorial in Washington, D.C., is quintessentially understated, and is all the more moving for its lack of heroics. Perhaps it is because the United States lost, but more important may be that the personification of loss through the individualism of names is more compelling than abstracted design or heroic statues of leaders who later may appear to be less commanding.

The opening this past summer of the Korean War Memorial in Washington, D.C., prompted reconsiderations of that war and its consequences. It was an important event, and one helpful in publicly solidifying the Korean-American relationship, and Presidents Clinton and Kim Young Sam reinforced the alliance.

A Korean friend suggested that one might also look at the Korean war memorial in the courtyard of the military museum in Yongsan.

Two monuments by two allies of the same struggle evoke two very distinct impressions.

The American memorial, long overdue, to the "forgotten war" almost abstractly personifies the gloom of that conflict, its suffering, but its virtual despair—a number of soldiers with intentionally depersonalized faces slogging toward some unidentifiable goal. In a sense, it illustrates that war depersonalizes individuals and more generally diminishes humanity. The ponchos, limply hanging from the shoulders of the troops, give them a profoundly melancholy, almost surreal, quality, quite unlike the capes of old, which were swashbuckling and romantic. If the Vietnam Memorial is saddening in its abstracted individualism, the Korean Memorial is visually heartrending in its personalistic story—a metaphor for the society as a whole.

The memorial in Seoul is quite different. It is in the heroic tradition, a larger-than-life rendition depicting the two sides of the fratricidal struggle symbolically in two individuals. Based on what is said to be a true story, two brothers from the opposing Korean forces meet on the battlefield, the South Korean soldier embracing his younger, captured brother. They say that when this statue was unveiled, some conservative groups in Korea objected to the symbolism of enemies embracing even though the family is the ultimate element of Korean society. But it speaks first to humanity, not politics, and is the stronger for it. The political symbolism of the Republic is still there; it is the southern soldier, as elder and significantly physically larger brother, who embraces the younger, more vulnerable and smaller northern sibling. In Seoul, we have the ultimate metaphor of war and reconciliation, its tragedy and humanity.

In a sense the two memorials illustrate how each society remembers the struggle. To the Americans-at-large, although obviously not those who fought in it, many of whom are still alive, the Korean War is an abstracted, depersonalized, event in an obscure place, evoking even for those who never heard of it a profound sense of sadness and disquiet but one removed from reality.

In Korea, nationalism is more evident, although subtle, but the emotions evoked are those of individualized and familial regret and despair—a visualized form of *han* (continuing remorse, anger) about which so much has been written. It is fitting that many modern memorials discount glory, emphasizing sacrifice and the horrors of war.

Koreans and Americans of a certain age like to talk about the alliance forged in blood in this war. And this is true. But the younger generations in each country may not share such impressions. The younger Americans may think of that war as remote both in time and place and melancholy, while younger Koreans may feel most its fratricidal qualities. If our two states base bilateral policies on old images that no longer resonate among the majority of their populations, the relationship is likely to be more fragile. The long-range interests of both need bolstering on their commonalities, however the memorials may say different things to different peoples.

November 1995

On Frugality

Frugality used to be considered a virtue. In many societies, in our preconsumption era, we were taught to save, not spend, and if we were to spend, to spend judiciously and wisely. This may have been based on historic memories made more manifest by the Great Depression. That period seems over as more people have greater disposable incomes, the economies of the world are increasingly dependent on consumer consumption, and many are not prepared to wait for a purported "next life" to reap their rewards for frugality.

Some time ago, the United States and Japan held talks on what was euphemistically called "structural impediments" to the relationship between the two states. This really was a recognition that our societies were organized in fundamentally different ways with different values that had impacts on economic performance including the balance of payments. Trade deficits were a manifestation of something deeper in the social fabric. To an outsider, the upshot of the talks was that the Japanese told the Americans to spend less, save more, and balance the budget, while the Americans told the Japanese to save less, spend more, and increase imports.

Are Americans frugal? We once were, but the Calvinistic tradition and the caution of many early immigrant groups seem moribund, and we no longer are. Our advertising calls for spending on products because they are simply new and improved, and what are deemed "necessities" inordinately multiply. Of course, this creates badly needed production, distribution, and sales jobs. But every occasion incessantly calls for spending. It is not only Christmas, on which now many sectors of trade and industry depend for their annual profits, but we have created Mother's and Father's days and Valentine's Day and now we see greetings cards on sale for Easter, Thanksgiving, and even the Jewish holidays. I expect we will have a continuous stream of such cards, and related presents, honoring one's favorite prisoner or epic battle or something. Anything for profits. When college students, who have no visible and personal means of support (except their parents), are sent unsolicited applications for credit cards, something is drastically wrong. We have taken an American cultural approach and exported it along with our products.

We are once again in Korea in the midst of a contretemps between the Americans and Koreans about "frugality campaigns." At an international meeting recently, some Americans strongly stressed this as undercutting free trade and international agreements. A distinguished Korean responded that he could not understand why the Americans were so upset about the present frugality campaign in Korea, because whatever its origins, whether publicly or privately initiated, it would fail. Koreans, he claimed, were anything but frugal. He had a point.

There have been a number of such campaigns in the past, where the Korean government has attempted to convince people to "buy Korean," much to the consternation of foreigners from a variety of countries. The Americans, British, and Germans have all publicly protested at varying times. But in the past such nationalistic practices have been widespread. In the United States, a slogan proclaimed "buy American," and in England "better buy British."

The Korean government claims that the present movement is private; the United States seems to doubt this. Whether publicly or privately initiated, it strikes a strong and responsive chord in Korea in the midst of very powerful and growing nationalistic sentiment. Some of those civic, nongovernmental organizations normally regarded as "liberal" in the Korean context (pro-environmental protection, women's rights, civil liberties, etc.) are leading this movement. They are important in a democracy. Even if the state did not approve, we could expect such movements to arise.

To an outside observer, Koreans are not frugal today. Money is to be spent (in spite of very high national savings rates), and in ways that astonish some Americans with residual moralistic notions of Ben Franklin's "a penny saved is a penny earned," which we seem to have forgotten. Koreans spend far more than Americans without residual guilt for almost any item or service.

Many Koreans have said that Koreans have a penchant for buying foreign luxury items, and are willing to pay much higher prices for them than for similar goods that are Korean made. I have often observed this, but whether this is only an upper-class syndrome is unclear, and why is less obvious. Is it solely for prestige purposes? In many cases it evidently is. There may also be an element of product or manufacturing mistrust, where locally produced goods were once shoddy. This reputation is hard to overcome even if Korean goods are now widely accepted abroad, because in some cases the standards for export and locally sold items have been different.

There seems to be a penchant among many Koreans for regarding foreign-made products as luxurious. There are two factors—one is price and the other is prestige. This is often true, but in other cases it is not accurate. But it is obvious to anyone with any overseas experience that the Korean public is paying higher internal prices for both foreign- and domestically produced items. Why, indeed, do the Koreans buy so much when they travel abroad? It is not now the unavailability of goods on the Korean market. Those days are gone with the openings in Korean retail sales. It is not even the duties charged, which have been substantially reduced. It is that both foreign and Korean products bought abroad are often cheaper than Korean or foreign products domestically purchased, and beyond any rational understanding. The internal pricing and distribution systems are gouging the Korean consumer, and this is something about which the Korean public should be concerned.

If, as the press charges, the Korean government changed its statistical reporting system in response to foreign pressure to obscure the issue of imports, this is both reprehensible and deleterious for both Koreans and foreigners.

The rise of Korean nationalism is obvious, and in these turbulent times it is to be expected that public pressures will exist for Koreans to buy Korean products. To appear to give in to foreign pressures (whatever the accuracy of that charge) is to exacerbate nationalistic sentiment resulting in increased antiforeign feeling and antiregime attitudes. Whether the government initiated, encouraged, or supported these activities is not known to me. It is secondary to another issue: the problem of the perception of the growing disparities in income internally in Korea. Of this Koreans are acutely aware, and it has important implications for policy and politics.

New Korean legislation, prompted by OECD regulations, now allows political activity on the part of labor. These income disparities as reflected in the continuing purchase of all luxury items should be of concern to those who do not want to see the development of class-based political parties and the political ferment that might ensue. Koreans might well consider the issue of luxury items, those produced both internally and externally, because Buick and Grandeur cars may equally reflect an incipient problem about which Koreans might well worry. To consider only one misses an important point.

May 1997

On "Rogue" and Other States of Concern

In the old, unlamented days of Stalin in the Soviet Union, when a person was no longer in favor, some faceless bureaucrat would ensure that all future references to that unfashionable individual would disappear from future editions of the *Soviet Encyclopedia* or other official publications. Those purged would be erased from authorized photographs. If a concept or idea was out of favor, then it was redefined in a pejorative way in the official dictionaries. Memory was officially to be ephemeral, pliable, and manipulatable.

The stupidity of such efforts was multiple. The concept of eliminating from history and historical memory those items deemed officially repugnant could not succeed; people were not so stupid, ideological fashions change, and regimes do not last forever. Those who tried to repress engendered profound disrespect not so much for the denigrated object or individual but for the regime and its bureaucrats. And as intellectual rigor mortis set in, policies were made on the basis of a false sense of reality. If the May Day slogans in Moscow were positive, but simplistic, attempts to mold minds, these simplistic negative manipulations were to alter the historical record.

The United States does not censor publications, although in the also old, unlamented days some local governments tried to prevent the sales of supposedly pornographic literature, which only increased attention and sales in other areas. We don't withdraw from circulation old editions of works with unfashionable conclusions or characters. And while some historical research is revisionist in the sense that it challenges accepted conclusions, the antirevisionist theories are never suppressed, although some may go unread. But we do seem to have the equivalent of May Day slogans, and it seems we also tend to make policy based on these simplistic approaches to often complex issues.

That certain adjectives are officially and constantly used to describe a state, a personality, a regime—almost anything—are a danger, for the policy-makers tend to believe in these characterizations, with the result that policy is consciously or unconsciously influenced or made on the basis of what, under the best and most enlightened of circumstances, must be a simplification of complex phenomena. In more usual times, this approach seriously undermines our capacity to face the issue in question with objectivity. Positive or negative adjectives, from "rogue" to "freedom-loving" or anything in between, simply mean that the possibility of nuanced thought and consideration are lost. There are two faults with this approach: the government deceives itself in policy formulation, and deceives the public, on which it depends for support in foreign policy.

Very recently the U.S. Department of State decided it would change in government-authorized references the designation of North Korea from a "rogue state" to a "state of concern." This was done, of course, in the light of the summit between President Kim Dae Jung and Chairman Kim Jong Il, and was an attempt to appear, if not positive about Chairman Kim Jong Il, than at least less negative. The Department of State had decided that it should not be too out of step with Kim Dae Jung. How could a listener to State Department briefings give credibility to a statement that one day negates the previous day's statement when nothing has changed?*

U.S. support for President Kim and his Sunshine Policy is not the issue. That is highly desirable. What is at issue is the seeming need for an authorized description or characterization of a regime, government, state, or individual in what is essentially a "sound bite" or a bumper sticker. This abrupt reversal would be amusing if it did not point out a serious issue. It is a ludicrous approach to serious thought.

And what is "rogue" anyway? It has several meanings: it is a cheat, a scamp, or a rascal, and obviously, if words are to have any accuracy,

* The Bush administration has reintroduced the use of the term "rogue state."

one would not want to deal with such a fellow so described. It also is used to describe an elephant that is destructive, uncontrollable, and is outside of the herd. One assumes that it may be in the latter sense that it has been used, but in that case it is the observer who defines the herd and control. And if a state is "of concern," then concern to whom and why? There is a profound sense of arrogance in both cases.

Koreans, south and north, are not immune from the tendency to orthodoxy in the use of sloganeering to describe a friend or foe. Think how Chairman Kim was ubiquitously characterized in the South in March 2000, and now today. This has been common. Korea has a tendency to demand orthodoxy, and it has been especially easy in dealing with North Korea, for the use of alternatives that were less then pejorative might have brought retribution under the National Security Law. From "puppet" to "imperialist," terms are used to encapsulate ideas, but they do not do so—instead they encapsulate emotions, and emotions are a dangerous and slippery basis on which to try to formulate foreign policy. And so is orthodoxy.

June 2000

On the United States as a *Yamche* Society?

Many Koreans seem to regard the United States as a *yamche* society. *Yamche* is a word for which there is no exact English equivalent. Sometimes it is translated as "stingy," but this is a bit too harsh. Parsimonious sounds too pompous. *Yamche* does have some of those elements but there is a cuteness or slyness involved in it as well. One illustration sometimes employed is when someone asks you for a match, and if you reply positively, then that person asks you for a cigarette.

If Koreans accuse the United States of being *yamche*, and they would only so do informally and quietly because they are too polite to do so otherwise, then this implies that Korean society is more generous and giving. And in some senses this is indeed true. Generally, in social relations where all the players are known to each other, Koreans are indeed generous. They are generous to a fault. Presents are brought and given on virtually every social occasion, and an appropriate exchange is anticipated because the equation of exchanges must somehow balance over time. This balance is not simply one of money, or even primarily of money in some relationships, but to appropriate levels of funds must be brought the differences in age, status, and relationships, and other unquantifiable elements such as loyalty, filial piety, and a general sense of etiquette. The equation may be obscure to a foreigner, but to Koreans it is very evident.

Americans, or more specifically Anglo-Saxons, seem to regard food simply as a necessity, and thus they appear to be *yamche* in eating. A "Dutch treat" is truly *yamche*, but there are more subtle forms as well. To Koreans, food is the heart of establishing relationships. A "pick-up" dinner in the United States may be socially acceptable among friends—it is not among Koreans. The meal in the United States in general (subcultures vary, as the Italian-Americans, for example, consider food as far more important) is regarded as a simple social opportunity, but in Korea it is symbolic of the relationship as a whole. The expression in Korean as one sits down to a display of what seems like a myriad of small dishes is "There is nothing to eat, but eat a lot." The academic literature tells the story of Korean students who went to countryside to help farmers and thought they were being magnanimous by not eating the farmer's proffered food because they did not want to deplete the farmer's resources. The farmers were insulted and did not want the students back unless they would partake of the farmers' hospitality. Even in the Korean language one uses different words for the one eating—the guest or honored person, or oneself.

Perhaps, some might say, the charge that the Americans are *yamche* comes from the individualism of American society, which is in stark contrast to the generally communal nature of Korean society. If one is individual, the argument might run, then the Korean social graces of mutual giving would be less important.

This misses an important point. Americans are some of the most giving and socially concerned of large societies, but they illustrate those attributes in ways the Koreans do not. The cumulative amount of money that Americans give to charities, churches, and appeals is staggering. If a sad story is on television about a family that needs help, thousands of dollars pour in from anonymous donors with no connection to the unfortunate person. This creates many problems as well. Many Americans are taken in by false or exaggerated requests through direct mailings or telephone solicitations that play on sympathies and compassion, and some are defrauded. American generosity in a collective sense is illustrated by its foreign aid program, which contains important elements of humanitarian assistance.

On the other hand, it seems that Koreans will give generously to those they know in social or familial terms or with whom they have some important tie. These might include a school or an alumni fund or scholarship program or church with which they have a connection. And of course many foundations in Korea have institutionalized giving programs in a different manner.

It seems that the charge of *yamche* cannot be sustained when one examines both societies broadly. Rather, one might say that Americans have a tendency to be *yamche* in individual circumstances, while Koreans have the same tendency in social situations beyond the family and clan. It is ironic that Koreans, then, are more communal in a microenvironment like the family, while Americans, in spite of their individualism, are more communal in giving broadly in societal circumstances.

July 1996

On Double Presidential Mistakes

The South Korean and American presidents in the space of a couple of weeks have each committed unnecessary blunders that will hurt the important relationship between the two countries. Both South Korea and the United States need each other for a variety of reasons related to complex factors in peninsula and regional security and trade beyond Cold War considerations. The security alliance between the two may be solid, but progress in the region and in the relationship has been set back significantly through each side misunderstanding the internal political dynamics of the other country.

That the national security objectives of each state overlap but are not completely contiguous should be obvious. Korean security priorities focus first on the peninsula and than on the region. U.S. security objectives are global, involving the nonproliferation of nuclear weapons and weapons of mass destruction, and then regional, and finally peninsula-focused.

Thus there are bound to be differences in priorities, but these need not cause major strains in or be destructive of the relationship. In spite of increased Korean nationalism and military and economic strength, the opinions and statements of U.S. leaders still carry considerable weight in the internal politics of South Korea, for they still provide added legitimacy; otherwise why would all potential leaders want to visit Washington?

Both President Kim Dae Jung and President Bush made serious errors that will affect the relationships on the peninsula and the ability of the South Korean regime to carry out its internal program over the remainder of President Kim's term, which ends in February 2003. Although at this stage we do not know how the statements of each president will affect progress on easing tensions with North Korea, it is evident that South Korean politics, already in a state of decline and frustration, will increasingly deteriorate as a result. The opposition will take the disappointing results of President Kim's visit as a means to stall internal reform in South Korea.

It is evident that the South Korean-Russian statement issued at the close of President Putin's recent visit to Seoul, while proper and intentionally noncontroversial, was unnecessary and ill-timed. It came too close to President Kim's visit to Washington, and the juxtaposition could not help but be treated as significant there. It reaffirmed the importance of the Anti-Ballistic Missile Treaty of 1972, which both the United States and Russia signed. This was therefore thought by the Koreans to be noncontroversial or at least acceptable to all parties. But since President Bush had been on record both during his political campaign and after taking office that he was prepared to abrogate the treaty and go ahead with a national missile defense system even if it violated that treaty, the joint statement was a clear signal that this would create problems with the new administration. It may be true that President Putin wanted a bald declaration against the national missile defense system, and this was a compromise, but President Kim need not have acquiesced in public, in any case. It has been clear for quite a time that South Korea was not interested in such a system if it would damage relations with China. Its priorities were focused on the reduction of North Korean forward-deployed artillery and other conventional weaponry aimed at Seoul, and no missile defense system would alleviate that threat.

When President Kim visited Washington, the statements by Secretary of State Powell and the joint communiqué were carefully and appropriately worded, but President Bush's offhand comments at the press conference that followed (and then Secretary Powell's testimony in the Congress in which he backtracked and joined President

Bush's caution and skepticism about the North) have caused consternation in Seoul. In effect, it was viewed by many in Seoul as castigating President Kim and distancing the United States from him. The respect with which President Kim was treated seemed considerably less than that of the Mexican or British leaders, and did not go unnoticed in Seoul, and many complained about it. Referring to the elder President Kim, Nobel Peace Prize laureate, as "that man" was insulting. President Bush seemed uninformed of the delicacy of the internal South Korean political scene. President Kim's popularity had dropped to under 30 percent. There is a political miasma in the South. Needed political reforms seem stalemated and the economy is not as robust as some believe and needs more restructuring. The Sunshine Policy toward engagement with the North is under attack from conservatives because of its pace and costs, yet it is the cornerstone of President Kim's historical record and program. It is clearly his priority objective. By distancing himself, and thus the United States and his administration from President Kim's program in such an obvious manner, President Bush has made the remaining two years of President Kim's term in office far more difficult. The economic restructuring that the United States has pushed will probably be set back. Political cooperation with the opposition will be more difficult. President Kim, already considered a lame duck with a variety of politicians vying for the leadership of his party, since he cannot run again, will be more ineffective. Conservatives in South Korea will point to the U.S. lack of support for President Kim as a rationale for a lack of cooperation with him. All of this was unnecessary and unfortunate, a result of each side misreading the other's internal agendas. It is true that President Kim pushed for an early meeting with President Bush, one that would take place before the planned visit of Chairman Kim Jong Il of North Korea to Seoul and Japanese Prime Minister Mori's trip to Washington. It turned out to be too early, before the new U.S. administration was organized to deal with this issue. Yet no one in the Korean government seemed capable of arguing with the Korean president that this was an inappropriate time for such a trip once he had made up his mind. Whether that North-South meeting will occur is now uncertain. Its cancellation would encourage attacks on President Kim from the liberals, while the president is already under attack from the conservatives. This debacle was unnecessary. Both Korean and American sides should take responsibility for a what may be a major roadblock toward easing tensions on the peninsula and in the reinforcing the important relationship between the Republic of Korea and the United States.

March 2001

On "Transplant Rejection Syndrome"

I met not long ago an old Korean friend who had returned to Seoul following his retirement after many years in the United States. He commented that although he, and many like him who went to the United States as adults, had no cultural adjustment problems in returning and adapting back into the Korean milieu, many Korean-Americans who were born abroad or who had been taken at a very young age had a great deal of trouble when they returned to Korea. He termed this "transplant rejection syndrome."

In thinking about this issue, the question arose as who was rejecting whom? The transplanted organ may reject the host, but the host may reject the newly transplanted organ. The question is relevant here.

Many Koreans who live in Korea resent Korean-Americans who show up here with a foreign passport and views and social patterns that seem antithetical to those that Koreans take for granted. They may have ease in social relations, but sometimes neglect the hierarchical niceties that are expected, especially from the young, which most of them are. They have an informality of social relationships that is frowned upon. In effect, they are expected to think, act, and respond like Koreans because they look Korean and may even speak the language. Yet although they have been brought up in a thoroughly Korean household, their peer relationships are usually American, and thus their approach to life may be quite different.

On the other hand, this Americanization that has taken place through primary, middle, and high schools often unconsciously puts them at odds with a society, although mobile and changing, that is still traditional in many social aspects. Thus the rejection may be mutual. American young people have a sense of social independence that may be too far in advance of their Korean social graces. These graces at least in part define the community, and it is the community that is the primary nexus of Korean existence, not the individual, as the Americanized Koreans have been taught and as they have experienced.

Korean society is built on personal contacts and relationships—the family, school workplace, and a mutuality of social class and even region. The younger Korean-American is outside the system, has little entrée into it, and if in, has few ties to sustain the relationship. He or she thus has difficulty in finding roles that are emotionally rewarding and financially stable.

The situation is worse for women. American-trained women expect to be treated equally these days, and to have professional opportunities and social relationships, but in Korea they may feel demeaned. If young, they may feel overly protected here or patronized, and if they assert their rights as they see them, then they may be rejected by the Korean males, and discouraged by the females. There can thus be mutual rejection.

Westerners also face discrimination—sometimes against them, but at other times in their favor. By not looking Korean, they are often not expected to act in a Korean manner, and their gauche activities are excused when in many cases they should not be. As a child unconsciously knows how to test the limits parental authorities set, and may use the free space to exploit the relationship with the parent, so a foreigner sometimes knows that he or she can get away with misbehaving on the pretext of ignorance. This is deplorable.

Of course, the natural growth of Korean nationalism and the past power of foreigners have given rise to a degree of antiforeign attitudes, most of which are more at the abstract level than directed toward any particular individual, except when that individual flouts the established conventions of manner and dress.

But it is the Korean-American who seems to suffer most. Korea is quite different from other states. In Cambodia following the UN supervised elections of 1992, the bureaucracy and the professions were staffed at high levels by multitudes of Cambodian-Americans and Cambodian French, who were welcomed because there was at that time a paucity of trained talent with which to administer a state trying to recover from the horrors of the past that had eliminated a trained generation.

Korea is completely different. Here, talent exudes from all corners of the society, and there is depth in all fields and at all levels. So what can the returnee offer to Korea that the Koreans themselves do not already have and that would gain the newcomer respect? Some facility in English, perhaps, and some knowledge of American markets or laws, but not much else, and those for only a relatively short period.

Korea is allowing in more foreign passport holders to work, and the professions are slowly being pried open from their clam-like closure. Most of those who come will be Koreans whose families have emigrated. But the task of absorbing those Korean-Americans and Korean-others who want to return here to work will not be easy and quick. But for equity and for social justice, this should be done. If such adjustment is not possible for Korean-Americans, does South Korea really think it will be able to absorb socially a large number of North Koreans who, when the opportunity allows, might want to come here but who have been trained in a society whose goals and culture are even more foreign than that of the United States? It is worth thinking, and worrying, about.

November 1996

On Law and Extradition

A few weeks ago the extradition treaty between Korea and the United States went into effect. It was greeted with considerable fanfare in Seoul, and it certainly deserves attention because it represents a marked positive change in attitude about the status of law in Korea among the official American community.

Issues of law have represented continuous points of conflict between Korea and the United States They have been most evident in the disputes about the Status of Forces Agreement (SOFA), which concerns in part which set of courts has jurisdiction over Americans who commit offenses while on Korean soil. In the agreement, however, it is evident that the United States has the most prominent role in terms of legal jurisdiction.

But the question of whose law and under what circumstances will it be enforced is based in more complex and basic questions of law and justice, perceptions of law, as well as the political role of law in Korea. From an unofficial and strictly personal American vantage point, the issue has simply been: have Americans trusted the Korean legal system? Evidently, at least until recently, they did not.

The essential questions evolved around the issue of whether the Korean legal system operated so that defendants were really considered innocent until proven guilty, and whether those accused have had appropriate and timely access to legal services, and could expect an impartial trial. Whatever the theoretical virtues of the Korean system may have been in the past, in actual operations the dependant was treated as, and in the overwhelming percentage of cases was found to be, guilty. Now, there are many problems with the American system of justice, as many minority members will rightly complain. And there are questions about whether the common law tradition of a jury trial by one's peers is a better system compared to the continental system, which Korea practices. Yet all considered, the U.S. legal system has improved and has been a major strength of American society.

Why did it take so many years for this extradition treaty to be approved? Not having been party to any negotiations and not privy to any document related to those discussions, one can only hypothesize about the issues involved. To the external observer, the issue has been the limited trust that the United States placed in the legal protection of citizens under the National Security Law. This law has come under criticism in the annual Department of State human rights reporting on Korea. The clue lies in the newspaper report on the signing that since crimes committed under the National Security Law of Korea were not considered punishable offenses in the United States, the extradition treaty would not apply in those cases. This issue of dual criminality was considered in a fall 1999 Senate Judiciary Committee hearing on this subject.

The National Security Law and related legislation were supposed to protect the state against North Korean and other subversion. Only in a very small percentage of cases have people been accused and convicted of spying. The law was so broad that virtually any modest praise of any North Korean action or situation, at various times the reading of any North Korean authorized publications (and any publication emanating from the North was ipso facto authorized), and substantial criticism of the South Korean government or social or economic system, and any unauthorized contact with the North would endanger not so much the South Korean state, but rather the South Korean individual who had been so rash. Of course, the law was selectively enforced, but because it was so encompassing it could be used as a tool of any regime in power. In spite of the political liberalization of 1987, the number arrested under that act has not substantially decreased.

There is a classic catch-22 in the Korean situation. Since North Korea hates the law and has continuously called for its abolition, then any South Korean, including those strongly opposed to the North but who champion human rights and call for the elimination of the law, are then potentially subject to arrest under the law.

The situation has greatly eased. After all, President Kim Dae Jung has long talked about changing the law and limiting it. The South Korean courts have also limited it to a degree. But it is still a feature of the South Korean legal landscape, and remains a concern of many. This is not to say that states should not have the means to protect themselves from subversion. They clearly should, but those who have followed the Korean scene know that for many years various administrations have used the law to enforce political control over its internal adversaries, most of whom were no doubt strong South Korean patriots.

The signing of the extradition treaty means that the level of trust between Korea and the United States in the legal field has grown. And this is a good sign. But the United States has done well to exclude from the provisions of the agreement the return of those who have violated a law about which most Americans would be concerned.

January 2000

On Rising Anti-American Sentiment in Korea

Many of my generation who fought in the Korean War think of the Korean-American relationship as one intimately forged in blood and sacrifice. A palpable emotional bond based on this shared experience is real and is still vigorous. It often unconsciously guides our analyses of the past, affects our thinking about policies, and influences our hopes for the future. As comforting as these feelings may be, they ill represent the total reality of both the past and the present, and may be dangerous to our future health. An emotion is not a policy.

Whether Korean or American, we of the Korean War era are a small and diminishing percentage of our respective populations. Although there is still a large well of good feeling toward individual Americans, an evident envy of and desire for some of the material aspects of what may be called the American way of life, and growing bonds based on study in and emigration to the United States, these have not prevented (and perhaps have even exacerbated) the rise of anti-American sentiment in Korea. There are many Koreans, anxious to keep the U.S. security umbrella open, who prefer to stress the positive for fear that negative or revealing comments on the relationship's difficulties may become a self-fulfilling prophecy. More likely, ignoring the negative does not induce not the positive, rather it invites proliferation of the erosion of understanding.

All evidence from public opinion polling indicates that anti-Americanism is rising in Korea. The reasons are complex, ranging from demographic through conceptual issues to increasing Korean confidence and the mistakes of both governments throughout the period of our relationship. Korea and the United States have been called partners or colleagues. In some sense this is true, but reality indicates that the U.S. relationship looms much larger in Korea than the Korean relationship does in the United States. As unfortunate or unfair as this may be, the evidence is overwhelming. Koreans have come to understand that the United States has acted, for better or worse, in its own national interests when dealing with Korea. But disillusionment with this knowledge that the United States was pursuing policies of realpolitik—previously withheld from the public by repressive Korean governments to ensure security support and economic aid—and that magnanimity toward Korea was not the sole or most powerful motivating force in the U.S. policy, has had an important effect. Polling shows most Koreans today believe that whatever benign policies the United States may have toward the peninsula are a result of furthering American, not Korean, interests.

The most basic and benign elements of the rise of anti-Americanism result from the growing mass of the Korean population who do not remember the liberation of Korea, the Korean War, and the American economic assistance that saved Korea in the war's aftermath. And as Korea has grown economically and in its position in the world, as exemplified by its membership in the OECD, by the quality associated with the myriad of Korean products exported, and by the increasing number of Koreans who have become international celebrities in the arts or academia, so has Korean nationalism grown. It has always been strong, for otherwise how could Korea have survived as a distinct culture surrounded by more powerful neighbors? This has been both a natural and even a necessary development. It has many positive attributes, including a far greater appreciation of traditional arts and virtues and things Korean. It has also meant deepening concern about foreign intrusions on this cultural realm. So as Koreans have geared up to meet and take advantage of the era of globalization, with all its advantages and dangers, they have done so with increasing indirect indication of their vulnerability by expressing fears of the foreign. Whether globalization, "cultural hegemony," or the IMF or foreign investment, all these potential dangers or problems are seen as surrogate indicators of U.S. influence. These spontaneous fears are evident in the strident nationalism of many civil society organizations.

The historical relationship also informs the present. The Korean literati, students and adults alike, have an understanding of Korean-American history lacking among most Americans of similar status. Koreans will trace the sorry record of our relations, noting that for over a century the United States has not acted in the interests of the Korean people. They say that the United States did not live up to the U.S.-Korean Treaty of 1882, which was designed to support Korean independence against imperialist dangers. They note that the United States sold out Korea to Japan in the secret Taft-Katsura agreement of 1905 and that President Wilson's concern for the self-determination of nations—expressed in the "Fourteen Points" at the Treaty of Versailles, which lead to the March 1, 1919, independence movement—was simply rhetoric. They charge the United States with dividing Korea, for suppressing popular and leftist movements during the military occupation of 1945-48, then for pulling troops out, and afterwards supporting dictatorships. They charge collusion with the military in the suppression of the 1980 Kwangju revolt. Each incident is carefully reexamined, reemphasized with some acerbic negotiations over trade, over the Status of Forces Agreement, over some military incident, or over the revelations of the Korean War Nogun-ri massacre. Some of these are taught in the Korean school system. As is the case with running one's tongue over and over a sore in the mouth or a cavity in a tooth, the situation feels worse by repetition.

Some of these complaints are justified, some are out of perspective, some met joint needs (such as security), and some are wrong, such as the charges about Kwangju in which the state sought support and the opposition deliverance. The positive aspects of the relationship are often ignored, such as the role of the United States in 1987 in limiting Korean military options and thus indirectly assisting the process of political liberalization, and in saving the lives of many Korean dissidents (including Kim Dae Jung). Yet they have created an atmosphere in which the tendency is for the United States to be portrayed in the press as overbearing. So in any negotiations reported in the media the United States never proposes, it always "demands." Even when the United States has no involvement, it is blamed, as in the Salt Lake City 2002 Winter Olympics and the Korean speed skater incident, in which the judge was not American but the venue was. This incident was interminably replayed on Korean television. When in doubt, it is the Americans who are wrong.

Yet there is also an unsettling ambivalence in the U.S. relationship that furthers anti-Americanism. States and most people do not want to be dependent. Koreans complain about U.S. dominance, and want the era of *sadaejuui* ("serving the great," or today translated as "flunkeyism") to be over, yet there is still a feeling of the need for the United States to play the "elder brother" role in Confucian international relations—a role denied in modern diplomacy even if it informally continues in reality. That role means the elder brother has special responsibilities for support and comfort of the younger sibling. So South Koreans wanted the United States to assist in improving relations with the North, and yet when its negotiations with the North in the early 1990s resulted in the Agreed Framework, Seoul was suspicious that the United States was abandoning them in favor of their "new wife"—Pyongyang. Park Chung Hee was greatly disturbed over the Nixon (Guam) Doctrine to fight no more ground wars in Asia, by the forced abandonment of the South Korean nuclear project (portrayed in a TV serial in the 1990s), and by President Carter's attempt to withdraw all U.S. troops from Korea and his expressed concerns about human rights.

There have been mistakes on both sides that have exacerbated anti-Americanism. There has been the demonstrated arrogance of some U.S. officials and some policies, completely insensitive to the political and social ramifications within Korea. The American sense of *nunch'i* is not well developed in such circumstances. Korean governments have lied about the attitudes of the United States (such as Chun Doo Hwan on Kwangju) and misrepresented or suppressed U.S. concerns about human rights and other issues. Korean rhetoric on trade issues has often been far less than reality, and the United States has not often displayed *yangban* propriety in these negotiations.

The forced imposition in the 1980s of American cigarettes into the Korean market, when they were considered a health risk in the United

States, and more recently of rice imports and now steel, all have been perceived as arrogant. Both sides have much to account for. The relationship has been strong because of perceived external threats to the interests of both countries, but it has been anything but smooth. Official announcements stress the positive, but underneath there has been ferment that has been apparent in the streets of Seoul, if not in the controlled media in Korea.

But as Kwangju and the American response, or lack thereof, are viewed as a watershed in the rise of anti-Americanism (as was vividly illustrated by subsequent incidents against U.S. installations in Korea), so in the past year we may be witnessing a new spark to relight those embers. The disastrous summit between presidents Kim Dae Jung and Bush in Washington in March 2001, the obvious antipathy of the U.S. government to serious North Korean negotiations (in spite of the rhetoric), the "Axis of Evil" State of the Union message in January 2002, followed by the revelations of a possible surgical nuclear strike against the North if it were to pursue weapons of mass destruction, the refusal of President Bush to certify that North Korea is in compliance with the Agreed Framework—all, to the Korean public, have placed the United States in the position of opposing amelioration of relations with the North. This has been an unnecessary and untenable position for the United States if it is interested in maintaining its position on the peninsula. So the past year, like Kwangju, may be another watershed in the rise of anti-Americanism. The Korean public once looked to the moral position of the United States in its policies in Korea, but over time, and exacerbated in the past year by the policies of the Bush administration, this moral position in Korea has been demolished by history and the "moralism" of President Bush and his concentration on "evil," and his polarity of "If you are not with us you are against us." But "moralism" is not a diplomatic policy.

The tragedy of the rise of anti-Americanism is that in spite of the discrepancy in the power balance between the United States and South Korea, we need each other. South Korea does need a protector, not only now but into the future because of traditional rivalries in Northeast Asia. It is, as they say, a dangerous neighborhood. The United States needs Korea, single or multiple, as a balance against the rise of any hegemonic power in the region. The obvious need for each other goes back as far as that original treaty of 1882. Neither side should forget this.

To eliminate anti-Americanism is probably impossible. But to stop its spread and diminish its influence is essential. Responsible actions on the part of both governments, keeping in mind mutual future needs, could make this possible. South Korea needs to act with internal political maturity that can be reflected in a bipartisan foreign policy with frank negotiations with the United States. Given the nature of political power in Korean society, this is very difficult. The United States also has a major burden, made more difficult because it is the only superpower today. A couple of years ago I was interviewed by a Japanese newspaper and asked what I considered at the time to be a strange question. The reporter asked what was the most important single thing that could prevent the United States from maintaining its superpower status in the twenty-first century. Without thinking, I immediately replied "arrogance." On reflection I believe that was accurate. And it is nowhere more true than in dealing with Korea. These are lessons that both societies might do well to consider if their national interests are to be maintained.

May 2002

8

North Korea
and Unification

On North Korean Tourism and the Environment

Now that tourism to the Diamond Mountains in North Korea is under-way and seems likely to continue, or as much as anything dealing with North Korea may be predicted, it is time to think carefully about the environmental issues that seem likely to develop.

Press reports indicate that North Korea was early concerned about this issue but received assurances that there would be no problems. Now, however, according to international reporting, in addition to the tours by boat now taking place, Hyundai is planning to spend about $100 million to build a performing arts center, shopping malls, and a spa, and later will invest almost $300 million additional to develop golf courses, ski slopes, and hotels in the region.

The Diamond Mountains are spectacular, as all classical paintings attest. A popular song is "Longing for the Keumgang [Diamond] Mountains." I personally have never seen them, and my only ac-quaintance with one who has was with an old Swedish woman living in Hong Kong who several decades ago told me how as a young woman she walked through those mountains in the 1930s, and how breathtaking they were. From all accounts, they are important natural assets that are worth preserving.

But the record of preservation of natural resources has been very poor on both sides of the demilitarized zone. Ironically, it is the zone itself, void of despoilers, that has retained some of the more interest-ing flora and fauna of the peninsula. The spectacular flooding that the North has experienced over the past few years has in part been caused, or at least strongly exacerbated, by the indiscriminate logging and destruction of the forests in the North, causing soil erosion. In the South, things have been much better with the reforestation program began by President Park Chung Hee, but even with the rise and influ-ence of civil society, environmental advocacy groups are still a rela-tively new phenomenon, and they, as well as the concerned ministry, have little power. The environmental dangers even in the South abound, as the environmental organizations here inform us, with in-creases in the population. The past destruction of the environment in South Korea has been legendary, and is lamented by much of the pop-ulation for whom nature has traditionally been important. The Korean government has recently indicated that they are willing to sacrifice part of some green zones for economic opportunities in the light of the financial crisis. This is likely to be a shortsighted policy of no return.

It is true that the peninsula is subject to strong pressures on the environment. South Korea is one of the most densely populated countries in the world, and environmental pressures abound—on water resources, green spaces, air, and urban encroachment. People try to escape from the crowded and aesthetically destroyed urban blight into the scenic hills. Their exodus from the polluted, dismal, and teeming cities has become almost legendary—just try to climb a local mountain on a weekend or drive out of a city on any road leading to the countryside. If the North Koreans had a chance, they might well do the same. An appreciation of nature has been one of the enduring aspects of Korean life and art, and some of the early European travelers to Korea remarked on Korean countryside picnics.

But Chung Ju Yong and Hyundai, together with a North Korean regime more interested in foreign exchange than natural preservation, should be careful. One may not think that a few thousand people for a few days will make a difference, but infrastructure, such as improved roads, will be needed, and after roads could come the detritus of South Korean life—hotels (even "love hotels"?), restaurants, *kalbi* shops, shopping malls, and tourist curio shops; now we see plans for golf courses and ski resorts. We have witnessed the destruction of the quiet of the Buddhist temples of the south by the proliferation of degraded amusements and hostels on their fringes. There is hardly a scenic view on a major road in the South that does not have some commercial establishment. Let us also not forget the cable lifts and their supporting needs. Greed is not environmentally pretty.

The press has previously reported on the environmental safeguards North Korea would like to impose. But more recent press reports indicate that expansion plans are underway. These plans are in conformity with the Korean government's Sunshine Policy, which is an advance over previous policies, but has a danger that the policy may be administratively pushed beyond what is in the longer-range interests of both countries and the environment. It is well to remember what a Thai preservation sign in a cultural or natural park area cautioned: leave nothing behind but your footprints in the sand.

Perhaps, given their limited options and predilections for nationalism, Koreans would go to the Diamond Mountains under almost any environmental circumstances. But let us not forget the parable of the fabled mountain that offered a magnificent view, but was very small at its peak, so only a few people could climb it and stand on the top at one time. The villagers at the bottom thought they could make more money from supporting services if they shaved the top of the mountain so that more people could stand at once. This they did, and then they did it again and again. In the end, no one came because the view was lost, but the villagers did not understand why they lost their incomes. There is a lesson here.

February 1999

On Flags, Hand-Holding, and Sports

Contrary to most of the world, I do not usually believe that international sports competition breeds international understanding. Although it is better than war and is often performed by those physically graceful or beautiful, it stirs up the juices of nationalism that could, and often has, led to much unpleasantness all over the world.

I did not therefore look forward to the Sydney Olympics with the sense of anticipation and international hype that seemed pervasive everywhere. I do like Sydney as a city, and the Australians I know are both charming and interesting. But watching the opening ceremonies produced mixed emotions; I was thrilled by one event, impressed by some, and distressed by the American commentary available to me in Washington, D.C.

To be negative first. The plethora of advertising that we in the United States were subjected to was an affront to the intended spirit of the games and the flow of the events, arousing an instant response—depression of the mute button on the remote or the shift to some other channel. Understanding the economics of television production does not substitute for good taste. The level of commentary by the Americans was often ridiculous, as when the sole "analysis" of the Central African Republic was that it was in central Africa. It also seems that the events on the screen are not sufficient in themselves but we must be subjected to constant talk by someone, and if it is not on the field or in the stadium, the network commentators will gratuitously supply it. Silence, rather than considered golden, is to be avoided at all costs.

The aesthetic, symbolic, and technological lighting of the Olympic flame was most impressive. It was imaginative and beautiful and a dclight to see. The recognition of the aboriginal population (and by indirection the wrongs to which they have been subjected) was both important and moving. The end of the staged initial events were far more impressive than the beginning, some of which bordered on kitsch.

For me, the event to which I looked forward with anticipation, and what prompted me to watch the whole opening ceremony in the first instance, was the procession of the united Korean athletes coming onto the field. Marching under one neutral flag emphasizing the "*uri*-ness" ("we-ness") of the Korean people without regard to political persuasion and propaganda, the athletes created what we hope will be the beginning of a new world—the melting of the ice of the last Cold War confrontation. It brought a lump to my throat and probably to those of many other foreigners as well. All the newscasts that I heard mentioned this as the most important aspect of the opening parade.

I was deeply moved by the scene, the athletes holding hands and walking in what seemed like friendship and unison, while the orchestra played a syncopated version of "Arirang" in the background. Although it only flashed on the American television for a short period, it was symbolism at its best, and could not help but portray to the world the important beginnings that have taken place on the peninsula over the past few months.

Some commentators, prompted by sources unknown to me, credited the outgoing chairman of the International Olympic Commission with this achievement. Whatever may have been his role, if anything more than approval of the event, it really must be ascribed to the changes in the whole peninsular environment that must be attributed to President Kim Dae Jung's Sunshine Policy and the summit meeting, as well as to the perception by the North Korean leadership that it was in their internal interests to reply positively to the overtures from the Republic of Korea. It is not the Olympic Commission that deserves the primary accolades for this important symbolic change, but the Korean leadership prompted by their peoples.

Fifty-five years is a long time for those living today to witness the separation of the peninsula with its mutual vituperation and destruction, although it is a moment in the history of the Korean people. This simple, united march onto the field of play by two previously antithetical elements of the same people solves nothing, as we all know, but it is another important step in the right direction. Symbolism is important. Although the June summit meeting was enthusiastically received on the peninsula and those concerned with Korea, it is the Sydney Olympics with a couple of billion people watching from every country that has television that will make an impression on the world. The simple march onto the field, the evident enthusiasm and camaraderie, however ephemeral, the flag with the emblem of the peninsula itself held high demonstrating a more positive sense of nationalism because it symbolized an ethnic and cultural unity, not one political in character, and holding of hands, the appropriateness of the background music, all conveyed a warmth that we who watched will long remember. To those who set the stage for this to happen, to those who arranged that this take place, we all owe a sense of gratitude and congratulations. To those who wish Korea well, it symbolizes hope.

September 2000

On the Large and the Small of It

We seem to like clear distinctions, so often we divide issues into two and use this bifurcation to discuss them. We often say, "There are two kinds of people, issues, problems," and so on ad infinitum. Perhaps this is inherent in Western dualism, where we like to divide everything into opposing positions: mind and body, good and evil, good guys and bad guys, right and wrong, truth and fiction, etc. This approach profoundly affected Western philosophy for centuries, and still is prevalent, even though we have grown, we think, more sophisticated. This very dualism loses nuances, however; more importantly, it is often evidence of naiveté and a need for reassurance because we then know there is always a good side and a bad side. This is also an element of politics. With all the trauma of the Cold War, it was in a sense comforting to know which countries you could "trust" and which were palpable enemies. Those in the middle, the neutral countries, were treated with suspicion. The end of the Cold War certainly has made life more complicated, if less dangerous.

There is an exception to this general dualistic rule, at least in some of the Western bureaucracies. That is, one never presents policy options to decision-makers in such dichotomous modes. The choice of only two options creates a literal dilemma that presents stark alternatives to policy people, many of whom prefer to hedge their bets or take the well-trodden middle path. Extremism in bureaucratic settings is often the avenue to involuntary exit. So in governments or large bureaucratic organizations, it is always better to invoke the triad—give the decision-maker three options. Those on both ends of the spectrum automatically seem so extreme that they create problems, and the one in the middle is the one that the originator of the paper prefers, and has so set the alternatives that it becomes virtually the only rational choice. This is, of course, bureaucratic politics and reflects politics at a national level, which at least in the United States moves toward the center over time. The Middle Way is a time-honored Confucian principle as well.

But in dealing with some substantive international issues there are often only two choices. The differences between South and North Korea in their negotiating styles comes down to a profound incompatibility of negotiating tactics. It is between two opposing views: either start discussing the fundamental questions facing both states, or begin with the relatively minor irritants or points of disagreement. North Korea says, in effect: let us deal with the major issues of governance (that is, accept our plan for a 'confederal' state) and then the smaller issues of reunification of families, investment, trade, and other elements will automatically fall into place. South Korea, on the other hand, essentially says: let us start to deal with the smaller issues, such as exchange of mail, reunification of families, and the like, and we can gradually build to the broad and fundamental issues of governance and political systems. The South wants what in the military are called "confidence-building measures," while the North wants the major issues resolved first.

Although I personally subscribe to the confidence-building approach, because trust between the two states is lacking, I recognize that for many this is quite disconcerting. If one goes for the "big-bang" theory of taking the hardest and most complex issues first, at least one knows where one stands. But the danger of failure is greater. Many years ago the Ford Foundation decided that it would support an attempted solution to urban problems by beginning in the most difficult of cities—Calcutta. It did not work. But the piecemeal approach of addressing smaller issues creates enduring questions rather than quick answers. In a negative sense, it is like the death of a thousand slices rather than quick and clean decapitation.

But if the search for the certainties that dealing first with the fundamentals resolves, it creates other problems. Incrementalism is not necessarily a bad thing, but it does require the stamina of continued, often tedious, negotiations and partial resolution of problems that might be avoided if only we could all agree on the large issues. It requires a kind of self-confidence often absent in politicians, and is subject to political complaints because it abdicates the high moral ground for modest gains. It implies statesmanship and imposes discipline, not simple jingoism or doctrinaire and pat, and often erroneous, "solutions" to much more complex issues.

In American slang there is an expression used to encourage dealing with broad issues or problems. We say, "Don't sweat [over] the small stuff," implying they will work out in the end if we cope with major questions. But this is one of those bits of local folklore that is misleading. We need to perspire over details. There is another expression: "The devil is in the details." Perhaps this is more to the point.

September 1999

9

International Relations

On Memorializing, If Not Righting, Wrongs

A few days ago the American press reported an event that is a heartening response to a sorry and inexcusable chapter in relatively recent American history. At the beginning of World War II, some 120,000 American citizens of Japanese descent were forcibly relocated from their homes on the West Coast to what can only be called concentration camps in remote areas of the western United States because some in authority believed they could be spies for the Japanese. Their homes and belongings were left behind until after the war ended, often to have been appropriated illegally by others while they were away. This was a case of blatant ethnic and racial discrimination. Although it is only one of many sad events in American history going back hundreds of years, especially the treatment of the American Indians and Afro-Americans, this one occurred in living memory, on a massive scale, and was the result of a single edict.

Even at the time many Americans realized this injustice. Eleanor Roosevelt, the first lady, visited one of the camps during the war. Belatedly, much too late, the Congress appropriated some monies as compensation for those who are still alive and their descendants. What was recent news was the dedication of the construction of a small memorial park close to the U.S. Capitol building that will serve as a living reminder of the event and reconciliation. The U.S. federal government contributed half of the funds required for the park, consisting mainly of the public land, while private donations raised the remainder of the funds needed to bring the park to fruition.

Museum-type memorials are a good thing, for they educate and can be a focus of learning and memory. But a living memorial, one that can be used every day as a part of a normal routine not requiring a special trip or adherence to visiting hours is of equal importance. No doubt, after it has been in operation for some time, many people will not remember that this park was designed as a token of reconciliation and for and by whom it was done, but some will, and no doubt there will be some plaque or memorial to remind us of the disgrace to American ideals and the effort of redemption.

Korean-Japanese relations during the Kim Dae Jung presidency have improved immeasurably. Up to this time, aside from the very fact of his election and its implication for the future of Korean politics, his efforts to reestablish cordial relations and the introduction of various confidence-building measures with the Japanese may be the single most important achievement of his administration.* Certainly, the thaw with Japan has been greeted in Tokyo and elsewhere with quiet and sincere enthusiasm.

Of course, dangers in the relationship abound. It is predictable that someone in Japan will no doubt say something inappropriate that will excite Korean nationalism, and some in the Korean government will have to respond in equally vigorous language. There is also the possibility that the opening of the Korean market to Japanese popular culture and automobiles may be seen by the Koreans as inundating them. But at least at the moment the relationship is historically the best it has ever been.**

Perhaps now is the time to try to convince both the Japanese and Korean governments, and equally important their peoples, that perhaps the model of a reconciliation park might be a good thing for Korean-Japanese relations. Suppose that the Japanese were to donate land in a major Japanese city for a park to commemorate the injustices that Japan committed on the Koreans during the colonial period, and further suppose that the Korean and Japanese publics were to provide the funding for a park that would be a small haven of rest, quiet, and contemplation for all who are in that part of the city. This could be a living memorial to the problems, but also to reconciliation, and it could be a reminder that never in the future should such events occur again.

Small gestures sometimes require big hearts. They also may require big initiatives and even risks to overcome bureaucratic inertia. But the concept of doing something that would remain as a testament to the problems of the past and the efforts to overcome their sorry results would be welcome. Perhaps some nongovernmental organization in Korea or Japan might bring this to the attention of authorities in both

* This has since been overshadowed by the South-North summit in Pyongyang in June 2000, and the Nobel Peace Prize.

** The textbook controversy over the portrayal of Japanese aggression in the Korean colonial period and World War II excited much nationalistic reaction in Korea. In the spring of 2002, the Japanese emperor, however, indicated his sympathy for Korea because of the origin of one of his Korean ancestors, a remark unprecedented in Japan and of great importance in Korea. The joint sponsorship of the 2002 World Cup by Japan and Korea may have played a role in the timing of this announcement.

countries, or perhaps some Diet member or National Assembly member could take an initiative. The fact that land is so scarce in Japan makes the task more difficult, but this would make the success even more meaningful.

We live by symbols and we create symbols to satisfy our deeper needs. Perhaps one definition of man might be that he/she is a producer of symbols. Here is a symbol that we all could help create. It could be an important reminder and lesson for those in the future.

October 1999

On International Conferences

There is no country I know more prone to international conferences than Korea. No country seems to top Korea in making such elaborate and careful arrangements for holding such international conferences. It matters not whether these are official, governmental meetings designed to deal with high-level international policy issues, or whether they are privately sponsored by universities, academic organizations, or nongovernmental groups. They all are done well, and in many cases the arrangements are meticulously planned and the entertainment is lavish. I know of no other country that treats its international visitors so generously at such gatherings.

There is a nexus between research and such meetings, and although one cannot prove, as some have written, that Seoul has more Ph.D.s than any other city in the world, it certainly has a plethora. There are so many that for some of the younger individuals, appropriate positions in terms of prestige and remuneration are becoming increasingly scarce. But these are the people who go to and present papers at such meetings, so there is naturally a vast store of talent on which to draw.

There was a time, however, when even the idea of holding any international meeting in Korea was considered preposterous. Hotels were limited, travel difficult, and the state was not yet receptive to such events. Korea was off the international academic map, and there were as well few Korean scholars who gave papers at international and professional meetings in other countries. It was true, as Cornelius Osgood wrote in the first English-language village study of Korea in the early 1950s, that there was no other country in the world so important about which so little was internationally known.

This has all changed, and sponsoring and attending international conferences has become a growth industry—even perhaps a profession. One might argue that attending such conferences has become a kind of subculture, where most of the participants are known to each other in advance, and see each other on the circuit of professional events in their field. When that field is directly related to Korea internally or internationally, or on Korean studies, we all know that we will see at these meetings most of the "usual suspects."

Probably no one knows how many such conferences are held in Korea in any one year. They may range from the huge, such as the international conference of dentists where some thousands are expected to attend, the Interparliamentary Union, or the International Political Science meeting in August; the prestigious, such as the World Bank and International Monetary Fund meeting some dozen years ago; to a small, specialized gathering of those concerned, say, with Korean linguistics. In each case, one may be sure that these conferences are conceived with two ends in mind: the professional content of the meetings should be appropriate, and the arrangements should be prestigious. So major Korean public figures will often agree to give a keynote address, and some large business concern will sponsor a luncheon or dinner at one of the best hotels. If the conference lasts a few days, the most difficult of one's problems is keeping one's weight down because one is so well fed.

These conferences never capture the international limelight, which is reserved for Korean-hosted sporting events such as the Olympics, the Asian Games, and the World Cup, but in fact far more people attend these relatively obscure meetings than the widely publicized sports ones. They also play a role in encouraging the tourism industry in Korea.

The funding for such conferences is extensive. Although it used to be a product of foreign support, now the great percentage of funds come from internal Korean sources. These may be from the Korean government through a ministry that has a certain interest in that subject, to the general foundations attached to many *chaebol*, to more specialized Korean foundations devoted in some manner to increasing international understanding. These groups also fund similar conferences outside of Korea, but in some manner concerned with the Korean scene.

These conferences are so well endowed because Korean international prestige is still considered to be at stake. So everyone wants the

arrangements to be perfect, if it is a general conference then the entertainment must be good, and at the close of the conference, the papers
presented are gathered together and published. These are distributed
to those who attended and sometimes to audiences beyond.

These international conferences in a sense are limiting, because
unless arrangements are made for simultaneous translation, which in
itself is very expensive in Seoul, then the conference is effectively restricted to those who can read a paper and become involved in the discussions in English. This is unfortunate, since there is a great deal of
important scholarship and critical views among those who, although
they have been taught to read English in the school system, do not feel
comfortable in writing or speaking it.

I am an unindicted co-conspirator in this process. If one believes in
dialogue on all types of issues concerned with Korea, then one wants
to foster the venues for such discussions, hoping that better understanding of the issues will occur, whether these may involve public
policy or arcane academic issues.

We should be attempting to identify those younger scholars and mid-
dle-range officials who cannot be included in the usual-suspects category. We need to ensure that new blood is introduced into the system.

When one considers how much is spent on these conferences, both
internal and external, how many jobs are dependent on support to
such meetings, and the funds infused into the economy, these efforts
become highly significant. I propose that economists should get together to have an international conference on the effects of international conferences on national economics. Such a conference clearly
should be held in Korea. If there were a company specializing in producing such meetings, then it would very likely be a growth industry
in which one might well invest.

April 1997

On Cassandra and Pollyanna

In a speech at my fiftieth college reunion, the former president of my
college was quoted as saying years ago that 'Cassandra sits in high
places today.' This was accurate because when he made that remark
the Cold War was in full flower, and fears of an atomic outrage were
rampant. The *Bulletin of the Atomic Scientists* listed the potential for
nuclear war as a hairsbreadth away. Europe was weakened by World

War II, and communism was on the move. It was a period in which many Americans were building private bomb shelters in their homes.

Cassandra was an apt analogy for that time. In Greek mythology, she was Priam's daughter and later killed by Clytemnestra, and when Apollo wanted to make love to her in return for giving her the ability to foretell the future, she became a prophetess but refused his favors. Asking for one kiss in exchange, she granted that and he spat in her mouth and told her that none would believe her prophecies. She then predicted the fall of Troy, which went unheeded, and became a synonym for predicting bad news and dire events.

Today, the problem is not Cassandra, but Pollyanna. Pollyanna is the eternal optimist, who views the world through, as we say, "rose-colored glasses." The name comes from a heroine of stories around the turn of the twentieth century who was unduly optimistic to the point of self-delusion. The U.S. economy is strong, the stock market continues to expand, and the popular belief is that this will continue. This is what politicians tell their constituents. Communism has collapsed and "democracy" seems on an international roll. The Asian economies (except for Indonesia) have basically recovered from their 1997 trials. Spending is up in Korea and consumerism has returned to Korean society. The Korean summit offers prospects if not for tangible returns in the immediate future, at least for reduced tensions and for the hope for better prospects. So if we have not yet seen Fukuyama's "end of history," all prospects please, as the saying goes, on the Korean peninsula and indeed overall in the world.[*]

But Pollyanna may be more dangerous than Cassandra. Dire predictions can cause dangerous misperceptions that can lead to policy mistakes, but at least one girds onself for the bad, if not the worst, and takes precautions. But a Pollyanna approach exposes one to the vagaries of the future with no built-up immune system to ward off the social, political, or economic diseases that may return to reassert themselves in some form.

With Pollyanna goes arrogance, which is a great danger for any society, but for no one more than the United States. As the only superpower, there may be a tendency to be so optimistic about the future role of that society that its leaders and their people may well ignore the dangers that are inherent in a multipolar world where technology

---

[*]   Until the tragic events of September 11, 2001.

outgrows restraint, and when the Cold War at least reined in local passions of ethnicity, race, and religion.

Globalization, we are told, will bring benefits, and so it will. But it also brings growing disparities of income internally in the societies and among countries and groups as a whole. The closer we become internationally, the more there may be envy among states and peoples. It may well induce more nationalism and xenophobia. Globalization may not breed disease, but it certainly spreads it. It brings shifts in labor requirements that throw the most vulnerable out of work in industrialized societies, and provides what may be only temporary relief for some who find employment in poorer countries. This may be ephemeral, for as we have learned only too well during the financial crisis of 1997, capital is peripatetic and moves with ease and rapidity that is sometimes frightening.

And market economies are accepted with alacrity because of the general failure of strict socialism even in countries that were not communist. But the unbridled optimism of market economies as solutions to humanity's economic ills is unfounded; it has not worked in many countries, most notably in Russia. Greed is not a social good. It seems evident that it is not helpful, especially when it comes to economics.

The obvious conclusion is that we need balance and nuance; the positive thinking associated with a Pollyanna together with the gloom of a Cassandra. With the latter we have intellectual armor with which to defend ourselves, and with the former the belief that events can be managed and that life will be better.

July 2000

On Korea and Japanese Influence

If there is one subject in the Republic of Korea on which it is even more difficult to do research on than North Korea, it is Japan, and especially the colonial period. With official approval, one can do research on the North; although Japanese subjects require no such concurrence, one may be subject to social ostracism if one's findings are positive for any aspect of that unfortunate era.

Japan is a sensitive topic even in contemporary relations, and even avoiding the issues of Tokdo Island[*] and others. For a foreign busi-

* Disputed by Korea and Japan.

nessman who has worked in Japan but just arrived in Korea to say to his new Korean colleagues, "Well, that is not the way we do things in Japan," it is not only the beginning but the end of the relationship. For a Korean specifically to call on the Japanese model in public is normally to be in trouble.

Yet there have been a few cases where state policies were in fact publicly expressed on this model. During the Vietnam War, Koreans said that as Japan had seen its economic rebirth as a result of the Korean War, so we Koreans would see our economic growth as a result of Vietnam. This was only partly accurate, but the sentiment was apparent. It was more to the point when the Koreans said that as Japan had gained international recognition as a result of the Tokyo Olympics of 1964, so Korea would do the same as a result of the Seoul Olympics of 1988. This turned out to be quite true. This was not a case of copying Japan, but using the Japanese analogy but based on Koreans' own capabilities.

The other public case in memory was the merger of the Democratic Republican Party and opposition political parties in January 1990 on the model of the Japanese Liberal Democratic Party, which changed leadership among its various factions but that time seemed destined to hold power forever. At least the Japanese case was quoted in the press as the model for the Korean merger.

Now, there is much to be copied, adopted, or adapted from Japan that would be useful to many societies, including the United States. In the United States, it seems that examples from Japanese management techniques, quality control, on-time procurement, or aesthetics are taken with due citation of the sources. In Korea, the model is sometimes surreptitious, and one is not supposed to know where the material originated.

Certain Korean popular music and television programs seem to have been created whole cloth from Japanese models, sometimes of a generation earlier, even if the originals are banned from local distribution because of a fear of being inundated by Japanese popular culture. One wonders how much the public is aware of this tendency. Of greater consequence is the annual cry for the Koreans to win the Nobel Prize for Literature because the Japanese have done so. It is only natural that competition with the Japanese is an important element of Korean life, given the past. One might argue that part of the spur to Korean economic success has been to outdo the Japanese and reestablish the pride that had suffered because of the colonial period.

Using the Japanese experience takes on various forms. A real shock to me came from a Korean friend who was formerly a minister in the government. He had to make some decisions on policy, and asked his staff to do a series of studies and options that he could use as background before he made his recommendations. In due course he received these studies and made his decisions. Only later did he find that his staff had not done the original research required, but simply had taken Japanese studies of similar problems in their bureaucracy and translated them into Korean as if it were their own work. He felt that he had been badly mislead because the requirements for each decision may have been quite different. He worried later whether he had done the right thing.

Because of the colonial period and the introduction of a modern bureaucracy in Korea and its dictatorial control, it is not surprising that Korean legal systems and administrative codes and regulations were simply translated from Japanese. Much of that corpus of material has continued in use. Although some may not be suited to modern, democratic needs, the situation here is significantly better than the case in Indonesia, where aspects of the contemporary legal code still are products of mid-nineteenth-century Dutch regulations that had never even been translated into Indonesian, and which most Indonesians could not now read. Some have written that the strength of the centralized Korean government was not only, and perhaps not essentially, a product of Korean history or the Korean military after 1961, but was in fact the heritage of the colonial era.

Another example is the organizational structure of the loan and grant aspects of the Korean foreign aid program, which directly has adopted the Japanese model. In Japan, the program has severe problems (the American problems with foreign aid are of a different nature).

There is much to respect in Japan. And those who know Korea know of Japan's historical debt to Korea, which is both deep and extensive and which many Japanese prefer to ignore or deny. Koreans seem to be able to absorb Japanese food with great pleasure and without guilt, given the number of Japanese-style restaurants and the Koreans frequenting them, although we know that Japanese cuisine will never replace Korean dietary patterns and it is regarded as an occasional, pleasant change.

Some Japanese bureaucrats or public figures have a propensity for making silly and insensitive statements about Korea or the colonial past, which exacerbates problems. But one hopes that Koreans can enjoy a good Japanese meal while not ingesting Japanese pop culture. Korean culture and society seem strong enough to withstand foreign influences. There is a vibrancy and vitality of the culture within the society. One should be able to discuss Japan and the past without fear of social retribution. By writing this, am I placing myself beyond the Korean pale?

April 1997

On Nationalism and the IMF

That nationalism has been growing in Korea is apparent to any observer of the Korean scene. We know that, as in any country, it has both positive and negative aspects. It has, for example, encouraged a greater sense of the importance and vitality of Korea's past, even though that appreciation may have produced some exaggerated results in which the excesses of enthusiasm transcended reality. Nationalism has quite obviously encouraged the revitalization of many aspects of Korean culture, and this has been positive overall. Yet nationalism has also been in tension with the stated government policy of globalization, so globalization in the eyes of some became more a movement to increase exports than to meld into an international community. Yet there is little question that the administration has moved to support the development of enhanced knowledge and understanding of international affairs and cultures, and not simply world markets.

The popular reaction to the financial crisis facing Korea has illustrated this nationalism. The revelations of the crisis—bad enough without the government's ham-handed attempts, first, to deny and then, to diminish its importance—and then the stringent conditions of the bailout by the International Monetary Fund, has produced not only the expected and immediate reactions of shock, anger, frustration, embarrassment, and shame, but also an intense antiforeign feeling. This strong emotion, always latent and sometimes overt, among a number of Koreans at all levels of society and incomes, is first directed at the IMF, and then at the United States as the principal force behind the IMF actions and financial contributor to that group. The group that will initially benefit from the bailout will be the foreign banks, including those in the United States, whose unwise lending has quietly contributed to the crisis and which will be materially assisted in this process. That Korea will benefit in the longer term does not assuage the immediate financial pain.

These nationalistic reactions have been extensively reported in the international press, especially in the United States. They have been portrayed more as a singular event, but they rather may be viewed in Korea as the culmination of a long history of latent frustration over foreign domination of Korea. Now, as the Korean press has sometimes reported, many feel that Korea is entering a period of IMF "trusteeship," much like the hated period following World War II when the great powers decided, without consulting the Koreans, that Korea would have to enter a long period of trusteeship under the United Nations before it could be independent.

The year 1998 is likely to be a most difficult year as these frustrations continue and grow. What has not been reported in the Korean press are the results of a national survey conducted in the early summer of 1997 and published by Strathclyde University in Glasgow, Scotland that shed light on the underlying attitudes toward the roles of foreigners in the economy.

In that survey before the crisis, 97 percent of the people rated the economy poor to some degree—as bad (57 percent) and not very good (40 percent), while 50 percent thought that present conditions were worse than those ten years previous. Seventy-five percent of the respondents thought the economic conditions of their own families were not very good—very unsatisfactory (12 percent) and not very satisfactory (63 percent). Forty-five percent thought that their family's economic standards were falling, compared to 14 percent who thought they were rising.

It seems evident, if the results of this survey are accurate, and they seem to be from other surveys dealing with similar subjects, that the burdens that the Korean people will have to undergo will further deepen the economic frustration that was already evident before the crisis began.

Equally important are the implications on public opinion of some of the terms of the conditionality that the IMF is imposing on Korea to open the Korean economy. These conditions allow potential foreign ownership of various aspects of the economy that to date have virtually been forbidden by Korean regulations. Korea was already under pressure from the OECD and the World Trade Organization, let alone from the United States and European countries, to open their service markets and allow a greater share in investment in Korean enterprises.

This survey asked a number of questions about foreigners' roles in the Korean economy. In response to the question of whether foreigners should own small enterprises, shops, or cafes, 58 percent felt that it was definitely not all right for them to do so, while only 4 percent felt it was definitely all right (a further 22 percent thought it was probably all right and 16 percent were not so sure it was right). An even greater number (65 percent), thought foreigners should not own big factories, 73 percent thought that they should not own small land plots, and 83 percent said that they definitely should not own large land plots. In each case, the number who thought that foreigners definitely should be allowed to own such properties varied between 1 and 4 percent. Although we do not have correlations of these attitudes by education or income, we do have them by age, and it is evident that, contrary to what might be expected, youth are somewhat less concerned with the role of foreigners than are those over sixty years.

We have, then, a public policy, no matter how needed, that evidently is at odds with popular opinion. As the IMF conditionality begins to take hold, we may then expect that the intensity of these attitudes will increase, and that there well may be major problems. As one influential Korean was quoted in the international press, there is likely to be a rise in anti-Americanism because of these events. After the bailout, Korean-American relations may need extensive reevaluation as the impact from economics may affect other aspects of the relationship. It is thus important for the United States to be especially deft in its public and private statements with the Republic at this time. It will require not only wisdom but, more practically, coordination among the various elements of the U.S. government and the Congress if this delicate situation is not to be made worse.

October 1998

Source: Doh C. Shin and Richard Rose, "Koreans Evaluate Democracy: A New Korea Barometer Survey." Glasgow: Center for the Study of Public Policy, Studies in Public Policy, no. 292. 1997.

10

Epilogue

On the Usefulness of Foreigners

A few weeks ago, *The Korea Times* asked me to write an article on recommendations on how Korea could survive in the new century. I have complied with that request with some trepidation, but that inquiry together with other writings in which I have been engaged on Burma (Myanmar) have prompted me to consider what role foreigners might have in commenting on events in another country—events that, even if the observers are fluent in the language, they may not fully appreciate because they remain outsiders. What, then, is the role of foreigner media writers on Korea?

The roles of foreigners will vary with the observer, but they also differ with time and topic and the society observed. Tocqueville writing during the early days of the American republic could record observations and analyses that Americans at that time did not recognize, as few had comparative perspectives and the country was in a state of formation. In mature but autocratic states, the role of foreigners, however unpleasant their observations may be to the ruling elite, are important for a number of reasons. In Burma, where an atmosphere of fear pervades and information is limited, even the high elite are often not informed of actual conditions in the country. So here one of the roles of the foreigner is, as the Americans ungrammatically say, "to tell it like it is"—that is, to provide the test of reality. The former head of that country once observed (in 1987) that they had been victims of their own propaganda for so long they could not plan, for none of the data could be relied upon because they were so inflated. Bureaucrats told the elite what they thought the elite wanted to hear, and as the press was muzzled, there were no voices for pluralistic interpretations of events. There are also other roles for foreigners—to analyze, suggest, cajole, assist when asked, and to be generally the sympathetic observer—but not sympathetic toward any particular regime or government, but toward the welfare of the people as a whole.

Even in the most stringent periods of autocratic rule, under the Yushin constitution, things were never like that in Korea. It was true that the press was severely controlled, and that certain types of news unpleasant and considered potentially dangerous to the leadership (such as reports of student demonstrations or revolutions in other countries) were downplayed or eliminated, but the elite and much of the general population did have international access to information, and although the government did try to manipulate statistics to support their case, those efforts were never as complete, even though control and surveillance were far more efficient than Burma. Even under the most stringent conditions, South Korea could never compare with North Korea.

Perhaps because of self-doubt and concern brought on by the Korean War and the constant state of tension (sometimes played upon by various administrations to suit their own political ends), the need for international support in its security relationships, as well as other social factors that indicate a sense of insecurity often compensated by strong feelings of nationalism, Korean institutions often ask foreigners for their views and give foreigners far more media attention than perhaps they deserve. After all, foreigners have often been wrong about Korea, and on critical occasions. Asking is quite different from paying attention to what foreigners think or suggest. Sometimes asking is only a ritual. An article by a foreigner in Korea will have far less influence than, for example, an article on Korea in an eminent international newspaper. The act of asking seems far more important than taking such advice, although the script will vary by subject, time, and individual. The role of foreigners, and of the English-language press more broadly, will only become vital to Koreans (as distinct from foreigners who happen to live in Korea) when that press says something new and important and does not mimic the Korean language papers. It will occur when the Minister of X in Seoul wakes up in the morning and asks him or herself, "I need to know what the English-language newspaper says about this important issue." To date this has not happened, alas.

But there is a usefulness in foreign observations and analyses that can be helpful and to which careful attention should be given. The foreign perspective is often important to achieve the ends sought by Korea or other states. I once told a minister in a foreign government that, while I would like to tell him how to run his country, to do so would be quite inappropriate and offensive, but to tell him how foreigners view his country and its policies, and their implications for the attainment of the state's own national goals, this was something on which one could comment and might be both appropriate and useful to those in authority.

So in Korea it is useful for foreigners to be able to discuss how foreign investors view the Korean political and economic scene, and what that means for Korean capacity to achieve its goal of encouraging foreign investment. So too when foreigners comment on the romanization system for *hangul,* it is worth listening to them, for romanization is not something Koreans need internally, but is important to foreigners and their reaction to Korea.

So, at the start of a new year and a new century (we will await one more year before we talk about a new millennium), one hopes one may be forgiven for commenting on things Korean, for such comments are designed to be constructive, and are devoted to the betterment of the lives of Koreans however much they may raise questions about events. As one ages, one tends to assume this avuncular role of offering comments and advice, but as with uncles, it is a role in which one attempts to be positive over the longer term.

April 2000

On Korea in the Twenty-first Century: Recommendations for the Future

Predictions are risky on more ways than one. In addition to being wrong on the record, one has other worries. Dante Alighieri in *The Divine Comedy* assigns soothsayers to one of the lower circles of hell. Many Koreans at the beginning of the new year consult the *T'ojong Pi-kyol* (The Secret Arts of T'ojong—a sixteenth-century manual of predictions) to find out their fate for the coming year. My assigned task, however, is to predict the future for a century and make recommendations. This is for a country, not an individual, and is one hundred times more risky, and so one must assume an even lower circle of torment awaits me. Even the new dragon year cannot assuage the dangers.

Yet there are things that ought to be said and condemnation risked. Recommendations are a sub-group of predictions, for they are based on an estimate of what is likely to happen and how to make the best of the situation. Koreans are not the only ones who seek comments on the new year, and from foreigners at that. A couple of weeks ago a Japanese newspaper interviewed me to ask my recommendations not on Japan, but my advice to the United States on how to enable it to maintain its preeminent position in the next century. I replied that the United States should avoid arrogance, which was its greatest danger as the world's preeminent power. I do not think that was well received. But the advice is, I think, sound when applied to relations in East Asia and specifically to Korea.

For Koreans (at least from this foreigner's perspective), the twentieth century was one of suffering. Colonized, divided, ravaged by war, pauperized, politically exploited by authoritarian leaders, economically uplifted but then struck part way down, it has been a period of trauma—of the development of a collective *han* (accumulated resentment and grief), and difficult to erase. The next century will be better.

So the search for reassurance in predictions and recommendations for success is understandable. That foreigners should be asked to do this is perhaps a sign of Korean insecurity—the assumption that foreigners somehow better understand Korea and the forces, internal and external, that impinge on its future.

This is a dubious assumption, for history reveals how wrong most foreigners have been about the developments in Korea when they were paying attention, which was not true most of the time. We were wrong about much in the military occupation of 1945-48 and were ill equipped to deal with it. We were also wrong about the Korean War, and then when Korea began its export drive, few foreigners thought it would succeed. Foreigners were wrong about more recent events in Korea as well—how else would supposedly astute international bankers lend so much money to Korea? And most recently, although all results are not yet in, we may have miscalculated the rapidity of the Korean economic recovery.

So our record should not allow us the luxury of hubris, and Koreans would be wise to examine carefully the *ex cathedra* statements of foreigners, and treat them with the caution they deserve. The only consolation is that many Koreans were equally wrong, and thus we have been in good company. But, as the Koreans say, "Under the lamp is dark," meaning that one can be too close to events to understand them.

But foreigners do have roles in providing different perspectives on societies, because they have distance and are often concerned about aspects of cultures that indigenous peoples take for granted. So the best book on the United States was written by a Frenchman, and the early western travelers to Asia provided glimpses of those societies on issues on which local writers and historians seemed uninterested or were beyond their ken.

So in the spirit of friendship one is prompted to offer certain observations on the Korean scene in the world context. The most fundamental element is that Korea is inextricably caught in a worldwide web, not only of cyber space, but of trade and relations. Globalization has brought interdependency, political as well as economic, and this is disquieting to many, as we have seen in the recent Seattle World Trade Organization conference demonstrations. This trade is not only in international commodities such as consumer products or primary materials, but of ideas, values, and culture. This will increase, rather than decrease, over the next decades. But as it does, it will produce an inevitable backlash from Korean nationalism, which itself has grown exponentially over the past couple of decades.

Nationalism is not necessarily a bad thing, for it helps forge identity and creates a greater appreciation of one's own heritage and deeper respect for the strengths of one's society. Yet clash it will with globalization, and it is likely to be a complex clash that is not easily characterized. It is probably simplistic to state that an older generation will attempt to keep traditional values while a younger one will opt for more international and popular culture. It is also likely that many youth will seek the preservation or reinterpretation of their own society as a positive element. The unscrupulous politicians of the twenty-first century may try to appeal to this nationalism for political gain, as many have done around the world. Here is a real danger that Korea (or any other society) would consciously do well to avoid.

In thinking of the future, it might be helpful to borrow from the lexicon of the economists and muse on what Korea's "comparative advantage" has been and is likely to be in the next century among the economic troika: land, labor, and capital. Certainly Korea's advantage lies not in natural resources, which are limited and are even less of an asset because of the intense pressures of population on both land and resources. This has been true since independence. Although Korea had an early advantage internationally in a skilled but underpaid labor force, kept in check by governments that sought this early form of comparative advantage, this disappeared over a decade ago. The third element in the economic troika—capital—is not that plentiful in Korea, and Korean industry and business have, as we all have painfully experienced, expanded through international borrowing and real estate speculation that finally resulted in the burst bubble of 1997.

So, then, where is Korea's strength? It lies in its people, or more accurately, in its educated people and its passion for education. Korea is known for this, and even the World Bank in earlier reports recommended that other states look to the Korean model of investment in education that would lead to the betterment of economic and social conditions in a society. This resonates well with the new world order, which is based on knowledge and information and its processing and manipulation. So the Korean stress on education and the world's emphasis on new technology and information management seem a nice fit for the future.

But is it really? A popular murder mystery of some years ago said that Seoul may have more Ph.D.s than any other city in the world. This may be hyperbole, but sometimes it really feels that way. Whatever the accuracy of the statement, we all know that in terms of formal education, Korea is far ahead of many developed countries. Korea has the highest percentage of its age cohort in tertiary education of any country in the world after the United States. Yet there is a mismatch between the extent of, and interest in, higher education and the type and quality of education received. There is still too much emphasis on rote memorization, and the role of the teacher or professor is too elevated, so that questioning such authorities stifles intellectual query, and innovation is insufficiently stressed. The social hierarchy of society as a whole is reflected in a type of intellectual hierarchy that in the pre-colonial past has been manifest in a tendency for intellectual orthodoxy. There has been a pattern of political orthodoxy since the division of Korea that has, one could argue, even stifled free inquiry and innovation in other, apolitical, fields. Koreans have complained that they have never won the Nobel Prize for Literature. Yet it has only been comparatively recently that Koreans were free to write about the universal themes and traumas on which such prizes are usually considered.

Whatever the causes, Korea has not been in the forefront of technological innovation in spite of its vast educated reserves that would be the envy of many countries. The number of patents received, the contribution of research and development to new products or systems or ideas, is far less in proportion than one might have expected. So if the 21st century is to be the information age, Korea needs to be a part of it through the encouragement of its widespread talent through basic reform of the educational system, which is still too rigidly controlled by a Ministry of Education that issues pronouncements and regulations designed more to encourage conformity than innovation.

If education is like a well-endowed house that needs renovation, politics needs rebuilding from its foundations. The politics of the start of the new millennium are travesties of the growth of other democratic institutions in the society. They are personalized and faction-ridden and archaic. We are now witnessing a restructuring of political parties before the spring 2000 elections; although the names may change, party politics are unlikely to do so. They are archaic. There needs to be a new spirit, and it will not come automatically with new and younger leadership, which obviously will soon occur given the ages of those at the acme of the political process today. But age is not the factor. The people must demand of politicians a new breed, willing to consult with people, consider national goals and interests beyond personal and party gain, and have a set of programs and ideals around which the like-minded will rally, not those solely interested in personal power. If reform of education and politics for the new age are internal requirements, the external environment is likely to remain highly complex and frustrating. Korea must also be prepared to deal with this effectively by preparing its people for the options it will have to face. In all probability, the historical necessity of reunification will occur in the twenty-first century, and probably closer to its beginning than at its end. But it is likely to be a slow, gradual process that in all probability will be better for all involved than some sudden trauma caused by regime collapse in the north. But even the change of regime, or of economic or social systems, does not necessarily mean the collapse of a separate state. Yet over time, with leadership changes and the eventual exposure of the North to the outside world, old antipathies can be eroded and eventually peacefully overcome.

Even should this happen, Korea still lives in a dangerous neighborhood. This has been true for the past 2200 years, and the next century is unlikely to see much change in the fundamental vulnerability of Korea, in spite of the development of new weaponry that theoretically should make old geo-political considerations obsolete. It is true that today, and into the future, the old patterns of physical aggrandizement are usually no longer relevant. But other, equally insidious, means of control and influence are available and about which Korea must remain intellectually vigilant.

The powerful roles of China and Japan, and perhaps after a decade or two, Russia as well, cannot be ignored. The rivalries between China and Japan are likely to grow more intense over the next generation, and Korea, caught in the middle, must play its role very carefully. An alliance with either party prematurely could be disastrous for Korea, either as a divided or united state. Three other options seem open and preferable. One is the development of a neutral position under such circumstances. This has many advantages if it could be maintained. A second position is seeking reassurance in multilateral security relationships, but in Northeast Asia at the present there are none. A third is reliance on a distant friend. This was the rationale for Korea's first foreign treaty with the United States in 1882. In the shorter term this seems still a desirable option if, as indicated above, the United States acts with discretion and collegiality with its Korean friends.

But national commitments are not forever, as the advertisements claim diamonds are. And any state that makes perpetual promises is not to be trusted. The United States let Korea down once in the past—the Taft-Katsura Treaty of 1905. Can the United States be relied upon during the next century? Although there is every intention to remain committed to Korea in the present U.S. administration, as well as the ones that can be predicted over the next decade, after that the crystal ball becomes more murky. Although the United States had reaffirmed it commitment to the Republic, and does so with what I regard as sincerity, no present administration in any country can offer commitments into the indefinite future. So it behooves Korea to do contingency planning, recognizing that such planning is not a substitute for active searching for relationships within the region, both bilaterally and multilaterally, for multiple and reinforcing reassurances.

The twenty-first century will likely be better than the last one, which in itself is not saying very much. Korea needs to face it realistically, eschewing both the arrogance that can accompany excessive nationalism, and the despair of interdependence and mutual reliance. Korea has the human resources to influence its future. We need not be fatalistic and let the accumulation of a century of *han* cloud an objective assessment of Korea's importance and confidence. After all, the century, nay the millennium, starts with a dragon year. And that is a soaring and hopeful sign.

January 2000

On Dynamos Driving Korea

No country in the contemporary world has a more remarkable record of dynamic growth than the Republic of Korea. Its vault in a generation from poverty to become in December 1996 a member of the OECD, the restricted club of industrialized nations of the world, is virtually legendary. Whether one measures this change in quantitative terms, such as the growth of annual exports—those in 1961 that equal those of about four hours today—or by the increasing recognition and prestige of Korean people and products throughout the world, the change has been phenomenal. Even its recovery from the financial crisis of 1997 has been swift and remarkable as well.

But Korea was not born anew, even though the analogy of the phoenix rising from the ashes has often been used to describe these changes. Miracles, on the Han River or otherwise, are symbolic, not real. Miracles of modernity are man-made, not materializing out of the ether. Modernity is still only one strand in a complex social web. Rather, there are important traditional elements of Korean society and culture that transcend the modern, that root the present in the past. Somehow, perhaps inadvertently, Korea has melded the requirements of globalization with respect for traditions that have given it depth and breadth.

Many will take credit for these remarkable changes. The Japanese could and sometimes do point to the colonial period that began some modernization, the Americans could call up their economic assistance under their security umbrella, and the multilateral banks and financial institutions might discuss the efficacy of their support. Each, of course, had multiple objectives that may not have been centered on Korean well-being. As foreigners tout their purported roles, Koreans will hearken back to their proposed changes in the late nineteenth century unfortunately cut off by colonization, and others will claim more recent strong authoritarian governments or democracy, or the ideology of capitalism or that of the "East Asia economic model," or Korean culture, or that all or some of the above have been responsible in some abstruse, unquantifiable formula. But each, whatever its accuracy, would simply be an element of disputed magnitude—only a piece, and one of unclear size, out of a complex jigsaw puzzle.

The rooting of this past melded with the inexorable demands of globalization and the ability of the society to manage economic, social, political, and even psychological change is remarkable. Korea may not be unique in this regard, but it is unusual on the world scene. Consider the trauma of the Middle East today and the search by those states and peoples for some acceptable amalgam recognizing the importance and efficacious role of tradition, as exemplified in Islam, in a globalized and secularized world. One then recognizes how far Korea has come. The still incomplete and agonizing struggles in the Middle East to find the "Middle Path" between the new and the revered, the requirements of a modern state that can no longer be kept insulated from the rest of the world and premodern rigidities, these are but modern examples of the intellectual and emotional wars that went on in East Asia over one hundred years ago, and have effectively been resolved by the post-Confucian societies, of which Korea is one. The Taliban may have been the most doctrinaire of the regimes that rigidly rejected modernity, but they are by no means unique. What is more remarkable is that in Korea, China, and Japan, the early introduction of foreign ideologies were also deemed to be subversive of the traditional order of the state and they were ruthlessly suppressed in the case of Korea with the massacre of Catholics, isolated in Nagasaki the case of Japan, and in China helped foment popular uprisings against Western influences as in the Boxer Rebellion of 1900. Yet these societies later recognized, perhaps inchoately, the possibilities and indeed the necessity of merging modernization and traditional elements of cultural identity.

Many years ago, a popular novel in the United States entitled *What Makes Sammy Run?* explored the motivations of a complex individual with a will to succeed. We should be asking the same question, but applying it to a national people, and then trying to account for the dynamic that characterizes Korean accomplishments. What made and makes Korea run? How did it move so far from so unpropitious a beginning? What in fact made Korea so dynamic?

Korea should not have succeeded. All the auguries were against it. The traditional economic factors of land, labor, and capital that are taught in economics courses in universities and are supposed to determine success were all negative. Overpopulated, impoverished, poorly educated, in an area without natural resources and even marginal in essential food production, it accomplished what everyone, including most Koreans, thought to be impossible. If one were rating the likelihood of national success in the mid-1950s of three countries with the approximate same per capita income and popula-tion—Burma, Thailand, and South Korea—Burma would have been the obvious first choice, Thailand second, and Korea would have not been in the running. Yet in 1997, just before the financial crisis, Korea's per capita income was about fifty times that of Burma and over five times that of Thailand.

To understand the dynamics of Korea, it is neither sufficient sim-ply to review economic criteria or even economic policies, nor is a re-view of political growth and sophistication adequate. Korean eco-nomic policies were often less than efficacious, state intervention into the economy produced first spectacularly successful and then equally dismal failures, and Korean politics has been ascending from the muck of the past in which it once was mired but is still less than a model to be emulated. One must search deeper into the society to dis-cover the origins of this modern dynamism.

Any such approach cannot not be without controversy and specu-lation, and foreigners who attempt this arcane task, aside from the hu-bris this entails, are spectacularly limited because forever they will be outside the dynamo they are attempting to observe. They have, how-ever, the advantage of that telescopic view that may help them to see a society from a distance—a view that is not obscured by the under-brush in which others must live.

Korea exists in a dangerous neighborhood, and has egregiously suffered because of its location. Although geography has not pro-vided security, ethnicity has. As a culturally homogenous people in a defined area and surrounded by states and societies eminently more powerful than they, Koreans have managed to keep their cultural con-tinuity under what must be described as overwhelming odds. First in the face of the monolith China, then in spite of a brutal Japanese colo-nial period, and then under the powerful influences of Westernization, Koreans have remained whole, as Koreans. No mat-ter how much factional politics weakened the Chosun Dynasty, and no matter how acerbic and often unproductive contemporary Korean politics, Korea as a culture and as a people have survived. This very will to survival, to better their former master, Japan, to overcome Chi-nese cultural hegemony, and to keep their culture in the face of insidi-ous popular foreign influences have been major factors in Korean success and Korean dynamism. The *uri*-ism, the "we-ness" of Koreans as Koreans, has been reinforced by the very threats to its existence. As a national society, Korea is a "Type A" personality—a driving force that demands to succeed.

But nationally this would not have resulted in progress were it not that this very Confucian society that for so long was criticized by international scholars and many in Korea itself as archaic, outmoded, backward looking, and virtually medieval, was in fact part of the reason for Korean success. The stress on education and the need for personal achievement—that honor also accruing to the broader community, the nuclear and then to the extended family, to one's institution—all these were part of that drive for accomplishment and success. There was inherent in Korean society an unarticulated need for personal efficacy and the pride that accompanied it. These forces, mostly unconscious, may have been and may still be the fuel for the Korean dynamo. How the state harnesses this energy has been important.

This drive and energy have bridged the cultural divides. As Koreans have rediscovered and treasured their own roots, they have adapted and even adopted the world's best cultural achievements, reaching international acclaim in the classic Western musical tradition, as artists, as academicians in all disciplines at the world's leading universities, and professionals as they migrated abroad contributing to the societies they have adopted. The determination to succeed has been profoundly important—the Koreans have been entrepreneurial not only in business but in the international arts and professions as well. Yet they have retained their culture, demonstrating that the traditional and the modern are not engaged in a Manichaean struggle between good and evil. Here is one of their salient strengths—the dynamism of intercultural excellence.

But, critics could charge, the admitted accomplishments of Korea were not without their detrimental upheavals internally generated, let alone those fostered from without. There have been at times various governments and social elements that have appeared to the outsider almost suicidal in their lack of regard for the benefits to their society and state. There have been the evils of corruption and environmental despoliation, of the pursuit of short-term gain at the expense of long-term benefits. Yet in spite of these factors, present in any society over time, the accomplishments of the Koreans on their own terms and in their own ways has been nothing less than phenomenal. In some sense, Koreans have succeeded in spite of their institutions—because of deeper strengths.

That is not to say that there is no trauma ahead or roadblocks on the ascending path. There are still needs to foster personal freedom and autonomy, of intellectual breadth, of social responsibility, and for the continuous reform of the institutions that shape society, such as education and governance. But there is little question that Korea is an example for the rest of the world. It is not a model, for the very uniqueness that made Korea accomplish so much means that its path cannot be explicitly followed. But if there is no specific model, there is a general lesson—that societies can rise from their own ashes and merge those important strands from their own traditions with other diverse ones emanating from pressures of globalization into a particular and efficacious tapestry of both internal excellence and international pride. This is the lesson from the Korean dynamic.

Originally published in *Dynamic Korea,* March 2002.

On Reflections in the Last Mirror

Some time ago I was sitting in a fashionable restaurant in Seoul, and my chair was placed so that it was reflected in mirrors both before and behind me. I had not noticed this when I sat down, but I soon became aware of it, and did not like it, but by that time it was too late to change my table as the restaurant filled. Thus I was forced to view myself infinitely projected in both directions in receding height and clarity, but nevertheless all too accurately. It was a sight remarkably disconcerting for one who dislikes looking in a single mirror. There was some irony to this event as I mentally reflected on the physical reflections and that my newspaper column had as its title "Stone Mirror." I was in some inscrutable manner being paid back in kind for my audacity in writing this column.

If one is narcissistic, one need not spend time looking in mirrors or at one's reflection in streams, however. There are other ways to allow one's ego a bit of freedom and to engage in fantasies of personal efficacy, if not aesthetic acclaim. I do not groom myself or dress for the public or my peers. Rather, I have thought that dressing and looking conservative, whatever one's political views, were means to avoid the superficial and concentrate on something internal. One did not want to stand out because of a loud tie or a particularly but ephemerally fashionable suit. Rather, one hoped to be remembered for an idea. There are, however, other forms of narcissism.

As I reflected on my multitude-of-mirrors experience, I had to admit that a narcissistic streak may have crept into an ego that I thought was singularly self-effacing. It was neither looks nor manner. As I had time to ruminate on the question while I waited at my table for my guests to arrive, I thought that perhaps writing a weekly column in a newspaper was in a sense an equivalent experience except with a set of finite mirrors—one's column illustrating the number of facets of one's personality one was willing to share with, or perhaps expose to, the reading public, and which the newspaper was willing to tolerate.

When I took on the task of writing a weekly column at the suggestion of *The Korea Times*, I had no idea of subjects beyond that of the first, which I had written for my own clarification. My charge was a weekly column (I was told that writers in the past had generally agreed that a weekly column was easier than a biweekly one—I am unsure of the logic of that remark but I have found that my fervid mind did easily produce items that eventually were printed and were dreamed up at a rate exceeding publication), and that the subject matter was to be anything on which I felt an inclination to write.

This was, in effect, and invitation to one's ego. Thirty years earlier, I had turned down an invitation from the same newspaper to write a column on my impressions of Korea. Although I know that some Koreans seem to have a masochistic delight in learning how foreigners criticize their country and customs, and foreigners may also have sadistic tendencies, I felt at that time this would be most inappropriate—a novice trying to interpret a hoary society far more complex than I could imagine.

This time, however, I felt, perhaps narcissistically, I had something to say even if I did not know what it was going to be. Perhaps the concept of my mortality began to creep into the unconscious. When one is young, one acts as if one is virtually immortal, but as one ages there is a desire to spread one's thoughts, even in 900 word-bytes, to a broader audience. This may be especially true for those, like myself, who have written extensively, but for audiences so specialized that if one found a reader outside of a very select subculture concerned with one's topic, one was always surprised. So a (relatively) mass audience was exciting.

Although ego-inflating, writing an English-language column in Korea forces a sense of proportion onto one's psyche. If you want to be widely read and influential, and affect policy, one naturally should write in Korean. Although Koreans do read the English press, they are relatively few in numbers, and those whom you wish would think about issues dear to you are too busy to spend time on another daily paper—no doubt they already read a multitude.

It is enjoyable, one must admit, to have people come up to you on the basis of an indistinct, small photograph in the paper, or on hearing your name, and remark, no matter whether from simple diplomacy or kindness, that they enjoyed one or another column. It may not last the requisite fifteen minutes that Andy Warhol predicted for fame, but rather a minute's recognition among a relatively small group. But it does provide even a momentary uplift of spirits after a particularly bad day.

As I read back over the titles of the columns, I am struck with how many sides of one's personality one has unconsciously revealed, or perhaps how many personalities have become apparent. A psychiatrist would have enough data to write a paper combining subjects with a study of the enthusiasms, concerns, use of language, imagery, and cultural perspectives. There is much breadth for analysis, even if the material and author lack depth.

But the time has come to end these pieces that have forced me into the market early every week to see which essay was chosen for that particular day. I must claim greater satisfaction than the reader in being able to write on such diverse subjects with such a free hand, or computer, and I thank the editor for his indulgence. Writing helps clarify ideas, and as Dr. Johnson said about hanging, it concentrates the mind wonderfully. It also forces more logic into argument. Even in the space of a few hundred words, perhaps because of the limited space, one is required to distill and, one hopes, amuse and share an impersonal dialogue at the same time. One never succeeds to the degree one would have hoped, but I would like to think that I have challenged and provided the reader with a few moments of morning respite from daily concerns, especially if washed down with coffee or *nokcha* (green tea). Would that I could have provided sugar for the coffee, but, alas, I am not sweetness, let alone light. I wish I could believe that I have enlightened discourse, but as a charming but hopelessly ineffectual hero of a Hemingway novel ironically says at its end, "Isn't it pretty to think so." Thank you for your attention all these weeks, and for letting me share my disorganized thoughts with you.[*]

June 1997

---

[*]   This column was written as I was leaving Korea to return to Washington, D.C. After that time, the column appeared on an irregular basis but has continued.

Stone Mirror

Reflections on Contemporary Korea

David I. Steinberg is Distinguished Professor of Asian Studies and Director of Asian Studies, School of Foreign Service, Georgetown University. He previously served as co-director of the Korean Area Studies program of the School of Foreign Service, Representative of The Asia Foundation in Korea (1963-68; 1994-97); Distinguished Professor of Korea Studies, Georgetown University; and President of the Mansfield Center for Pacific Affairs.

Early in his career, as a member of the Senior Foreign Service with U.S. Agency for International Development (USAID) of the U.S. Department of State, he worked extensively on development in Asia and the Middle East serving as Director for technical assistance in Asia and the Middle East, Director for Philippine, Thailand, and Burma Affairs. During this period he spent three years in Thailand with the USAID Regional Development Office.

Before joining USAID, Steinberg was Representative of The Asia Foundation in Korea and Washington, DC, and Assistant Representative in Burma and Hong Kong. He has resided for seventeen years in Asia and has travelled and lectured widely throughout the region.

Mr. Steinberg is the author of over ninety articles and twelve books and monographs, including, *Burma: The State of Myanmar* (2001) and *The Republic of Korea: Economic Transformation and Social Change* (1989).

David I. Steinberg was educated at Dartmouth College, Lingnan University (Canton, China), Harvard University, and the School of Oriental and African Studies, University of London.

EastBridge

Signature Books
Doug Merwin, Imprint Editor

Signature Books is dedicated to presenting a wide range of exceptional books in the field of Asian studies. The principal concentration is on texts and supplementary reading materials for academic courses, on Asian literature in translation, and on the writings of Westerners who experienced Asia as journalists, scholars, diplomats and travelers.

Doug Merwin, publisher and editor-in-chief of EastBridge, has more than thirty years experience as an editor of books and journals on Asia and was the founding editor of East Gate Books, an imprint of M.E. Sharpe Publishers. Mr. Merwin was born in Peking and lived in China off and on until 1950. He earned an undergraduate degree in Public Law and Government and a Master of Arts degree in East Asian Languages and Cultures from Columbia University.